Praise for *Brides of 1941*

Using letters discovered in the back of a closet, Bonnie Park weaves together three generations of women in a remarkably honest family history. Moving deftly between a Chilean copper mine, an elite East Coast college campus as the U.S. enters WWII, and her own Vietnam-era coming-of-age, her narrative honors women and the families they hold together. In a larger sense, the book speaks to the power of writing to sustain human connection. As a reader, I am grateful those boxes of letters fell into Park's capable hands.

> - Amy Williams, PhD, Associate Professor of English

A true story told with spirited honesty, Bonnie Park shares the intimate past of her parents, Robin and Buster, but also owns up to her own personal history. She will have every Baby Boomer reminiscing about the wild times they survived in college during the 1970s.

> - Joan Mills, owner, College Process Consulting and retired
>   Guidance Counselor, Park City High School

This candid exposé reveals events leading up to one young man's weighty decision to join the Army National Guard in 1939. From that point, the die is cast for Nathaniel Forrest Bedford's WWII military career. A veteran to be remembered as one of Mountain Lakes, New Jersey's most memorable and decorated. I salute him and this true story of his early life and service.

> - James L. Prescott, Navigator, USS Biddle (CG-34), 1977 – 1981

I've known Bonnie Park as a remarkable and innovative community organizer and manager, but I never dreamed she had such a unique ability to write. She is a gifted researcher, historian and storyteller, and her *Brides of 1941* is a terrific tale.

> - Sally Elliot, Elected Public Servant, Community Activist,
>   Co-Chair Friends of Park City Ski Mining History.

Rich in detail and poignancy, Bonnie Bedford Park's *Brides of 1941* is an insightful tribute to the Greatest Generation and how their lives influenced generations to come, one meaningful moment at a time. Her story makes you realize that it's only after the loss of our parents that we truly appreciate their journeys and reflect on how lucky we were to have them in our lives. Thanks for capturing all of it, Bonnie.

- Sueanne Peacock Sylvester, resident, Real Estate Agent, and creator of "Love Mountain Lakes" Facebook page.

These letters took me right back to my father's stories of Amherst (Class of 44_W*) and Smith pre-WWII. My own days at Smith included many of the same traditions from this era, perhaps most importantly, the cultivating of smart, creative, and independent women, which is the lifeline that connects all "Smithies." I felt a palpable connection to Bonnie's mother through these letters.

- Beatrice Peck, B.A. Smith College (1974), J.D. University of Utah College of Law (1988), Business Attorney

*"44_W" denotes a graduating class disrupted due to WWII. During the war years, large numbers of young men attending college awaited their call to service and left school. Some would eventually return, others did not. The "$_W$" qualified their place in what would have been their graduating class at an elite school where, post-war, fond memories, lifelong friendships and allegiance to the institution endured.

Bonnie Park's novel *Brides of 1941* takes us on an ancestral journey through letters kept by a strong American family. Long after reading this story, memories of history, early sacrifices and remarkable advancements in twentieth century medicine linger on.

- Gina LaRusso Agy, RN, Public School Nurse

In a tribute to her parents, Bonnie Park weaves kindness, compassion and empathy into a well-researched piece of personal history. An inspiration for anyone who wishes to memorialize the joys and heartaches that formed the tapestry of one's life.

- Jan McCosh, J.D., in House Counsel, Synergy Development

To Liz !

Brides
OF 1941

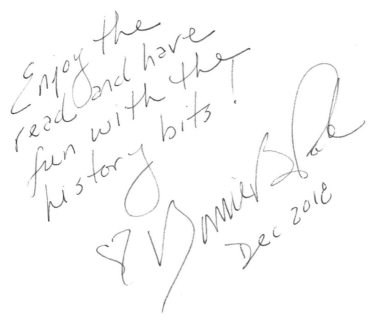

Enjoy the
read and have
fun with the
history bits !

♥ Danica Blah
Dec 2018

Brides of 1941

Bonnie Bedford Park

SPIKY PIG
PRESS

Published in the United States by

Spiky Pig Press

spikypigpress.com

ISBN: 978-1-7326140-0-0

Library of Congress Control Number: 2018908801

Book cover art by: Michelle Rayner, Cosmic Design

Interior design by: Katie Mullaly, Surrogate Press®

All spelling, capitalization and punctuation in the original letters have been preserved to honor the authenticity of the written correspondence.

"When we long for life without difficulties, remind us that oaks grow strong in contrary winds and diamonds are made under pressure."
Dr. Peter Marshall

I dedicate this book to the soulful spirits buried in the pet cemetery
of my childhood home in Mountain Lakes, New Jersey.
They opened my innocent eyes to the "Circle of Life."

And to my playful and loving parents (pictured above)
who taught me to care for all of God's creatures, and Mother Earth, too.

Table of Contents

Prologue

My forebears were not extraordinary Americans, but they were Americans with opportunity—people of social conscience with admirable core values. Except, let's be honest. In the arc of a life, what person isn't peppered with a few family members of variable character. Relatable, flawed human beings stir the pot with conditions and situations not to be talked about.

Except, sometimes, in letters.

Occasionally in the body of a note, the addressee is specifically instructed, "Don't repeat this, for goodness sake." And if it doesn't bear repeating, it's probably worth hearing. Whether verbal or written, there are no take-backs with words that cut deep, and the written word is physically etched with greater permanence. Forsake not my mother's voice ringing through, "If you can't say something nice, then don't say it at all." You must recognize that 1942 vintage quote from the movie *Bambi*. Good advice brought to you by the wonderful world of Walt Disney.

"Letters are among the most significant memorial a person can leave behind them," so said Johann Wolfgang von Goethe. Yet it's fair to say that our generation and beyond will not be leaving boxes of letters. Unless one is of celebrity status, our best shot at passing along a legacy of moral code, principles, ideas and ideals might be reflected in a personal journal, a blog, or a handful of printed emails that escaped evolving Internet technology.

Just as letters are a lost art, penmanship is endangered. Some kids lost out in the twenty-first century educational debate that placed emphasis on keyboarding over the curlicues of cursive. For them it spells trouble scripting their individual identity on an election ballot or deciphering the U.S. Constitution past the "We the People" part.

From start to finish in compiling this book series, I have honored my late sister Dianne as a partner in its production. Stick with me for a minute and I will tell you why.

Dianne's life took a very wrong turn at age forty-five. Sitting stretcher-side in the back of an ambulance she conversed with her husband for the three-minute ride from my parents' house on Crane Road in Mountain Lakes, New Jersey, to the emergency room at Saint Clare's Hospital, barely over a mile away. He rolled "code blue" (hospital speak signaling cardiac arrest) through double doors into the void of a sterile overly lit hallway. A heart attack victim in denial, he classically dismissed the signs as indigestion for too long, an all too common mistake with deadly consequences. At age forty-nine no one saw it coming. Prayerful hands clasped over mouth and nose, hyperventilating, Dianne might have wished for a small paper bag in which to breathe.

Abandoned in the wake of emergency responders, the chilled air swirled through her; lost souls flying in search of a living host. The antiseptic smell of the waiting area didn't register. Like playing a surreal scene in a psychological horror, she observed others perceptibly tense and anxiously awaiting updates on loved ones. The news of a flat-lined EKG gobbled Dianne up into complete shock and disbelief. "What do you mean he's dead? He can't be dead. I was just talking to him!"

Semper Fi, or *Semper Fidelis*, "always faithful," he learned honor, courage and commitment in the Marine Corps Reserve. How could this be happening?

Dianne's throat constricted with the realization he'd left her and their two children behind. The emergency room physician stood flatly in his green scrubs tackling, with facts, the most onerous responsibility of his job. Had it been the discovery of cancer to speak of, there would be "odds"

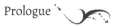

for and against the ultimate outcome. A menu of treatment options, too. This news was unalterable. She fixated on the doctor's mouth as he spelled it out. The ER team had given their all in the resuscitative effort for a full twenty minutes, admittedly longer than normal because of his young age. "Honey, trust me. With no oxygen for that long, you would not want him back in the condition he'd be in." The absence of cognitive function tipped the scales in favor of letting him go in peace.

Neither friends nor family fully recognized it, but Dianne's inner self changed like a fractured gem that day. I flew home to New Jersey for the funeral; welcomed at the Crane Road house due to my nine-month-old breastfeeding travel companion. He delivered sweet smiles like little crescents of eclipsed sunshine in an otherwise dark universe. The morning of my return trip to Utah I scripted with lipstick the color of toasted almond on the upstairs bathroom mirror. "Know that you are loved." Years later when I mentioned it, she remembered the note but hadn't a clue that it was *my* message. Like some spirit meme'd it?

It was just a matter of time before she shattered.

Bound by a financial straightjacket, she and her children moved in permanently with my parents. And even though multi-generational family living under the roof at Crane Road was a source of pride for our dad, taking care of his own in a time of need, it was more of a shame for Dianne. Upon the death of her husband, the structure of her perfectly nuclear family unit (dad, mom, two children) blew up. She raised her young teens with the help of our parents in a town highly regarded for its excellent public schools and opportunities for recreation.

But this scene drastically deviated from the script of how her perfect suburban life was expected to be written.

A weathered-gray wooden sign pitched in the front yard distinguished "Birch Bay," the name my parents chose for their home. The Borough of Mountain Lakes stood out as a magnet for the "best set" in the 1950s. The racial makeup? Strictly white. Well-educated, white collar, predominantly registered Republicans.

At the corner of Crane Road and Cove Place, the lakefront property along the shore of Mountain Lake was bordered by an expanse of wooded habitat dominated by stately oaks. A small stream, its origin unknown to me, fed the lake. In 1953, my parents moved into the custom home my dad took two years to design. In 1999, a widowed Dianne (then a Coldwell Banker agent) sold it as "A Nature Lover's Paradise."

On the main level, all who walked beneath the bright cathedral ceiling of the living room faced a wall of glass. Picture windows framed the second story view. Birch trees circled the perimeter of the cove, hence the name, Birch Bay. A small island buffered the main lake. Wakes on the water below trailed mallard ducks, geese, swan, muskrat, turtles, frogs and fish.

Half the basement, built of solid concrete block buried into the earth, offered protection from fallout radiation should disaster strike. On the peaceful lakefront side, a Dutch door opened no more than fifty feet from the dock where fishing, boating and ice-skating circled the calendar.

When the time came for my parents to move out, they let go of insignificant material objects and kept forty-six years of memories. Dianne owned the mission of shuttling the letters revealed in this book, and its sequels, from the back of one closet to another. Crane Road to Franciscan Oaks Retirement Community, the continuing care complex anchored at one end by St. Clare's Hospital, where her husband died six years prior.

Eight years after that move Dianne completely rattled the family tree when she chose to leave this earthly realm. Her psychic self-destruction was invisible, at least to me. A simple suicide note included, "Tell my family I love them." Now a spirit guide of sorts, she is one of many ancestors cheering me on as I write. Though it's possible some might prefer their story remain in the grave.

The parents Dianne and our brother, Bob, knew were quite different from the parents that raised my near-Irish twin Dorothy, and me. Divided by a decade, we were two families in one. Household economics that governed our growing years were disparate between the 1940s and 1970s, but by no means desperate. Though as an anxious and impressionable teen they felt that way to me.

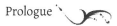

"Your generation is the first to start at the top and work its way down," warned my father, Nathaniel Forrest "Buster" "Buz" Bedford. The peas literally jumped when my dad rapped his knuckles at the head of the dinner table to emphasize this point. If seated close enough, I was tempted to poke the glabella furrows deepening between his brows. Instead, I embraced the image of Mr. Spock and a mind-meld into the hopeful Vulcan message, "Live long and prosper." Big words and Star Trek. Cool.

The CBS Evening News with Walter Cronkite routinely preceded our family dinner. I penciled my algebra homework curled up on the orange convertible sofa in the TV room serenaded by rat-a-tat-tat gunfire; newsreel footage from the Vietnam War. Buz, thoughtfully puffing on his pipe, offered parallel counsel on defending democracy. He explained elementary war strategy like a single-wing game play on the football field. Oversimplified objectives: Power-block the North Vietnamese on the battlefield. The South Vietnamese must not fall under communist control. Then came the most concentrated air offensives of that war: "Operation Linebacker I and II." In name, it naturally appealed to my father's love for football. (No surprise Nixon was an ardent fan, too.) He'd say, "B-bug," (Dad's pet name for me), "it takes a full team effort to win." The turn of phrase "carpet bombing" was defined visually. Long bursts of M60 machine gun fire gave way to great swaths of land erupting in flames.

While we watched the news, my mother, Roberta "Robin" Skinner Bedford, bustled making dinner in the kitchen. When the spitting, whistling pressure cooker released its steam, the brown rice was ready, and dinner was on. Robin sat at the table perpendicular to the right of Buz—nearest to the kitchen, of course. My place was to her right where, if my elbow found itself resting on the table, she would stick it with a fork. My mom was all about good manners through effective behavioral modification. Buz's incessant reminder to sit up straight called us to attention as he dished out dinner. Following posture correction, the passing of plates and grace, "Lord bless this food to our use and us to Thy service," a discussion of current events seasoned by the evening news would ensue. Do you get the picture? A lot of learning took place here.

The early 1970s economic stagnation led to a deep New York recession. In the trickle down from his clients not paying their attorney, dad got behind in my monthly clothing allowance of twenty-four dollars. At that time, in a different place, it might seem a generous sum, but in the town of Mountain Lakes, New Jersey, not so much. After all, he was a partner in a small law firm with a prestigious New York address at 115 Broadway, NYC. Each morning, splashed with Brut by Faberge, he retrieved and unwrapped a freshly pressed shirt from his bureau drawer and put on a dark suit and tie. Stifled in the East Coast humidity (never complaining), he rode the Lackawanna Railroad in an air conditioned "club car" with other companionable "Lakers" on the commuter path into "town." It seemed to me, if he went to work, he should get paid. His clients were not deadbeats, they just suffered the recession themselves. The bottom line? Lawyers get paid by their clients, not their employers.

The going rate of seventy-five cents an hour for babysitting added up to peanuts no matter how many babies I sat, but it's what a girl did in the day. No daughter of his was going to pump gas for a bigger paycheck at the shiny new white-and-green-banded Hess Station on U.S. Route 46, the commuter link to Manhattan. I missed my calling to squeegee windshields and give away toy truck collectables. I longed to wear the bright white Hess button-down shirt with my name embroidered in green to match the patch.

To the extent that personal fashion correlates with self-esteem, both went in the toilet early in my high school career. At the time, faded bell bottom jeans and T-shirts shrouded in Buz's WWII army shirts worked well enough. I helplessly fretted over the fate of friends in the Vietnam draft lottery. Dianne's clean-cut and kind twenty-three-year-old friend David, an Army Staff Sergeant, started his "tour" on his birthday in September 1969. As a light weapons infantryman, he served honorably with the 11th Armored Cavalry Regiment. Then he connected with a booby trap in an "incident" that occurred six months into that tour. David made his way home from Tay Ninh (South Vietnam) sooner than expected in a flag-draped box. He'd held on for seven weeks. Amputation of his gangrenous leg didn't save him. David's funeral delivered the reality of the Vietnam conflict to our doorstep.

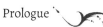

A turning point when I first came to understand the heart wrench of "casualty" and meaning of "ultimate sacrifice." In Honors Biology, dissection of the requisite fetal pig led to an anatomy exercise of dissecting a human leg. The wafting of formaldehyde stench was filtered out with thoughts of David's demise. The serious study of anatomical structure and function was lost on me. I could not get past the ulcers on the necrotic limb we sliced with scalpels. My imagination ran away with the story of its host.

I give Buz and Robin credit for tolerating my passive resistance to the war. And they did not over-react to my screaming neon handiwork; hippie pop art posters with an obvious Peter Max influence, shouting things like *Flower Power*; *Shoot speed, not people*; and my personal favorite, *Nixon, pull out like your father should have*. I laugh out loud remembering the silent looks exchanged between my parents. Out of earshot, they laughed, too. Chalk it up to the youngest child syndrome. As the "baby" in the shadow of three older siblings, I got away unpunished in my fidgety defiance. In retrospect I must admit that Buz and Robin were pretty hip. And my friends liked them, which proved that they really were.

I don't recall my father talking much about WWII. Rather, I didn't listen during those wonder years. The war in which he served was relegated to high school history curriculum. But the ghosts were afloat. With tribulation I slept in Buz's down-filled WWII olive drab mummy bag at Girl Scout camp. His army helmet, a Japanese flag, and a short-wave radio were among the memorabilia scattered from basement to bedroom in our house on Crane Road. His pungently musty canvas pup tent pitched in the back yard, spider eggs cornered in the peak, furnished an untouchably creepy atmosphere for sleep outs and requisite ghost stories. I've bequeathed a fearless fetish for poking spider sacs to my own children.

The letters came to light when Mom and Dad "crossed the bar." They celebrated seventy years of marriage in June 2011. Mom died five months later and my dad, with the soul of a southern gentleman escort, followed peacefully in his sleep five months after that. In a cleaning frenzy, I reached the back of the closet, and, in a cosmic coincidence, found the letters, delivered years before by the hands of Dianne.

My mom often spoke of writing a memoir. "Bedford's Bedlam" would be the title. The content an exhibitionistic monologue of living with my dad and us kids on Crane Road, Erma Bombeck style. Our grass grew greener over the septic tank, just like Erma's. (Pity the neighbor boys who mowed the acreage for three dollars a pop and ruined their shoes in that cesspool mess.) Humor kept the family afloat. For example, when I was in the sixth-grade I hosted my first "boy-girl" party in the Crane Road basement. While playing a game of spin the bottle, my mom yelled down the stairs and told us to quit moving the furniture. It may be that's what scraping glass on linoleum sounds like one floor down. Or was it a subtle way of letting her parental presence be known without busting the bash? My party guests spontaneously combusted into flying-eyebrow mimed surprise. We stifled hysterically nervous laughter, then turned the volume up on Tommy James and the Shondelles. Atop a Naugahyde vinyl boat cushion, the twist of a curvy green glass Coke bottle was effectively silenced.

Mom's book could easily have launched with this generational saga beginning with her parents, my grandparents. All the characters, including Robin and Buz, their parents, aunts, uncles, cousins, and family friends took hand to pen, pen to paper, paper to envelope. Letters stamped and sent boat mail, or airmail, traveled great distances in the run up to U.S. involvement in WWII. Their own written words spilled the action in their heads and hearts. They cut through a slice of white society like multi-layered wedding cake that's anything but plain vanilla. As geographically stretched letters unfold, we learn by their example how family environment and social climate shape our beginning. Then discover how the very personal business of decision making, at the turning points of life, shapes our destiny.

Sincerely,

Bonnie Bedford Park

November 11, 2018

The Main Characters

Chapter One

A news clipping, *St. Petersburg Times*, March 30, 1941

"Confidentially Speaking..."

The engagement of Miss Roberta Lelia Skinner, daughter of Mr. and Mrs. Thomas Wayne Skinner of Rancagua, Chile, to Forrest Bedford of Pelham Manor is to be announced this afternoon at a tea for 100 friends of the young couple in the Carpenter suite of the Waldorf Astoria in New York City. No date has been set for the wedding.

Miss Skinner attended the Emma Willard School and is a member of the graduating class at Smith College, Northampton, Mass.

Mr. Bedford, a former resident of St. Petersburg, is the son of Mr. and Mrs. Nathaniel L. Bedford. He graduated from Shorecrest School, the St. Petersburg High School in the class of '34, the Lawrenceville School and Princeton University, where he was a member of the Tower Club and prominent in athletics. He attended Columbia School of Law and is a member of Princeton Club of New York and of Squadron A. At present he is on active duty with his regiment, the 101st Cavalry, stationed at Fort Devens, Mass.

Left to right at my parents' engagement party: Forrest "Buz" (my dad) with a nervous smile and hands to match. Roberta "Robin" (my mom) under a Cinderella spell. My adorned "Grammy" Bedford, while giving instruction, missed the cue to look at the camera. My "Grampy" Bedford, in practiced calm.

Backstory: My Mother's People

Chapter Two

B efore I jump to the chummy prose of letters, allow me to reach into the past and waltz you forward through the scaffolding of the family tree: my grandparents and how my parents started out.

T. Wayne, age 24

Lelia, age 22

The residence of my maternal grandparents "T. Wayne" Skinner and Lelia McLatchey Skinner sat pitched along a barren mountainside in Sewell, a mining town in the Andes Mountains east of Rancagua, Chile. Both well-educated American citizens, my grandfather T. Wayne was a Columbia College School of Mines graduate, class of 1911, successfully employed as a mining engineer for the Braden Copper Company; my grandmother, Lelia, a proud alumna of Woman's Medical College of Pennsylvania, class of 1912.

The rites of matrimony were solemnized on July 20, 1916 in Keuka Park, New York, by Marie McLatchey, a gospel minister who also happened to be Lelia's mother (my great-grandmother). The newlyweds made a pivotal career decision to work in Chile with Braden Copper Company. While T. Wayne kept busy in the mining operation, Lelia had touchstones all around "Campamento Americano," the residential section of the Chilean mining camp reserved for foreign personnel. She arrived by steamship and rail from New York as a new bride in 1916. Sewell, the Chilean city of copper in the clouds, elevation, 7,000 ft., was the brawn of the Braden works where copper, the number one metal in demand to supply ammunition for both World Wars, was mined at full speed. A narrow-gauge railroad line between Sewell and

Digging out the narrow-gauge rail to the Teniente Mining Camp, Sewell, Chile. (*Bedford Collection*)

12

Rancagua was the only way in and out of the camp. Wooden sheds protected rail tracks and passengers from wind and drifting winter snows, as well as the threat of avalanche. Most of the houses were stacked two and three stories high, narrow and long, made of wood, and connected by hundreds of staircases. "Ciudad de Escaleras" (city of stairs) is a fitting moniker for a community with stepped pedestrian pathways layering the hillside. The echoes of my grandparents' footsteps are there, coming and going from House #71. Today the camp is preserved as an uninhabited UNESCO World Heritage Site. Still a standout, in an international trade kind of way, the Chilean state-owned copper company, Codelco, profitably digs deeper. A century after my grandparents arrived, El Teniente endures today as the world's largest underground copper mine.

Three years into the marriage, a pregnant Lelia disembarked the steamship *Santa Luisa* in New York on April 20, 1919, following an eighteen-day voyage from Valparaiso, Chile. Then it was onward to the Commonwealth of Pennsylvania to have her baby in her (and her husband's) birth state. There my twenty-nine-year-old grandmother settled in awaiting her labor and delivery confinement. Was it uncertainty over their unborn child's U.S. citizenship that preceded the ocean crossing? A Chilean birth certificate, written in Spanish, a conceivable hassle factor for life? Or she was disquieted over the words she'd studied in *Genesis 3:16: "In pain you will bring forth children."* For want of clear-cut answers, I believe it was my grandmother's trained eye that informed the decision. To deliver their firstborn anywhere lacking proper hygiene and sanitation would be out of the question. Here, in PA, she found peace of mind and a sense of security while in her *delicate* state. Why? It was familiar territory, and she knew people.

How?

In 1909, she'd launched from the McLatchey nest in the hamlet of Keuka Park, upstate New York, to attend college in Philadelphia. In a move that would be completely unconventional (actually out of the question) for a college kid today, my great-grandmother, Tryphena "Marie" Baird McLatchey, relocated by her side. What for? Marie (like her father) was a

Presbyterian minister. This move allowed her to resume evangelistic work in the city while my great-grandfather, William Miles McLatchey, remained in Keuka Park working (like his father) as a farmer. The mother-daughter team took up residence, as boarders, in a three-story single-family brick home at 2221 West Thompson Street, in the Sharswood section of Philadelphia. (New then, and part of a much-needed transformative neighborhood redevelopment project today.)

It occurs to me, in historical perspective, that during Lelia's ambitious college career, the two women bonded over a right-place-and-time experience. City living in the company of other bold civic-minded women suggests to me the dynamic duo took to the streets garbed in long dresses bedecked with chest sashes and floral hats. These were busy years for suffragettes! I'd lay odds my great grandmother, then in her early fifties, bold and blessed with a preacher's voice, capitalized on her day in the sun and Deuteronomy, too. Picture throngs of sign wielding women in the streets of Philly: *Fight on and God Will Give the Victory!*

Left to right: Alta McLatchey Dixon, Rhea McLatchey Huntington, parents William Miles and Marie McLatchey, a pregnant Lelia McLatchey Skinner, Frank Huntington with son Roy, and Bill Dixon, New York Harbor April 20, 1919.

In April 1919, seven years after graduation, Lelia steamed into port on the *Santa Luisa*. With a bun in the oven, it was another six-weeks before my mother's arrival. Conceivably my grandmother bided time in New York State and Pennsylvania, catching up with her mom, dad and the family clans. Logically the game plan for Lelia was laid out to land at the hospital of the Women's Medical College at the end of May. When labor was imminent, I imagine caring and quite talented women skilled in obstetrics, possibly some of her own classmates, gathered round like it was homecoming weekend sans the requisite football game and marching band.

My mother "Roberta" was welcomed to this world on May 31, 1919, in Philadelphia, the first of three Skinner children. As a matter of historical fact, Congress passed the Nineteenth Amendment to the U.S. Constitution four days later, giving women the right to vote. Though it was not ratified by the necessary thirty-six of the forty-eight states until August 1920, it is a "first wave of feminism" fact that culturally anchored the time of my mom's birth and underscores the staggering changes in women's rights that occurred in her lifetime.

With a stated travel objective to "dwell with husband" handwritten on her passport application, Lelia and five-month-old Roberta set sail in October 1919, headed for summer weather in South America to rejoin T. Wayne. Now, I suppose to "dwell with husband" might have been a politically correct objective for a young mother in 1919, especially in the eyes of a customs official. But can you visualize a 1970s Gloria Steinem with pursed pink frosted lips, bug-eyed behind her big-ass aviator glasses reacting to that statement? You'd think a woman with a college degree, predisposed toward equal rights pre-roaring twenties, deserved a loftier reason. I do. Steinem, a mere fifteen-years younger than my mom (and a Smith College grad, class of '56) is credited as a pioneer in the "second wave of feminism." Trust me, the virtue of veracity bloomed at the Crane Road house when it came to Steinem's cause.

Let me add to that. In an empowering sort of way, my siblings and I were wowed into believing our grandmother was a practicing physician.

Did she hang out her shingle and make house calls, too? Nope. We were tricked! I have evidence that Lelia was employed as assistant house physician at Vassar College for one year, then held a position with Goodrich Rubber Company as medical advisor for woman employees for a few more. Once married, her professional medical career went out the window. If you read these letters like I do, you'll see she ran herself ragged as a schoolteacher and property manager of sorts. Yet, on the subject of medicine she was our family pioneer. Lelia advocated preventive health care a century before its time, embraced homeopathy, too. Across continents she freely prescribed advice on health matters related to her children, and rather progressively minded her own health and that of my grandfather. Her coat of arms? Well educated, raised to be upstanding and honest, with lofty expectations for her offspring. What did I gain personally from my relationship with her? Preordained facial bone structure. Chubby cheeks and a face of innocence. As much as God knew what trouble I got myself into, it was hard for others to believe I was guilty of anything.

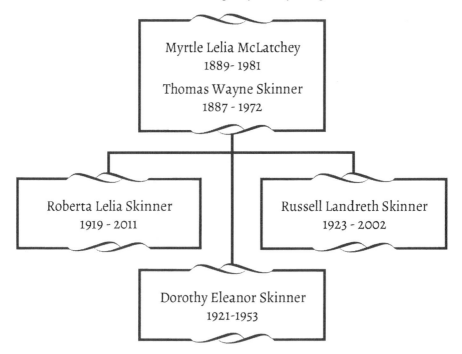

A simple family tree makes T. Wayne and Lelia's lives no less complicated.

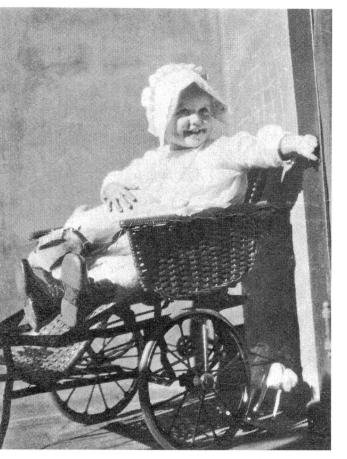

Two-year-old Roberta Lelia Skinner with awfully big shoes to fill.

It's reasonable to assume my pregnant grandmother could not fathom an eighteen-day steamship ocean-crossing adventure with a two-year-old in tow. Consequently, Rancagua was the birthplace of Roberta's younger siblings, my aunt Dorothy and my uncle Russell. I never met either one. Happily, I now know their stories. Sad as they are.

Let me be factually precise, dig further back in history, and sift through the shifting sands of the family landscape.

Clan Kinship of the 1800s

Chapter Three

In 1920, a life well-lived ended at age *ninety-five* when Lelia's maternal grandmother (my great-great-grandmother) Lois Courtney Baird flew toward the gates of heaven five days after Thanksgiving. Lois, a woman who birthed six boys and six girls in twenty-one years deserved to rest in peace. Her farmer turned minister-husband, (my great-great-grandfather) Lorenzo Baird, waited twenty-five years for the good Lord to invite her on up. *Seven* of their twelve kids flanked him like color guard for the heavenly reunion. They, too, preceded her in death.

Lelia's paternal grandparents, the McLatcheys went ashes to dust long before the Baird clan. They were nowhere to be found by 1920.

Do not fill your gray matter with the names of family members I regale in this chapter. Just reflect on their stories of hardship and courage. If your ancestry is anything different than my Euro-American heritage, odds are your family stories are more daunting or downright horrible. Which is exactly why they should be remembered. None of us can help where we came from. But history, independent thought and the dignity of free will could be usefully applied to level up our collective ethical awareness and common future.

The father of Wm. Miles, (my great-great-grandfather, William, Sr.) served as an elder in the Presbyterian Church in the township of Tionesta, Forest County, northwestern Pennsylvania. (On the eastern border of what would become the wild and scenic Allegheny National Forest.) A well-re-

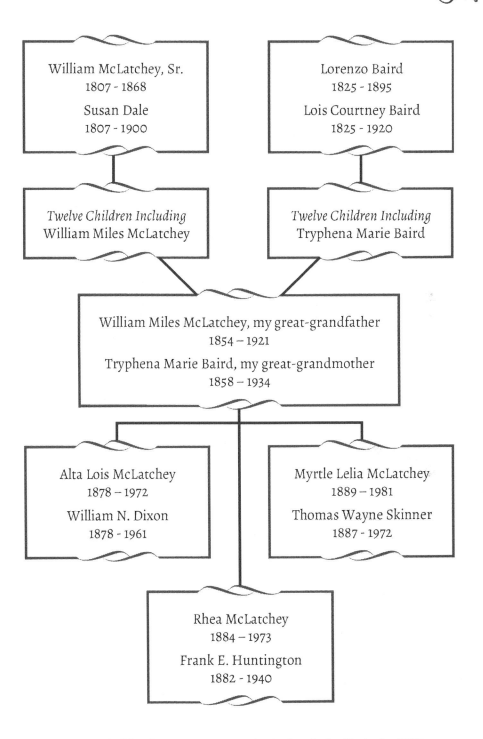

William McLatchey, Sr.
1807 - 1868

Susan Dale
1807 - 1900

Lorenzo Baird
1825 - 1895

Lois Courtney Baird
1825 - 1920

Twelve Children Including
William Miles McLatchey

Twelve Children Including
Tryphena Marie Baird

William Miles McLatchey, my great-grandfather
1854 – 1921

Tryphena Marie Baird, my great-grandmother
1858 – 1934

Alta Lois McLatchey
1878 – 1972

William N. Dixon
1878 - 1961

Myrtle Lelia McLatchey
1889 – 1981

Thomas Wayne Skinner
1887 - 1972

Rhea McLatchey
1884 – 1973

Frank E. Huntington
1882 - 1940

The extended family tree, my maternal side, fought for life in the 1800s.

spected farmer and horticulturalist, his grand finale fell on the Fourth of July 1868, at age sixty-one. His demise? Tuberculosis. At the time he passed, Lelia's dad (my great-grandfather Wm. Miles) was just thirteen.

By comparison, my great-great-grandmother, Susan Dale, clicked off another thirty-two years, celebrated the turn of the century, and died November 2, 1900, at an awe inspiring *ninety-three* years old.

As progeny of generations of pioneering Pennsylvania farmers, William Sr. and his wife, Susan, had good reason to propagate a dozen kids over twenty-three years. Because they were a tight-knit family, I am compelled to stay true to the record of their offspring: six boys, six girls, plus one angel (absent of name or gender) in heaven. A miscarriage? Possibly stillborn. The result of an unforeseen congenital abnormality that, today, might be repaired surgically, in-utero.

At the time Lelia's dad (my great-grandfather) William Miles was pushed into the world he was the eleventh child welcomed into the loving family. Yet the lad lined up under the McLatchey roof as number nine. Why?

Two of the twelve children, four-year-old Charles (1835-1839), and thirteen-year old Mary Jane (1837-1850) died before 1854, the year my great-grandfather Wm. Miles was born. At forty-six years old, his mother Susan was no quitter and went for a living ten. A baby brother, Louis Allen, arrived when she was *fifty!*

Then tragic horror struck. In the sunny summer of 1864 the "strangling angel of children" infiltrated their home in Tionesta. June to September, "black" diphtheria buried three in the *Presbyterian* Cemetery at Tionesta. Their seventeen-year old daughter Nancy Ann, "Nannie," their fifteen-year old daughter Sara Marilda, "Rillie," and "baby Allen," then nearly six, died gruesomely. It was not labeled the epidemic of 1864, but do you agree it qualified as such for them?

Triage in the parlor? Vigil in shifts?

The travesty went something like this: Within each child, a thick dark membrane of bacteria slowly grew around their tonsils, down their throat. They gasped for air, then suffocated.

Nanny died in June. Rillie about six weeks later. Like brave young women of sisterly solidarity, sweet Rillie "did not wish to live without Nannie." Allen, *already compromised due to tuberculosis contracted from his dad* (my great-great grandfather), didn't stand a fighting chance. He followed his sister Rillie to the grave one month later.

Proof that the strangling angel didn't discriminate based on age, three older siblings; twenty-five-year-old John Dale, twenty-four-year-old Elizabeth "Lyde," and twenty-two-year-old Samuel "Sam," took sick to bed and fought for their lives, too.

A fourth, thirteen-year-old Joseph Fremont McLatchey, was not expected to survive. By the grace of God, *he outlived all his siblings.* He died in 1936, an elderly eighty-four-year-old taken by a cerebral hemorrhage. His death came two years after family members captured his reminiscences, in 1934, without which I would know little about this branch of the family. The McLatchey roots are found in this book: *Out of the Past of the Wm. McLatchey Family.*

As much as the disease was a mystery in the summer of 1864, parents today all know the word diphtheria. More than a fine word choice for a spelling bee, the trifecta vaccine combo of DTaP has been routinely used since the 1940s. But ask around. You will quickly discover few people know how diphtheria toxins eerily manifest and kill, the way I just described it.

Can you handle one more drama bomb? A historical refresher of other calamitous events of the 1860s? The Civil War.

The diphtheria of my great grandfather's heroic older brother, John Dale, manifested differently. Here's how. Three years earlier, at the age of twenty-two, John enlisted during the "late Rebellion," August 1861, in Company G, Eighty-third Pennsylvania Volunteer Infantry. He served (and survived) in the Union Army during the whole of the Civil War, including the bloodiest battles of America's bloodiest conflict; Antietam (1862) where he was first wounded, and Gettysburg (1863). It was the Battle of Laurel Hill, part of the Campaign of the Wilderness (Ulysses S. Grant's Union Army vs.

Robert E. Lee and the Confederates, May 1864) where, on May 8, brother John was shot in the right shoulder.

Recuperating at home alongside his debilitated siblings, *diphtheria infested his bullet wound*. Weeping ulcerated lesions, red and gray, grew like horror movie gore.

It's lucky John Dale, then the eldest surviving child, had the smarts to swab out my great-great grandfather's throat. He used whisky, medicinally, to cut the mucous that might have choked and buried his father alongside Nannie, Rillie and Allen in the Presbyterian cemetery.

As another of the four McLatchey children to barely pull through the siege of diphtheria in 1864, John Dale's honorable discharge from the Union Army followed that September.

My great-grandfather, William Miles, ten years old at the time, was *the only child living at home who escaped the contagion*. Enough to convince me luck plays a far larger role in destiny than most people realize.

Moving beyond that dark past, let's get back to the launch of the roaring twenties, and the whereabouts of Lelia's folks. So sorry, but it starts with the death of her father (my great-grandfather) William Miles.

An obituary published March 21, 1921 in the *Democrat and Chronicle* newspaper (Rochester) revealed this:

> Penn Yan, March 20, 1921 - William McLatchey died at his home in Keuka Park on Friday night [March 19] after a long illness with heart trouble. He was prominent in the affairs of the park and had been a resident there for a great many years. He was 66 years old and leaves his widow, who was Miss Marie Baird, three daughters, Mrs. W. N. Dixon of Missouri, Montana, Mrs. Frank Huntington, of Schenectady; Mrs. T. Wayne Skinner, of Ranchgue, Chili... The funeral will be held from his late home on Monday afternoon at 2 o'clock and the interment will be in Lake View Cemetery.

Evidence that newspapers don't always get it right, permit me this editorial correction. There is no *Missouri, Montana*. It is Missoula. Though to cut them some geographic slack on that point, the wide *Missouri River* is the longest in North America. It gathers steam in western Montana at the confluence of Jefferson, Madison and Gallatin Rivers, and flows all the way to the Mississippi, north of St. Louis. As for *Ranchque, Chili,* for me it conjures mouthwatering spicy ranchero Tex-Mex fare. You already know more than the obit columnist. It's *Rancagua, Chile.*

More than misstated places on the map, it serves as a reminder that these were the days (long before #MeToo became a pivotal hashtag) when a woman's identity was defined by marriage. As a matter of social protocol, *Mrs.* Skinner, *Mrs.* Dixon and *Mrs.* Huntington took their husband's first and last names, just as their own mothers had before them. The salient point, and the names to remember, are my great aunts (my grandmother's older sisters)—Auntie Rhea Huntington and Auntie Alta Dixon. They complete the triangle of three McLatchey women who counseled until the day came to give my mother—the bride—away, and then some.

The Mystery of Ida Homker

Chapter Four

It's a matter of principle that I honor and share the short story of Ida, my biological great-grandmother. Her son, my grandfather Thomas Wayne (T. Wayne) Skinner, came with little family load compared to the breadth and depth of Lelia's clans, but no lack of drama. Grandpa was the only child born to Frank and Ida. He was raised as an only child in Dunmore, a borough of Lackawanna County, Pennsylvania, near the city of Scranton.

I am among the few people on the planet to appreciate, well over a century later, the hard-working news reporters of the *Scranton Tribune* writing to produce a New Year's Day edition in 1895. No over-served champagne on their watch.

This is the one small discrete item that opened my eyes and cracked my heart:

> "Mrs. Frank Skinner, one of our most respected ladies [in Elmhurst] quietly and peacefully passed away at 6 o'clock. She was an exemplary member of the Methodist Episcopal Church… She leaves a husband and one son."

Afflicted by one of any number of ever present nineteenth-century maladies, it's lucky for my mom (and me) T. Wayne escaped the deadly disease du jour. Church ladies brought relief gently "holding the space," as it were. Then, at the peaceable time the Lord chose to lead Ida to still waters, the women hovered like heaven sent angels. Cooking and cleaning (without committee appointment, like we'd expect today) they prepared for Ida's proper sendoff. Average life expectancy was forty-five-or-so years at the time. To die at thirtyish? She factored as a one-woman variable in quantifying the "average."

No one over-thought the subject of grieving children. The "five stages of grief" were yet to be identified. Age seven at the time, I imagine T. Wayne as a rangy boy. Quiet on the outside, he thrashed from within, left to make his own meaning out of it, glad to have his dad. Resolved to be a good boy? Destined to make his mother proud.

Nearly two years later, T. Wayne gained a stepmother. Did the betrotheds tap into some universal spiritual principle when they picked the date? It was the shortest day of the year when my great-grandfather, Frank, and Miss Sophie Brown exchanged vows on a Monday, the winter solstice, 1896. I have every reason to believe my grandfather was taken with Sophie Brown. To me, her name rang like a classic western movie starlet. I have faith the days got brighter for both men of the house. The essence of a nuclear family lovingly restored under the Skinner roof. Had my great-grandmother, Ida, unselfishly encouraged Frank from her deathbed to find another good woman? One who would guide T. Wayne, and look out for the boy should anything happen to Frank? Railroad work paid well, but train track tragedies were commonplace. Often deadly.

Like any man working the rail system, my great-grandfather, Frank, had stories. All aboard to catch a murderer? It's a disarming account that began when a section hand on the Erie Railroad made disparaging remarks about a rail-worker's wife. Both men were Italian immigrants. They hailed from the same village on the island of Sicily where they escaped *la miseria* of poverty. Wielding a stiletto, the incensed husband stabbed the big-mouthed section hand deep into the vitals of his gut. The perpetrator ran off through the woods. The victim writhed in pain then bid *adieu* dead in his tracks, on the tracks, where his own brother found him.

Back at the Elmhurst station, my great-grandfather Frank and a fellow rail man were tipped off by Italian workers who recognized the killer when he'd purchased a ticket to ride. Turned gumshoe, the men jumped stealthily on the same train. As the locomotive sped along, they moved through the mix of unsuspecting passengers. A well-performed handkerchief trick worked magic as a fine substitute for handcuffs. My great-grandfather dodged the murder weapon, and a bullet, too. It's true. The outlaw carried a new, fully-loaded 38-calibre revolver. The gun was confiscated with the stiletto, without incident. As reported in *The Citizen* newspaper of Honesdale, Pennsylvania, *"Police and detectives…. Were much pleased over the quick capture, for it saved them a lot of hard work."*

In his off-hours my great-grandfather Frank engaged politically as a Republican, volunteered as an election delegate, and served time as a legislator in the Pennsylvania General Assembly. As a Free and Accepted Mason of the King Solomon Lodge, No. 584, he, like his brothers, believed in a supreme being, a higher power. What exactly is Freemasonry? It is not a religion per se, rather it is a fraternal order open to men of all faiths. They worshiped side by side in the name of Christianity, Judaism, Islam, Hinduism, you name it. A person got to heaven through up-worthy acts of charity, moral living, voluntary civic duty and self-improvement. It's roots as a service organization date to the Middle Ages. In North America it dates to the 1700s. The likes of Benjamin Franklin, George Washington, and Paul Revere were Free Masons.

Whoa. Time out for toleration and liberty, too. No religious wars or church-related sex scandals, where everyone, no matter what higher power they pray to, is compelled to do good. Call me naïve, but let's just sit with that for a moment. The magical cornerstones of civility? Common sense and compassion.

Eventually the Women's Suffrage movement led the fraternal order of Freemasonry to call for Co-Masonry, but for T. Wayne's stepmother, Sophie, the timing was off. Her work was prescribed in the Women's Missionary Society of the Presbyterian Church. Elected as president of the local society in Dunmore, meetings were called in the Skinner living room where principled women eagerly gathered to plan saintly activities.

At age seventeen, my grandfather left the family home in Dunmore. He set up residence in Keuka Park, New York with a plan to further his education. On campus, he found gainful employment as a stenographer at Keuka College, a four-year spiritually centered liberal arts school. His job kept him on campus year-round. Putting two and two (with a pinch of kismet) together, the mystery of where my grandparents met was solved. Geographically speaking, Keuka Park is situated just four miles east of Jerusalem, New York, where the McLatcheys lived at the time.

I do not know the exact circumstances of their introduction, but I do know about this attention-grabbing calamity. In August 1905, my grandfather, T. Wayne, *fell out a third-floor window of the college building.*

Defenestrated? Meaning someone threw him out? Or was he showing off? Even worse, drunk? It's hard for me to imagine my gray-haired grandfather (a slow-mover at age eighty-one, when I first remember meeting him) performing stupid kid tricks. I pray it was not a suicide attempt.

I foresee grandpas of tomorrow dazzling their "littles" with preserved action sequences of their youth, shared on some device that is yet to be invented.

For the benefit of hometown friends in Dunmore, *The Scranton Republican* reported, *"...word of the accident was received in a telegram to his father, who hurried to his injured son."* The bodily damage? *"While serious, will not prove fatal."*

That news had to be the scuttlebutt about Keuka Park. Then maybe this: A synaptic connection fired through the prayer chains of my great-grandmothers' Skinner and McLatchey? A young T. Wayne, worthy of priority attention in the eyes of the savior?

I have absolutely no proof but wager this incident could be the single event that brought Lelia, just weeks short of sweet sixteen, to his side.

Presumably the romance simmered, then gathered steam as both achieved serious educational goals. Their marriage, ten years later, on July 7, 1916, in Yates, New York, was solemnized by the rites of my great-grandmother, Marie, in her capacity as a "Gospel Minister." Her husband William

Miles, and possibly stepmom, Sophie, witnessed the event. My hero of a rail-man, great-grandfather Frank, died in 1915. He looked down on the party beside T. Wayne's birthmother, Ida, from above.

It's safe to say some young couples married hastily surrounding WWI, which the U.S. had entered in April that year, but not my grandparents. T. Wayne, then twenty-eight years, and Lelia, twenty-six, took their own sweet time. Honoring *"in joy and in sorrow, in sickness and in health, as long as we both shall live,"* they stayed true to their vows. They celebrated their "double-nickel" anniversary in 1971, married for fifty-five years. T. Wayne died six months later.

How exactly did I discover the identity of my biological great-grandmother? T. Wayne spilled it, scripted in pen on the groom's portion of my Skinner grandparents' *Certificate of License to Marry*. History tells us a mass immigration of Germans landed as early settlers of Pennsylvania, fortified by Hessian prisoners who stayed after the Revolution. There, Ida Homker was blessed to be born into melting pot magic.

Love or Money

Chapter Five

Asnewlyweds Lelia and T. Wayne epitomized this adage: the reason people move is for love *or* money. In their case it was both. It explains why they found their way to Chile. They'd also studied *The Book of Genesis* and understood this expectation: *"Be fruitful and multiply."* Their progeny of three soon blossomed on the ancestral tree. It occurs to me that God's specific plan led to a life they probably hadn't envisioned when it came to chasing three tots teetering on the brink of very steep stairs in a South American mining camp.

It was my great-grandmother, Tryphena "Marie" Baird McLatchey that lured Lelia and T. Wayne from Chile to sunny California. Following the death of her husband (my great-grandfather William Miles) in 1921, Marie moved far from the ancestral pioneer roots in the northeast. It's possible she felt spiritually uplifted in this stunning geographic shift where she found safety in the service of the Lord. Long Beach served up a booming population that needed salvation as much then as it does now. It was more than a seaside resort town at the time. A burgeoning industrial center for shipping, automobiles and aircraft sprang up in proximity to the seaside port faster than anyone could say "economic development." The presence of the Pacific Fleet brought sailors to whom she could teach short prayers of strength and courage; prayers for forgiveness of their sins, too.

Marie's listing in the city directory publicly advertised her widow status. She lived in an understated two-story, sixteen-unit apartment building at

359 Obispo Avenue, Long Beach, in what's known today as the Bluff Heights Historic District. The street is pleasantly populated with Craftsman-style bungalows. Doubtful blue-collar roughnecks who toiled on drill rigs had much presence in the neighborhood, but following Royal Dutch Shell's oil discovery in 1921, derricks quilled the viewshed fast and thick on "Porcupine Hill," better known as Signal Hill in the annals of Long Beach. There, native tribes historically spoke with smoke as far as twenty-six miles across the sea, where indigenous people on Santa Catalina Island interpreted news from the mainland.

At Marie McLatchey's beckoning, the Skinner family of five rode out of Valparaiso, Chile in December 1924, aboard the motor-ship *Geisha*. The boat, pointed north, slowly rolled over ocean swells at a steady fourteen knots. My mom, then five years old, held the ship's rail close to Aunt Dottie (age three). Albatross followed, a mariner sign of good luck. Uncle Russell (age one) flapped in Lelia's arms. Christmas on board made it a challenge for Santa. Sea shanties took on a jingle bells bent. On New Year's Eve, no merrily inebriated reveler sang the Scottish tune *Auld Lang Syne*. Although Robert Burns wrote the lyrics in the 1700s, Guy Lombardo and His Royal Canadians would not popularize it as a signature piece until 1929. A "Passenger Lists of Vessels" informed me they debarked in San Pedro harbor to celebrate New Years' Day, 1925. I have no way to know if corned beef, cabbage and black-eyed peas appeared on their dinner table that night, but years later that meal became traditional fare at the Crane Road house. Intentions for good luck and prosperity in the coming year were set with the silverware.

As *Geisha* kissed the slip, and dock hands hurriedly secured multiple mooring lines, I imagine a magical moment went like this: T. Wayne and Lelia toted the kids down the gangplank and stepped onto the wharf. Setting eyes on her grandbabies, the thousands of relationships Marie previously experienced in her lifetime fell away into the sea foam and the pages of a new chapter began. Odds are my mom and Aunt Dottie followed orders to "take Grandma's hands." In "flying V" formation, they dragged her lagging between them, straight to the edge of the dock. There, Marie's rediscovery of the world through their eyes began. Whatever they witnessed in the lapping water (rainbows of an oil slick?) was met with intrigue. Curious kids don't waste time. Any exhausted parent understands they naturally gravitate toward danger and (theoretically) learn from the experience without getting killed.

Likely, an engineering degree and real-life work experience with Braden Copper led my grandfather straight to a position he'd already accepted pre-voyage. It's possible, as a company man, he ranked enough to re-locate to North America. The young family took an apartment in the same complex as matriarch Marie. All are listed at 359 Obispo Avenue a year later in the 1926 Long Beach Directory. For my mom, the Horace Mann Elementary School, less than two blocks from their apartment, planted the seeds for a lifetime of learning, the way it still does today.

Like their neighbors, they adjusted to the environmentally lacking boomtown in familiarity that breeds invisibility. The stench of fossil fuel production permeated the air. Their linens, hung out to dry, turned gray flapping on the clothesline.

Maybe it was greener pastures and cleaner air, but for a reason unknown to me, the 1930 census placed Marie and my grandparents further north in Alameda County, the Bay Area. They'd beat it out of southern California before March 10, 1933, when a magnitude 6.4 earthquake shook Long Beach. Land owners at the time could build a house and drill for oil on their property smack dab in the middle of a residential subdivision. That explains an elementary land use principle in its early twentieth century infancy: zoning. In the aftermath of the quake, fingers pointed to frenzied and unregulated oil drilling as the cause.

In Oakland, my great-grandmother Marie, then seventy-two years old, rented dwelling #194, at 3945 Fourteenth Avenue. T. Wayne and family lived in an adjacent unit, #195, around the corner, at 4030 Park Boulevard. What were the demographics of this area, as measured by my personal random sample of the Fifteenth Census of the United States? Some married, some single, one divorced, Marie was the only widow. Everyone "white." They came from a smattering of states across the country, notably none from the south. In a worldly way, other citizens were documented from Armenia, Canada, France, Russia, Turkey. My aunt Dottie and Uncle Russell represented Chile as their unique place of birth, where they spoke English in the home. Census data also told me each residence had a radio set. All except for my great-grandmother. I suppose her Bible kept her company in the evening, and she ran around the corner when the family tuned in Sunday nights for entertainment underwritten by Chase & Sanborn or Maxwell House Coffee. Gathered around, I imagine they watched the radio speaker as though something might poke through the grille cloth. Joe Penner appealed to my mom and her siblings, in a Pee Wee Herman character kind of way, though historically Eddie Cantor has bigger, broader name recognition today. Cantor lit up the comedy fun factor performing in front of a live studio audience no one could see, pre-dating canned laugh tracks. The census rats out the fact that neither Dottie, then nine, nor Russell, age seven, could read or write. In the 1960s, I learned to read from the same basal readers they did well before I turned seven: *Dick and Jane*. Their tardy start was surprising since ambitious standards for educational achievement were set for my mom and her siblings at an early age. Kids can't ignore those expectations when they come from both sides of the family tree.

I know this to be true from personal experience.

Oakland's unemployment rate in the early 1930s hovered north of twenty percent. You've heard the stories. People were not only jobless, they were homeless and hungry. Mulligan stew made from scavenged vegetables was a staple for families living in places the likes of "Pipe City," a makeshift village where residents dwelled in jumbo sanitary sewer pipes, resembling whiskered rats. A shave and a haircut even cost too much.

Understand that pipes laid out for human habitation remained *above* ground. Fortunately, those were apartment dwelling days for the Skinners. My mom never piped up with firsthand stories of her personal deprivation.

How long did my grandparents feel the undertow of the Braden Chilean operation while they lived in the U.S.? Nine years. Then it unleashed as a riptide. In South America, T. Wayne was paid well, and my grandmother could contribute to the bottom line, too. The copper handcuffs of the El Teniente Mine commanded their return to the mining camp in a *selling-their-soul* sort of way. Guided by family values, each generation was raised to go beyond their parents' lot in life. Money to fund excellence in education as their children's key to a world of opportunity was paramount.

I cannot imagine what explanation they offered the kids. Harsh as it sounds, how does a parent logically legitimize abandonment? Lelia and T. Wayne escorted my great-grandmother Marie and all three of their children back to the northeast. Why? Amsterdam, New York was the home of Marie's middle daughter, Rhea Huntington. There, specific instructions were spelled out in legal doctrine; T. Wayne's handwritten Last Will and Testament. Lelia's Last Will and Testament, too.

Adios Mis Hijos

Chapter Six

Lelia's Last Will and Testament detailed my grandparents' joint real estate holdings nothing short of an impressive nine parcels of land designated by Lot, Block, Tract, Book and Page number in the Los Angeles County records. Due to lack of any evidence, I say with greedless gratitude there is no reason to believe they ever took to drilling for oil. Though it would have been another option to crack the nut on the cost of college for the kids. Should Lelia meet her demise, the parcels were... *"to be equally divided between our three children, Roberta Lelia, Dorothy Eleanor and Russell Landreth Skinner."* Did she have jewelry? Yes. A modest collection. A pearl necklace, diamond pins and rings (probably her wedding bands) were to be divided between the daughters. They'd get her Cascade pattern Towle Silver Service, too.

Sterling flatware was of such material importance then, for the generation to follow, and for some still today. A "must" for the best set. Overrated in my opinion and, if you have any, you know who polishes the stuff. In my house, it's me. I have a mismatched medley of forks, knives and (never enough) spoons derived in bits and pieces from the ancestral tree. A handful of sterling serving pieces inspire holiday table chatter. The deciphering of engraved scripted initials channel family surnames and personalities of Thanksgivings and Christmases past.

Because jewelry and flatware were bequeathed to the girls, their brother Russell was to inherit Lot #114 in the hamlet of Keuka Park, Town of Jerusalem, New York.

Does that dividing of assets pass the smell test? It stinks if you ask me, but in 1934 that's how the division of earthly possessions was sorted between a son and two daughters.

As a preface to the last Will and Testament of my grandfather, let me drill in for a minute on the risky business of mining. It's wet, cold, dark and dangerous, which is the reason mining disasters become media events. Do you recall that rescue of thirty-three Chilean miners in 2010? (If not, you should refresh yourself, watch this film: *The 33*.) The entire world held their breath! In the first half of the twentieth century the occupation was far more dangerous. It's no surprise T. Wayne built a diversified portfolio of insurance detailed in his Will like this: New York Life (seven policies), Sun Life Assurance of Canada (five policies, plus dividends, plus double indemnity in case of accidental death), Equitable Life Assurance Society of the United States (three policies; one in a group plan kept up by Braden Copper Co.), one Prudential Insurance Company policy. That's sixteen policies! Do you fully comprehend why he had them? By tragic example, read this excerpt about the fate of a family friend, relayed in a letter written by Lelia, sent to my mom from Campamento Americano.

Poor Mr. Spectzen was killed by an ore train in the mine last Thursday. One leg and one arm were cut off.... He died instantly – what a blessing he didn't live a few hours to suffer.

Did he really die instantly? Quick yes, not instant, but death was certain as he bled out fast on the tracks before help arrived.

Mining disasters were one dark demise, but air travel also came with risk. Thoughts of erratic weather over the Andes were unsettling. A plane crash straight into a mountainside would leave no survivors. Should he and Lelia met their death simultaneously, my grandfather, Thomas Wayne Skinner, *being of sound mind and memory* scripted this playbook of educational expectations (and how to fund them) in his Will and Testament dated February 3, 1934:

Sufficient money from the insurance proceeds to be paid the Emma Willard School to cover the expense of Roberta Lelia Skinner for the remaining three years of her course there; [1934-1937]; and for Dorothy Eleanor Skinner for the next four years [fall 1934-1938]. For their higher education, subject to their approval, would suggest Smith College [the expense also to be met from insurance].

His sound mind continued flowing through the tip of his fountain pen:

For Russell Landreth Skinner (now barely eleven years old) *Taft's School for preparatory and Yale or Harvard for higher education.*

T. Wayne's Will, attested by Rhea's husband, Frank Huntington, and their twenty-three-year-old son, Roy, included a bracketed notation. A mindful afterthought? The date they hugged the kids close and departed for summer in South America was revealed:

[There may also be additional airplane insurance in case there is any available before starting trip Feb. 13, 1934.]

From that day forward, hearts, hands, and prayers reached out to guide the peripatetic path of my mother, Aunt Dorothy and Uncle Russell. My grandmother, separated from her circle of three children, took to transactional writing—a written conversation. She inked letters with what I perceived as shifty perspective in a therapeutic exercise. By necessity, she relied heavily on the kindness of her older sisters and their spouses. Auntie Rhea and Uncle Frank were imposed upon for the well-being of the three kids due to geographic proximity in New York state. My Great Auntie Alta and "Uncle Dix" Dixon offered reinforcements from Big Sky Country (Montana), where Dorothy spent three summers, and my mom learned to love the West in a matter of months.

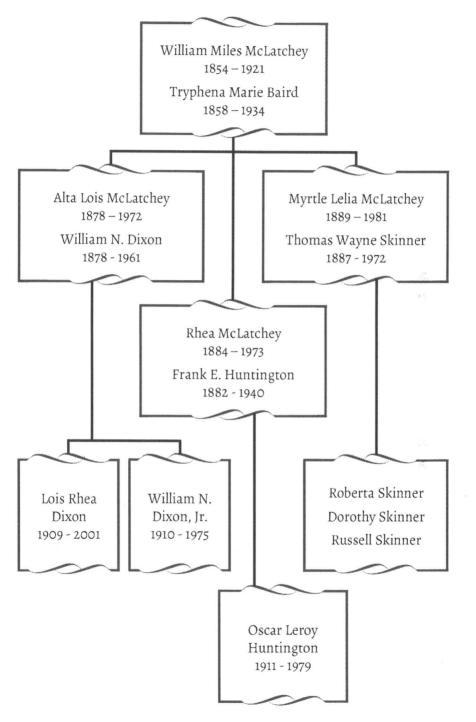

The McLatchey clan grows into the twentieth century.

Confederates Be Damned

Chapter Seven

My paternal grandmother, Ethel Nicola Delinusha Bedford, hailed from Monastir, Macedonia. That's a seemingly exotic family factoid that stands out to my own kids. Not so plain vanilla in their predominately British/Scot (and newly divulged German) heritage.

Grammy immigrated in 1898, at the age of twelve. She buffed her English as a domestic worker, then attended Northfield Seminary for Young Ladies, in Northfield Massachusetts. Christian doctrine was the school's educational emphasis. Underprivileged women from diverse backgrounds were welcomed and educated there. The curriculum included practical skills, too. Domestic chores and farm work.

Nursing the sick was a most attractive field for women in the early 1900s, made popular by Florence Nightingale, the idolized angel of English hospitals, founder of the Red Cross Society and modern system of trained nursing. Grammy would have graduated from Northfield Seminary in the class of 1903 but, after two years of schooling, she discovered hospital courses as a practical option, and means of support, for a single girl. At Grace Hospital in New Haven, Connecticut, she excelled beyond the changing of bed and body linens and learned to dress bed sores, burns and ulcers. She observed the behavior of wounds as she applied fomentations and poultices. Somewhere in the line of duty, administering medications and ventilating sick rooms, she met Grampy. He happened to be a patient at the time. One who would charm her with his southern gentility, wit and wisdom.

As I knew her, "Grammy" Bedford was a soft squeeze with a signature scent of sweet gardenia and a delicate demeanor to match. She spoke in whispery words, which (like E.F. Hutton) were remarkably effective in getting others to hush, lean in and listen. Customarily she wore (evolutions of) pillbox hats and white gloves. It never occurred to me, as a young girl, the fashion influence of Jackie Kennedy had anything to do with it. Her floral aura lingered on the two or three rolled one-dollar bills she surreptitiously slipped into my elfin palm on every visit to the Crane Road house. Even my piggy bank took on her smell.

Holiday spectaculars at Radio City Music Hall were her treat, and not in a one-off way. The Christmas and Easter shows, marked on my mom's kitchen calendar, months in advance, were religious Bedford family tradition. In my naivety, I believed the "Mighty Wurlitzer" pipe organ, first-run movie premiers, and the glittery kick line of Rockettes in clone-like synchronicity were a part of every child's life, as much as Santa and the Easter Bunny. For holiday dinners, Grammy turned out specialty items, impeccable kid fare; plump macaroni with a blend of gourmet imported cheeses and baked egg custard, both set to perfection—recipes that possibly reached back generations. The happy colors of Ambrosia compote eyed through prisms of cut crystal bowls included generous fruit sections stewed in sugary syrup with coconut! I assumed she'd be around forever, until suddenly she wasn't.

Grammy died when I was nine, two days after Thanksgiving, 1966. It was my first experience with grief over the loss of a flesh and blood family member, though I had cried my eyes out over many furry ones.

I was the self-appointed caretaker of our pet cemetery in the woods bordering the edge of our yard at the Crane Road house. After raking clear the giant oak leaves that blanketed the sacred grounds, I would heave acorns that dared to sprout new life where great sorrows were suffered. My Bedford grandparents took particular interest in my cemetery tours. The soul that lay beneath each circle of rocks had a story; the plot map seques-tered in my head unfolded for them. The parallel universe of pet loss proved comforting when Grammy died, because I knew good company awaited, wagging (and otherwise) to welcome her beside Saint Peter at the pearly gates.

My remarkably efficient Grammy had wrapped up Christmas shopping before Thanksgiving. I was comforted by a "Granny Doll" that found its way into my arms, the gift chosen with intention to remind me of her love. A flowery maxi dress, long brown hair and "granny glasses," the wire rims made popular by none other than John Lennon, becoming on both men and women at the time.

By contrast my paternal grandfather, Nathaniel Lynn Bedford, was born in Macon, Georgia. Straight out of the womb his life began father-less. To banish what you may think is careless misfortune, do not label him a bastard. My paternal great-grandparents, Kate Lynn Robert, age seven-teen, and Nathaniel Peter Bedford, age twenty-one, were a handsome, young couple in love. They wed in Macon, Georgia, on November 25, 1884. Evidenced by the birth of my grandfather, ten months later on September 14, 1885, the newlyweds were legitimately blessed. Excepting this tragic fact. Nathaniel Peter died on May 25, 1885. His bride of six months was left behind heartbroken and five months pregnant. Family lore holds pneumo-nia seized upon him after helping to fight a house fire.

My great-grandmother, Katie, remarried at the age of twenty-six, to a dentist sixteen years her elder. The Twelfth Census of the United States in the City of Savannah, Georgia, revealed that my grandfather Bedford, at the age of fourteen, worked full-time as an office boy. Two younger half-siblings (William, one year, and Evelyn, two months) occupied his mother's time, another (Hawlie) yet to be born. There is a wicked stepfa-ther story here in the family tree. I lack the details, but it led to this. At the age of sixteen, Nathaniel Lynn Bedford ran away from home and occupied himself as a cabin boy on an unnamed sailing vessel.

"Grampy" Bedford had little formal schooling but, according to my dad, became self-educated through his love of reading. I am proud to say this guy was no dummy, and altogether street smart, too. He gained employment as a traveling salesman for the American Book Company, a manufacturer of books and educational materials. Their book list, primarily texts, ran the gamut of subjects at every educational level. To wit, this title from 1912 grabbed my attention: *Where Have My Profits Gone?? AN EXAMINATION OF VARIOUS WAYS BY WHICH PROFITS ARE LOST, WITH AN EXPLANATION OF MODERN METHODS OF PREVENTING SUCH LOSSES.*

It doesn't take an *Amazon* search to understand books like this are perpetually authored, shifty topic that it is.

Later, as a graduate of the Guaranty Bond School, Grampy Bedford thrived in the world of business finance. When people asked me what he did for a living, I would confidently reply, "He's a businessman." Since I didn't have a clue what that meant, I felt relief when the conversation ended right there. But I can tell you this; Juicy Fruit was his chewing gum of choice, well before Jimmy Buffett suggested it in song. A roll of Butter Rum Lifesavers, kept in a coat pocket, satisfied a sweet tooth, too. And in a moment when I was so hungry I might have eaten the leather seats off his Mercedes, he magically served up a fat dinner roll slathered with an emergency ration of Hormel's canned Spam in the back of the car.

To me, his face looked rather like a snapping turtle, though I never told him so. He often contorted those facial features into devilish expressions with unending entertainment value. As a bit of a trickster, he feigned a heart attack at a family reunion when our Pontiac station wagon pulled in more than an hour late for the gathering. Unlike Fred Sanford (Redd Foxx) á la the 1970s sitcom *Sanford and Son* using that transparent ruse "This is the Big One," Gramp played the part a little more seriously, laid out prone on a picnic bench.

It can be a little scary what a kid remembers about their heritage. But most importantly, I know I was well-loved.

Backtracking a bit, my grandparents wed in 1907 in New Haven, Connecticut, Grammy then twenty-one and Grampy, twenty-two. The

Thirteenth Census of the United States, 1910, positioned them on St. Johns Avenue, in Jacksonville, Florida. Here is a sad fact. For census purposes, they were asked the birthplace of their respective fathers, and mothers. "Un" (the abbreviation for "unknown") is marked *four* times, indicating that *neither* of them could report where their respective parents were born. It's reasonable to believe Grammy wasn't certain how to name the birthplace of her parents in the conglomeration of territories that preceded the crumbling of the Ottoman Empire pre-WWI. As for my trickster grandfather? Was his intention to cast off a defective past? A skeleton-free Confederate closet to begin his own blessed family?

My dad, Nathaniel Forrest Bedford, was born on May 21, 1918, in Jacksonville, Florida. My grandparents made their home with "Forrest" (later nicknamed "Buster" and, later still, "Buz") in St. Petersburg Florida from 1924 through the 1930s. Here they flourished in the winter resort where they were among the core of year-round permanent residents and my grandfather struck success. It was in St. Pete that Grampy Bedford was recruited to help evaluate the profitability of the Gandy Bridge, a pipe dream proposal to span Old Tampa Bay for six miles, from St. Petersburg to Tampa. To catch my drift, check out the 1924 "Gandy Bridge Song" on YouTube.

Grampy also helped finance the construction of the Don CeSar Hotel, the "Pink Castle" in St. Petersburg, during the economic boom prior to the Great Depression. And while on that topic, let me digress to say I believe the Great Depression had less of an impact on Buster than the recession of the '70s did on me. Family photos bear witness that my dad was well-dressed. As far as I know Gramp never got behind in his allowance of two dollars a week for general spending. As a teen he drove a top of the line 1932 Plymouth chick magnet.

The short story on Grampy and Grammy during my dad's growing years is this: In 1925, my grandfather hit a home run in real estate and development under the moniker *N. L. Bedford, Inc. Realtors*. He had a pulse on the booming Florida land market, and understood location, location, location. By 1928, he'd hoisted himself up a notch to *N. L. Bedford Co., Inc. Investments*.

Fourteen-year-old Buster poses with the Bedford's '32 Plymouth Roadster.

Grammy rolled up her sleeves to participate in Red Cross work and that of the Women's Club. The latter included social functions, playing bridge, planning and participating in fancy luncheons. The table center-pieces? Local flora; pink and yellow snapdragons, sky-blue lupines, pink and yellow roses, white sweet peas. The pastel theme carried across a room-ful of starched linens with tall wax tapers of pink and blue, and short taste-ful nut cups. My research revealed this worthy Women's Club endeavor; an educational survey of illiteracy in the state, *both juvenile and adult,* tied to the 1930 Census.

To understand the magnitude of illiteracy was a starting point. Schools at the time were separate and unequal based on race. An immigrant herself, I hope Grammy played like a crusader. My grandfather's success under-scored how far a person could climb simply knowing how to read and write.

In the months leading up to Black Friday 1929, N.L. Bedford adver-tised in the *Tampa Bay Times* classifieds under the bold section heading: *Investments, Stocks, Bonds.* He sold himself, providing financial information *as to the value of any securities either in St. Petersburg or any part of the United States...without charge by writing or calling* him personally. Like a data magnet, he wanted his finger on the economic pulse wherever he could find one. His abiding faith? *Everything that could be done, should be done to expedite trading and exchange.*

Educating my dad by example, Grampy was not all business all the time. The causes he supported with volunteer time and money included the Boy Scouts, YMCA and Community Chest. In their own world of real life *Monopoly,* the "Community Chest" committee consisted of business and civic leaders looking to make positive impacts for the greater good.

One radiant afternoon, Grampy played hooky with my dad to go fishing. The two piscators hauled in *forty-two* Kingfish, a feisty variety of mackerel, on a boat out of Pass-A-Grille. (I know that doesn't exactly sound sustainable. Likely they fed the hungry with fishes and loaves, too.) More than angling for fun, as the elected President of the Pinellas Fish and Game Conservation Association, my grandad became a leader among a group of prominent anglers. In 1934 they took a conservationist position against gill nets and seines used for fishing. That was impressive action to protect natural resources. Did it get political? Like drilling for oil and gas in the National Monuments and recreational lands of the west are political fighting-words today? Of course it did.

The hospitality and charm of the South left an indelible mark on Forrest's way of being—his love of fishing, insatiable. His would-be older sister, Eugenia Lynn, lived a short life, 1909 – 1917. Family lore has it that Eugenia's petticoat was licked by fire as she chanted *"Jack be nimble, Jack be quick,"* leaping and laughing as an eight-year-old would, over a candlestick. Her life ended tragically, engulfed in flames. For that sad reason, my dad grew up an only "replacement" child, cherished by his parents with double the love and doting due to the void left by Eugenia. And practically speaking, since I never knew her, I grew up with yet another mythical aunt.

But then I gained an "aunt" (in truth, a first cousin, once-removed) unexpectedly. In an unpredicted kerfuffle of life, my grandparents took in Grammy's niece, Victoria. She, too, immigrated from Macedonia with her father and brother to escape land disputes and ethnic identification in the western Ottoman Empire. At the time of her arrival in the U.S., circa

1916, she was three years old. They lived in New York. It was the death of her father (Grammy's brother, Stergios) that landed her in the Sunshine State at age sixteen. In the 1930 Census she was officially accounted for as a "Bedford." According to family lore, Grampy urged their niece to take the Bedford name because it would be easier on her than carrying a "foreign" name.

Vicky notched into household order, five years older than my dad. Educational expectations for her were the same as any Bedford. She graduated from Rollins College, in Winter Park, Florida. Then went on to become Art Director for Binney & Smith (the Crayola Company). As an internationally recognized finger painter she authored books on two artful subjects: finger painting and papier mache.

Who was Victoria Bedford to me? A surrogate aunt who stepped in for those I never knew and, in a nutshell, everything an aunt should be. At the Crane Road house, we called her "Honeychild" (How southern is *that*?) I never knew it to be a "code name" but used it in youthful innocence. I did not know Grammy was not all that fond of her. Why? The insurmountable loss of her natural born daughter was too much. I was shocked to learn my sweet-scented Grammy had a bitter bone for Vicky. Face to face, she once cracked these curdled words: "Why didn't you die instead of Eugenia?"

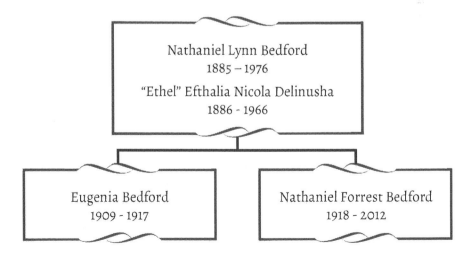

Nathaniel Lynn Bedford
1885 – 1976

"Ethel" Efthalia Nicola Delinusha
1886 - 1966

Eugenia Bedford
1909 - 1917

Nathaniel Forrest Bedford
1918 - 2012

Looking back, the best possible education was provided to my dad, blended with athletic and cultural opportunities from an early age. (The fact that I was paying back college loans until the age of thirty-five is not lost on me. But that kind of fiscal responsibility fostered a *stick-to-itiveness* attitude in finding gainful employment better than a kick in the pants.)

At the remarkably young age of seventeen, my dad worked one summer for New York stockbrokers W.H. Goadby & Co., a registered firm on the New York Stock Exchange. Downtown, at 74 Broadway, Manhattan, he calculated bond yields on a slip-stick (a slide rule) for the M.I.T. trust funds, dabbling on the side in investments for himself and my grandparents.

In 1935, N. L. Bedford and Co. Brokerage House suspended business in St. Pete, the collateral exhausted because of a sharp drop in their holdings in the New York stock market. My grandfather capitalized on his former work experience with the American Book Company. The 1940 census reveals his gainful employment as an executive in the printing business. It would lead to my grandparents' uprooting from Florida. Their subsequent relocation to New York gave them reason to tail Buster in the northeast.

My grandfather Bedford was retained as the Special Assistant to William Sherman, the President of Standard Register Company, Dayton, Ohio as that firm expanded into the Connecticut and Massachusetts markets in 1941. Ironically, at the outset of U.S. engagement in WWII, the federal government pronounced business machines as non-essential to the war effort. Then somebody's light bulb went on to recognize that pieces of paper moving desk-to-desk were vital in a time of war; efficient record keeping, to track manufacturing of munitions, procurement, troop movement and such. Standard Register's pin-fed platen, with those little holes tracking each side of continuous business forms, was an innovation that increased speed and efficiency. Grandfather Bedford was, for the second time in his adult working life, in the right place at the right time.

The Boatmail Begins

Chapter Eight

My mom's captive letter-writing journey began in 1937 at the age of eighteen, her freshman year at Smith College (Northampton, Massachusetts) underway. She resided in Wesley House, one of many residential houses (in lieu of dormitories) on the Smith campus. Each house, with its own unique character, was something like the Hogwarts campus of Harry Potter fame, I suppose. She did not labor tirelessly in her schoolwork, as you will see for yourself. I am convinced for every hour I spent in my college and university libraries, she spent twice that chasing the New England social scene in the escort of Ivy Leaguers. And according to her own penmanship, a "townie" named Louis who wanted to marry her.

As planned, my aunt Dorothy traced my mom's footsteps. She attended Emma Willard preparatory school in Troy, N.Y. Then in 1938, "Dottie" followed the chosen higher education institutional path at Smith. The party path, too. Freshman year, she resided in Haven House, a classic New England architectural statement: clapboard siding and muntin windows, a double chimney and full width steps leading up to a broad covered front porch. Ripples and bubbles of single-pane glass failed for insulation against Massachusetts winters, most notably when blustery *nor'easters* rattled through.

As for my uncle Russell, nicknamed "Skeeter," his destiny wandered way off course from the plan T. Wayne laid out in his Last Will and Testament. More about Skeeter and his floundering later.

My mom pigeonholed my grandmother as a "worrier" as far back as I can remember. I accepted that label as gospel. Why? I'd come to know Grandma long distance in the 1960s, through the receiver of a black rotary-dial Bell Telephone. Shy child that I was, I'd anxiously coil the phone cord around my shrimpy fingers while she chatted me up about my animal friends. Had I overshared about the pet cemetery? She seemed to worry about them dead or alive. But in 1937, Grandma was especially fretful for good reason, as evidenced by the following letter she wrote to my mom.

L.M. Skinner, Rancagua – Sewell, Chile – Dec. 3, 1937

Dearest Roberta,

My school has finally closed for the summer and I hope at least for the next 11 weeks of vacation I can get letters off to all you children on every boat. We rec'd your type written letter last week. I think you are doing pretty well with typing. Was especially glad to see your expense acct. check so well. Yes, I think you should send Daddy a monthly expense acct. because otherwise we don't know how much money we need to keep sending up there. Smith won't send monthly statements to parents as Emma Willard did. They have too many students to attempt that.

I have just sent the Xmas check for all you children to Auntie Rhea. We allowed $30 for our gift to you and $15 for your shopping for friends and relatives. Can you make that stretch do you think? You know in your freshman year I don't think you ought to be asking to go for weekends to Boston and other places. It takes your mind off your studies too much for one thing. You know those <u>big colleges</u> just kick freshman out, also soph's, if they don't do good work. They do that on purpose at all colleges just to limit the student body and keep only the ones with the best standing. So freshman and soph's better apply themselves pretty studiously to their work and not be getting low grades – or out they are liable to go. All colleges plan on a lot of freshmen not returning for their sophomore year. So attend to your studies the best you can this year <u>especially.</u> Daddy and I would feel disgraced if you were to be told *not to return to Smith next year. And then another thing, if Smith won't let fresh-man go to other cities without written permission – if they won't take the respon-sibility for freshmen, how do you think Auntie Rhea would be willing to take that responsibility? You have several years ahead of you to be taking joy excursions over weekends. Do try and apply yourselves, all of you, and make the very most out of your college years that Daddy and I are making such a life sacrifice to give you chil-dren. You can never fully realize - until you are a parent and have children of your own to do for and expenses to meet – just the struggle we are making. It isn't for you alone, so don't take it personal – it is for all three of you. We are doing so many things to try to bring in extra money for school expenses – that one thing crowds us after another – as soon as one thing is finished it means rushing into something else to attend to that. And we don't feel we have time to do justice to anything. If you think your college life has one thing crowding into another, wait until you get out into the world and a living to make. One thing comes on top of another. All year we have had to sit up until 11:30 or 12 o'clock to try and get things turned off. That's why we haven't had time for letter writing. Every minute of my time Saturdays and Sundays goes with doing laundry and bookkeeping that I have to let slide from Mon. to Fri. I never in my life was pushed as I've been the past two years. I may be able to quit work and come up and rent a house in Northampton and make a home for you and Dorothy. You need a mother's companionship as well as parents need yours. I could just weep that you are nearly ready to go out into the world on your own and we haven't had your companionship. There is a music course of six weeks offered at Smith summers. How would you like to arrange to stay there, if the dormitories keep open so as not to have to bother Huntingtons? We would also like you to be able to take typing and shorthand during vacation.*

Bye Bye Hugs and kisses. Mother

Every mother knows what it feels like to be "pushed." But in my experi-ence, it happens when children are underfoot. (Worse when they are sick!) As a full-time working mother, a friend once asked me, "How do you do it?" My answer. "I just never stop."

But I held an important card up my sleeve. One my grandmother lacked. I was *present in the company of my children*. Not every moment, but

49

enough to make parenthood feel like the blessing it is. As much time as I spent being with my kids, it's evident my grandmother spent double-time occupied with worry about hers.

L.M. Skinner, Rancagua – Sewell, Chile – Dec. 29, 1937

Dear Roberta,

This will be a hello and goodbye as I've been out sprinkling in the garden and came in to write four letters for the mail and I've had forty-eleven interruptions on the phone.

Well Xmas is past thank goodness – but we have New Year's ahead of us yet. The holidays make us so sad. Naturally parents are remembering their own at the Xmas season more than at any other time of the year. I try to busy myself with the Xmas work for the American and Chilean children so as to keep my mind from wandering too much to you children – but I still can't help recalling you three and to the kind of Xmas I wish we were spending with you all together. Oh, I do hope after I earn money for another two or three years, to help Daddy with the tuitions, I can then go to the U.S. and take a house and make a home for our children for two or three years. So you can feel you have a home of your own. These are my dreams and ambitions.

My grandmother goes on handwringing: *We do so want you to be happy, along with your hard work. Because we realize college is hard work.*

It's clear to me Grandma pored over the most recent Smith Alumnae Quarterly as if it was her only source of news from Northampton. The sole *objective* news source, at any rate. One photograph grabbed my grandparents' attention. That of my mother's academic advisor, Miss Virginia Corwin: *We weren't particularly struck with her looks... rather strict and hard. It might be a good idea for you to have a talk with her and ask her if she can point out your weak points...so she will get the impression you at least are trying your best.*

Make the *"impression"* my mom was trying? Like a brown-noser? Miss Corwin was a professor of Religion and Biblical Literature. Strict and hard, she wouldn't be fooled. Quite possibly she'd already judged Robin as high-flying and self-indulgent. My grandmother revealed her deepest fear, then signed off: *"Oh, we just wouldn't have you put out of Smith for anything... Worlds of love and best wishes for a New Year filled with happiness, Mother and Daddy"*

Any one of us can relate to the "forty-eleven" interruptions my grandmother spoke of. It happened then, and arguably happens at an accelerated pace today. But do you hear the steeled sadness in her voice? Those of us who do our own yardwork understand how thoughts take over in that short wrinkle of time made for hand sprinkling in the garden. For Grandma, as cheery and colorful as her summer bedding plants may be, it is Christmas. Three years have slipped away and there is no way to iron out getting that time back. Family photographs to prove they are near and dear don't, and won't ever, exist.

A Fine Young Man

Chapter Nine

The preserved letters of my dad "Forrest" began like intricately woven needlework samplers. I'd never go so far as to laud him a Renaissance man, but with his start as an unsophisticated kid from Florida, he "prepared" at The Lawrenceville School, and under the influence of Princeton became a combo jock/cultured intellect underpinned with Southern gentility. He chose a major in economics for the simple reason that the world and U.S. economy were in bad straights in the late 1930s. Extracurricular interests during his college years included girls, athletics, beer drinking. And more girls. So he said, to impress.

For a lifetime my dad exuded the sporting ethos of Princeton football—teamwork, effort, loyalty to the extent it was contagious. Travel to Tigertown for Princeton football Saturdays, September through November, amounted to more than an occasional family outing. And it was inexplicable how a college football game could manifest the big top energy and excitement of a Ringling Brothers Circus, but he made it that way for me. Like warning drums in advance of a sacrificial ceremony, percussive beats rang around Palmer Stadium and spilled out onto Nassau Street. Throngs of fans dressed in orange and black stepped in time toward what appeared, to me, to be an enormous ivy-draped coliseum.

It all started when he played 150-lb. "Tiger" football as a kid himself, long before thick necks were over-developed to stand out clear across the quad, when helmets were made of hard leather. His nickname, "Buster," derived from the fighting tiger position he held as fullback on the squad. Time and again I'd heard that explanation in my youth. Like a big cat he basked in the glory of legitimized *bad-assary*. But the core values of the sport were life lessons; preparation, commitment, perseverance, fair play. I envied his trained instinct to tuck a shoulder and roll into a fall with grace. I bear witness to the fact that this skill served him into his 90s. Though he would occasionally trip and fall, he never succumbed to increased mortality due to a broken hip or any other fracture common to the elderly. Let me add to that. He understood the value of core strength long before television personality Jack LaLanne, "Godfather of Fitness," began preaching the virtues of exercise and diet to the American television viewing audience in the 1950s. My dad used the "B-bug, I'm tough as nails," shtick as far back as I can remember, proving LaLanne had nothing on him (except a thirty-inch waist, bulging biceps and blue bodysuit to advertise *every* physical attribute).

My dad's bit went like this. Braced with tight abs, he'd invite me to fist him in the gut. Core strength was old news to him. Tough as nails, yes, he was, and I do believe it all started with his love for Princeton football.

Friday night

Dear Folks,

Gee but that was a hard one to lose! We scored a touchdown in the first five minutes of play when Bob Downey recovered a Lafayette fumble on the kick-off and we ran right straight through on line plays to a score.

I respect the fact that many people restrict their football consumption to nothing more than an annual Super Bowl bash. Craft beer, clever commercials, (concussions?), nachos, wings and a halftime headliner dominate the conversation. But a touchdown in the first five minutes of play, on a recovered fumble, is an electrifying game opener even for a neophyte.

The opposing ground forces hut-hut hiked, tackled and passed up and down the field of play for four quarters, then: *With four minutes left we had pushed the ball down to the Lafayette 10-yd. line.* The Tiger offence was stopped short on the fourth down, with five yards to go. Then what? Game over.

Lafayette threw a long forward pass just over my head... a lateral on the end made it good for 90 yards and a touchdown.

There is one good thing about this game, though. When the Yale and Rutgers boys start to compare scores and think that the Princetons are just soft pickings they are going to get the surprise of their sweet young lives. With two weeks to rest up before the Yale game we are going in at full strength and with plenty of fight. The same goes for Rutgers.

Although I was not injured in the game this afternoon beyond a few bruised muscles, I am so tired out that I can hardly sit up in my chair. Before closing though, I want to tell you that I put the Everglades Club Bonds in the black box and saw to it that the check was deposited to my account. It was lucky that I didn't send you the check before because the dumb bank had not deposited it, but here it is enclosed and everything is O.K.

Your loving son, Buster

Buster wearing his game face.

Cartoonist Charles Schulz, creator of the *Peanuts* gang, released a compilation of syndicated cartoon strips in 1974, titled *Win a Few, Lose a Few, Charlie Brown*. In many respects, my dad was a kind-hearted soul like Chuck, but one thing for sure, Buster did not want to come up with a loss against conference rival Yale.

It's a sporting fact that the Princeton Tiger vs. Yale Bulldog rivalry dates to the year 1873. Respectably one of the oldest athletic events in the country. If football isn't your thing, compare it to the likes of the Kentucky Derby or the Westminster Dog Show. Historically big, even if the viewing audience is a niche market. Buster captured the nip and tuck snippets of the upcoming Big Game weekend for his parents who would not be there.

"I just barely managed to make weight for the Yale game tonight, but I succeeded and we arrive in New Haven at 11:30 A.M. on Friday."

Why did he have to "make weight?" Not unlike the brute force sports of boxing, wrestling and weightlifting, it's about equalizing the competition. Weight limits are inflexible. In the case of the 150-lb team, the boys prided themselves in moving the ball down the field with speed and agility.

If you're not a sporty sports fan, all you need to logically understand is that faster play captivated spectator interest. Anyone who's eaten pizza in a pub during football season knows watching big lumps of body mass slowly muscle their way to a first down gets monotonous. If a play is worth watching, everyone will turn to mind the big screen for the replay.

Afterward, Buster reported the rumpus like this: *"Football game was the most thrilling I have ever seen. It was nip and tuck the whole last half and Yale was just lucky on its timing. A few more minutes and we would have had the winning touchdown."*

Yep, you win some, you lose some.

On a social note, a Jacksonville lass by the name of Fran Wilson was supposed to be Buster's date for the dance that night. His folks were to collect her at the train. Then he explained, *"Fran won't be able to come down to New Haven, so you don't have to meet her."* Consequently, the senior Bedfords skipped motoring to Connecticut and were absent in the "Yale Bowl," home stadium of Bulldogs, when the Tigers lost. *"Awfully sorry you missed it,"* wrote Buster. Then cheerily added, *"Met several girls at the dance last night and still think that Yankee gals haven't got that certain something. St. Pete carried the day."*

Doubtful anyone from St. Pete was there in the flesh. No matter. The contents of his perpetually refreshed mailbox kept him entertained. *"Have had loads of letters from home this week including Peggy Laughner.... Will tell you all about it Friday."* The "home" he spoke of was St. Pete. He was umbilically attached.

Mind you, we'll hear more from "home" via Peggy Laughner, later.

Then this P.S.: *"It has been so cold down here that I have been wearing fur-lined gloves to football practise."* Buckskin, lined with bunny pelt? Admirably, Buster spent little energy writing about the weather, never filling newsworthy space on his stationery with superficial fodder. Football season delivered unfailing sunshine, low humidity, and a snap in the sweet smell of fresh fall air.

In Buster's letters home, the content was thematically mixed. They boiled down to some combination of this: sports, girls, entertainment, school, and family finance.

For example, *"I've spent so much time writing about football and the state of my health that I have completely neglected the subject that we are all most interested in, really. Well, since my bruised and aching muscles are somewhat recovered from Friday's encounter, I will turn my subject matter towards studies for a change."*

True confessions? *"As you might expect, all the time that I have spent at football practise has somewhat detracted from my grades, but I am fully convinced that when the season ends in three weeks things scholastic will take a definite turn for the better..."*

He went on to talk about his coursework; Politics, History, French, Philosophy and Statistics. It revealed this: *"About my hardest subject is Philosophy."*

As if that course load wasn't heavy enough, for entertainment he attended *two* different productions of Hamlet and then spent time stretching his gray matter over the following compare and contrast composition for a letter home. Unbelievable.

"I haven't had time to give you a complete criticism and comparison of Howard's and Gielgud's "Hamlet," but I will make a few outstanding comments now and tell you the rest later. Personally, I feel that Gielgud's production is grossly overrated in comparison and that Howard has not obtained his just share of the glory. In all except the first two scenes, Howard's settings are superior. His costuming is better throughout, and I believe that his supporting cast is better. My chief adverse criticism of Howard is the continual fluttering of his hands. John Gielgud starts out wonderfully at first sight – his quiet reserve – that of a man who has received a terrific shock, is perfect. You think "Here is Hamlet in truth!" But as the play goes on, although his acting is forceful throughout, one finds fault with his excess emotion and with the continual thrusting out of his neck as if he were waiting for someone to cut it off. All in all, I would recommend Howard to the person who had never seen "Hamlet" acted before, Gielgud to the critic who goes to study a man in the part of "Hamlet," but admit that both were done well and were worth seeing, there being little to choose between."

I hoped these words were, in part, something constructed for his philosophy class, studying words, deeds, and death in the mix of a well-spring of Shakespearean universal themes: religion, government, politics, social life and the like. A discovery of Hamlet in truth for a professor's grade, not just his mom and dad.

Lord knows Shakespeare never qualified as something I'd ever write home about when I was in college. Yet, I can appreciate the energy around a good Shakespearean Festival.

To add more to my dad's overachieving fine young man persona, he signed off with furrowed brow and this fiduciary note. *"Please let me know when you expect to come down next and I will have your bonds ready for you. Or if you think it advisable, I can send them into N.Y. by registered mail."*

I must admit, this parent/child financial management role reversal was a head-shaker. How is it my grandparents relinquished control to Buster to manage their investments? I've sorted it enough to determine he was moti-vated. Why? Simple carrot and stick theory. He was their sole beneficiary.

February 1937, sophomore year at Princeton, a Charlie Brown-like Buster attended a Saturday night performance on Broadway without mention of a date. His review, prepared and shared with his parents went like this:

"Went to see "A Point of Honor" at the Fulton Theatre last night and enjoyed it very much on the whole. It got off to a very slow start in the first scene, but about the middle of the second scene it began picking up speed in a hurry and finished with a bang. The author handles the plot very skillfully, making a hero out of Benedict Arnold, a brave and loving woman out of his wife, a bitter, envious woman out of his sister, and a villain out of his father-in-law. According to the play, if it hadn't been for his sister's meddling in his affairs and disrupting his plans, he would have been recognized as a hero instead of being made a traitor."

U.S. History taught me that Benedict Arnold was a Connecticut Yankee and Revolutionary War hero turned Red Coat. He ran off with the British as a "Turncoat." This production was a comedy, which I presume explained how Benedict Arnold made out as a hero. Evidence that truth exists in historical context and whatever eyewash is applied.

Lightening it up with a sports report, Buster signed off with a P.S... *"I threw the javelin for an hour yesterday afternoon and was pleased to find that my form was quite good and my shoulder vastly improved. By toughening it up slowly for the next two months I hope to have it in good enough shape to make the North Carolina trip this spring. We meet the U. of North Carolina on April 7 and Duke on April 10."*

How does a young man learn to throw a spear? My dad encouraged his number one son, my big brother, in the backyard of the Crane Road house. What happened? It doesn't take a detective to identify the mark of a javelin that's pierced the metal slide of a playset. Like a peep show all the kids in the neighborhood took turns circling an eyeball around the perfectly perfo-rated hole. Imaginations ran wild with bloody "what if" scenarios had a kid been on the slide at the time.

Here's what Buster said about his politics exam on Tuesday.

"Three hours and a half is a long time to write on one subject...With luck, I should get a pretty good grade. Some other fellow may have hit it, too, and that might lower my standing."

Blasted four-eyes who ruin the curve.

"But any way you figure it, I feel that I know a lot about the subject in spite of the grade I get on the exam, and the knowledge gained is the important thing."

He came off like such a suck up. My style? Cram. Then, superstitiously, put notes under my pillow. Sleep, get up early to cram some more and sit for the exam. I ruined the curve. Yes, I did.

Okay, not every subject.

Now, here's a bit of whining I could relate to. He wrote, *"There is nothing happening here but work, work and more work – everybody is doing it, and I am working hardest of the lot."*

As a college student, I religiously questioned the rationality of having to pay the registrar's office a tidy sum, and then work, work, work for no pay.

As for my dad, he was not one to conform to habits of the all work, no play norm, evidenced in this next escapade.

"John Early, one of the members of the skeet team, asked me to come home with him for the weekend since our match Sunday afternoon was at a field fairly near Summit, N.J., where he lives. He got dates for us Saturday night and we went sledding and skiing at the country club. It was the first time that I had ever tried snow sports and I thought that it was loads of fun. I actually skied all the way down a hill without falling down."

In my youth, a much older Johnny presented as a tall, bald Caucasian version of Geoffrey Holder, the "un-cola nut" Trinidadian guy with the deep voice and hearty laugh; that 1970s pitchman for 7-UP. If that doesn't ring a bell, recall the top-hatted voodoo villain, Baron Samedi, in the first Bond film to star Roger Moore, *Live and Let Die* (1973).

On November 12, 1938, Princeton faced off with Yale in the *first ever intercollegiate skeet shoot* held in this country. Johnny held his mark as the second-high gun. Though it wasn't enough for a Princeton victory, surely there was a sterling silver "loving cup" trophy with large handles involved. One that rarely, if ever, got polished. Several like it adorned shelves in the Crane Road house, staged in fifty shades of tarnish.

Sunday morning, the two young men attended church. If they prayed for a sporting win, the Lord let them down. *"We lost our skeet match with the New Jersey Game Wardens because Johnny and I were the only two members of the first team to show up. The other three fellows were substitutes... After the match we went back to the Early's for dinner, then came straight back to Princeton to get back to work. It was a keen weekend and I didn't lose much time that I would have been able to use for studying, either."*

Then this head scratching news: *"I finally had a letter from Theo Saturday. Everything is fixed for the Prom. I'll let you know what time I will be in for the car Friday."*

Prom! To me it sounded as though Buster and some guy named Theodore might be planning a double date for the dance. I was wrong. Theo *was* his date.

Don't get me wrong. It could be Theodora? Theophila? Theodosia, notable name of the wife and gifted daughter of Aaron Burr?

Genealogists revere doozy christenings of this kind. Recall my great grandmother on my mom's side, baptized "Tryphena," for which she was nicknamed "Phene" as a kid, before she latched onto "Marie" as an adult. I haven't mentioned her sister, "Tryphose," nicknamed "Phose," fell next in line, middle of the Baird family pack of twelve. Primed for reincarnation on someone's internet list of most popular baby names. Or not.

Prom, with Theo on his arm, was apparently nothing to write home about. Neither Theo, nor Fran (the dance date that never happened after the Yale game), were ever mentioned again. Likewise, the girl Johnny Early set him up with the night before the skeet match remained a mystery. What *do* I know? Buster wrote of the women in his life one at a time. He was all out with school and sports. Johnny Early remained an enduring friend for life *because of* school and sports.

For my mom? Chasing men became a sport unto itself.

Circling back to the commentary on Philosophy, my dad spoke a truth that resonated with me when he wrote: *"Dear Folks...Had my Philosophy exam this afternoon, but didn't do particularly well in it. That stuff is the devil and all to get hold of to begin with, and worse to put back on paper. Some parts are very interesting, but others are so darned obscure that it is enough to bore you to tears."*

Anyone who has studied philosophy knows Truth is a tricky topic. Put your thinking cap on and keep up with me here. Objective truth is one we all believe in. But then mess with the doctrine of relativism, and we learn the truth exists in relation to society. Or culture. Or, God help us, historical context. Trump and the Truth, anyone?

Enough on the schoolwork, let's hear about another swell gal.

"This morning I received an invitation from Mrs. Campbell, Mary Jean's mother, to come down to Baltimore on Feb. 26 and spend the weekend. I think that I will go. If it is O.K. with you, I will ask Mary Jean up to the Harvard hockey game and swimming meet on Saturday, Feb. 13. That is about the only time that I can see will be vacant, right now."

Not so fast. Mrs. Campbell was putting Buster up to a Mary Jean encounter? Then with polished southern manners, of course he planned to reciprocate. I doubt my dad went to Baltimore, but I do know this: *"Mary Jean seemed to be quite pleased with Princeton, and wrote me that she also enjoyed the car trouble because it enabled her to take her first subway ride. She is a darned sweet kid and in another year will really be going around plenty. It's lucky that I met her this year."*

Here's hoping he was also lucky in what might represent a post Great Depression trading strategy, late 1930s. The family secret? *"According to your broker's statement which came yesterday you are the proud and happy (I hope) possessor of 1,300 Rossia Int'l; 300 Budd Wheel; and 100 U.S. Steel. Your debit balance is $5,065.13 including interest to date. I have also received your receipt for the $5,000 check sent to Goodbody and am saving both the receipt and the statement.*

If Budd and Rossia were doing as well as Steel none of us would have any kick coming. I don't think we have any kick coming anyway."

Speculation in the market? U.S. Steel, a safe bet, but with the others they took "the kick" straight to the knee. A February 1937 article in *Fortune Magazine,* titled "Pioneer Without Profit" told the story of Budd Wheel in a marginalized moment. If the Bedfords were in for the buy low, sell high long run it would all work out after the war. As for Rossia Int'l? I have no proof they lasted beyond 1942.

More recent history tells us Goodbody eventually blew it, too. How? Due to surging trade volumes in the late 1960s, a paperwork crisis in the then paper-based securities industry emerged. It's hard to imagine today, trading of stock certificates amounted to pushing real paper around. Merrill Lynch came to the rescue of customers of the Goodbody brokerage and prevented a snowballing loss of confidence among investors on Wall Street.

Kick the can of Wall Street down the road to Main Street half a century and subprime lending reveals the avarice of greedy ass hats. I ask, were their mothers proud?

Sad to say, they probably were. It was all about the money, honey.

The Big Taboo

Chapter Ten

A penny for your thoughts on the taboos of talking money. I grew up not wanting to talk about it. I blame that on the 1970s recessionary years and some damnable dinner table discussions. And you will recall my dad forewarned about my generation starting at the top and working its way down. He lived long enough to watch the occupy Wall Street movement on Fox News, fully resigned to the fact that we were people of the so-called 99%.

Am I over-generalizing when I say we Boomers were taught talk of money is inconsiderate, or at least awkward? A subject not tolerated in polite society? Off limits? Except within the family unit, I suppose. Or to commiserate about cost-of-living topics ranging from gas at the pump to college tuition. I don't have to point out that dollars and cents are already a recurring theme. And will continue to be.

The good news is this is history, these are facts, and I like sharing them. Possibly for cathartic reasons, but there is more to it.

Looking at the past to gain a perspective on family economics then and now contextually frames that subject into a circle-of-life theme. Read on and draw your own conclusions. Reflect on the roots of your own family's financial rollercoaster and your personal relationship with money. Heck, bring it up for book club discussion as a social experiment to see how your friends react!

From where I sit, there is no better way to learn than from a bad example—unless you don't know you have learned from a bad example. Especially when it comes to managing money.

Savvy? Let me explain.

I was not raised by Robert Hall shoppers. Who is Robert Hall, you ask? It was the name assigned to a low overhead department store, the nation's leading "no-frills" clothing chain. The Robert Hall happy, sappy radio jingles, touted offers of lay-away with months to pay. I sang along bobbing restraint-free in the back seat of our '62 Pontiac Tempest convertible, the way kids used to when wearing seat belts was optional (if the car had seatbelts at all—many didn't). Robert Hall stores stocked the neon banded double-knit polyester dresses of the day. Racks and racks, in all sizes, under industrial fluorescent lights. It wasn't so much a matter of pride, it just never occurred to my mom to shop there.

Until the recession hit in the mid-1970s, shopping with the Bedford family occurred in dignified department stores and specialty boutiques like the Buster Brown shoe store. Mr. Grobois, an immigrant merchant on Main Street in Boonton, the town next door, fitted my shoes with great care as a little girl. In some variant of Russian dialect punctuated with agreeable white-haired bobbing head nods, he emphasized proper fit in quality leather, patent leather, and PF Flyers, too. (My brain forever hard-wired to think of him wherever the smell of leather lingers in the air.)

Lay-away was not in my family's vocabulary. Robert Hall ranked with the other notable variety stores of the '60s, like Woolworths and Kresge's (forebear to Kmart). All of them served *penny-saved-penny-earned* people. Under my mom's wing, purchases in those haunts were pretty much limited to children's toys, the likes of Trolls, Twister, Silly Putty and Gumby, for a friend's birthday party present. My mom was shocked when, as a teen, I preferred ShopRite's store-brand yogurt over Dannon. She was a brand loyal *Skippy-over-Jif* kind of consumer. The emotional slap of Proctor and Gamble's *"Choosy Mothers Choose Jif"* was unveiled after the nest was empty.

Then in my young adult working life, when she found out I wore plastic heels from Kmart (they were inexpensive, and I didn't need shoe polish), she told me I'd ruin my feet. Mr. Grobois would be appalled, and so was she.

All of these conversations boil down to dollar-and-cent fundamentals.

In the end she was right about the Kmart heels, though I denied it when she pointed out the bunion on my right foot. By then the die was cast. Yes, I had regrets. Today I am a quality shoe snob favoring wide toe boxes to accommodate that deplorable protuberance. My footwear, always function and comfort over form, is strictly purchased when on sale.

Thankfully, financial literacy is part of the public-school curriculum today. And parents are possibly better equipped to have "the money talk" with their children—or not. With any luck smart financial decision-making will go over better than sex education in the 1960s and '70s, fueled in response to that free-love social movement of yesteryear. Are moms and dads ever fully prepared to bring these lessons home? One of my favorite authors, Malcolm Gladwell, says this: "We learn by example and direct experience because there are real limits to the adequacy of verbal instruction." Sadly, for my mom, when you are raised by "boat mail" verbal instruction is about all there is. Take this, for example.

L.M. Skinner, Rancagua – Sewell, Chile – Jan. 12, 1938

Dear Roberta,

I was just starting this boat letter when your air letter has just popped in and I've read it over, saying you need money.

Only pennies in her pocket? Indicator of a swell Christmas break.

I know your laundry bills are coming due – and lighting bills also – but I don't know what all else.

A house elf to lighten the laundry load?! In a generation shift, I pedaled to the laundromat. Pockets of quarters as ballast, I pinched a plastic basket in the rat-trap of my ten-speed. On the way home, jeans and t-shirts wrinkled in the crimp of a bungie cord. No sock left behind.

I think your vacation sounds interesting. Am glad you had a chance to see something of New York. And it was nice you had an opportunity to return to Lake Placid.

Lake Placid had hosted the Winter Olympics six years before. My mother toasted this undoubtedly festive white Christmas in the famed resort village. Meanwhile, Dottie traveled to Illinois where she celebrated the holiday with an Emma Willard prep school bestie and her family. Fun factor priority check: one of these places is not like the other.

Dottie's dilemma was that she had to find *somewhere* to light when the boarding school closed campus for the school break. Then my grandmother beat her brains out, *"kicked like a steer"* over the expense of a rail ticket to Chicago. Why? She anticipated Dottie would *"go back to Missoula to Auntie Alta's next summer."* For Grandma it was a purely practical matter. If Dottie could layover in Illinois for a week or two in summer, en route to Montana, there would only be one train ticket to buy. More than that, the imposition of Dottie spending weeks on end with Auntie Alta and Uncle Dix would be that much less.

Why didn't my aunt Dottie spend this Christmas vacation at the home of Auntie Rhea and Uncle Frank Huntington in Amsterdam, New York? It made practical sense. Their place was convenient; only about forty miles from Emma Willard.

Grandma divulged this family secret. It explained two things. First, why Dottie went to Illinois. Second, why my Grandpa Skinner buckled to pay for the rail ticket:

Daddy figures Auntie Rhea isn't as fond of Dorothy as she is of you and he hates to force Dorothy upon them. (Don't repeat this to the Huntington's though – for goodness sake, will you?) It isn't that he favors Dorothy or chooses to do more for her or give her more trips than you but it's just that it worries him to have to feel dependent on the Huntingtons for a place for Dorothy to "put up during vacations." One cannot exactly blame Dorothy for not being crazy about being there either, where she realizes they care less for her than for you.

A backhanded way to say she's grateful my mom stands in with Auntie Rhea and Uncle Frank. But how very sad for Dottie.

We just haven't the money that we could be shooting three children all over on the railroad for such a short vacation as Xmas was... look at it reasonably 'til you're finished college and a little bit of these tremendous expenses let up.

Then more dollars and common sense.

You speak you would like to come down to Chile and see us next summer. You know for the terribly short time a student has when you get down here, it isn't anywhere near worth the cost of the trip – better to wait until you are finished college.

The party line of parents in Campamento Americano was this: The cost of passage from the U.S. was nothing short of eight-hundred dollars. Concealed behind the force multiplier of practicality she convinced herself and Robin it was best to delay a visit. To lessen the blow, Grandma rationalized like a travel agent.

Being in Chile's winter time you couldn't see any of the southern part of Chile which is the most beautiful part – one can only go there in January and February as it pours and rains during all the other months especially in June – July – August and Sept. They can't even use automobiles and you couldn't cross the Andes to Buenos Aires, which one would want to do if you were making a trip down here – you should see all of South America – both coasts. The East Coast is by far more interesting than this West Coast. So we have always felt it would be far wiser for you to wait until you've finished college and can spend six months at least and come in Chile's summer time. You need to be able to speak Spanish before you take a trip down here, also. So there's something to work on. I certainly hope you can all three come down to Chile, some day after we get you through college, with your degrees.

With the intercontinental journey scrapped, Grandma picked up with an arithmetic lesson. Basic as balancing a (now primitive) checkbook she advised: *You know you ought to subtract your expenses from your balance each month, so we can see just how much balance you have for the following months.*

I don't know whether you had a debit balance of $8.90 (in the hole) to begin your January 6 – February 6 account with. I hope you weren't there without a cent and owing $8.90 at the beginning of January.

By all indicators, the high-end holiday ate a hole straight through the bottom of my mom's pocketbook.

Well - you're learning how to keep expense accounts, and that's something. Practise makes perfect.

Except money *management* basics are lost on my mom. Rather than calling her eldest daughter on the carpet to reign in, she described the pitiable circumstances of her lot in life. Then signed off.

I have an infected thumb now (well, on the mend at present), but I can hardly write with the bandage on. I think I got dirt in a crack in the skin – working in the garden... Almost 6 weeks of my vacation is over and where the time has gone to I don't know. It isn't really a vacation. I still have to run two jobs all through the summer – the laundry and the guest houses so no wonder the time is flying. I just dread the thought of 40 weeks of school opening - three jobs on my hands is too terribly heavy. I just can't seem to get rested a bit, feel just as tired out as I did when school closed and this year's school work is going to be still heavier than last.

I hope you can read these hen tracks. Hugs and kisses, Mother

Two days later, an emergency check was sent airmail, to the rescue.

L.M. Skinner, Rancagua – Sewell, Chile – Jan. 14, 1938

Dear Roberta,

I'm sending this air to send this check you were asking for. It hurts me to pay .40 and .50 [cents] for air letters. The rate has been reduced from the States to .40 – but from this end the price remains unchanged. Your second semester tuition has been sent, so you won't need to be anxious about that... Since you wrote saying you *were at rock bottom, I thought I'd better hurry this $50.00 along. Will it cost you $1 to get this cashed?*

Can you think of what you can do this summer?

Like get a job?

Have you made any inquiry about that music course offered at Smith for six weeks in summer? We don't want you to drop your music entirely. You'll get so you can't play at all if you go without doing something with it. That would be something for you to do and a place to hang out – without being around Amsterdam at Auntie Rhea's all the summer.

Love Mother.

P.S. You must always endorse your checks just as your name is written on the face of the check, otherwise they won't cash it for you. Always look at the front before you endorse it on the back.

Malcolm Gladwell was spot on when he said, "We learn by example and direct experience." And in more ways than we know, or want to admit, we are guided by those who have gone before us.

Henny Penny

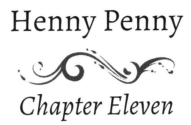

Chapter Eleven

L.M. Skinner, Rancagua – Sewell, Chile – Feb. 8, 1938

Dearest Roberta,

We didn't receive any letter direct from you on the last boat.

Nope, just that air letter that asked for money.

Auntie Rhea enclosed one of your little typewritten notes to her, written after you had gone back to school the first week in January (when you had been there only a few days) and you said you had so much to do. I know what that is with any daily schedule here, to have one thing after another crowding me and not enough hours in the day to get things turned off, so I can make allowances for you not writing. We received a regular volume from Dorothy.

I think about my own unsettled working-mother gut managing my children every school break. I had lots in my favor: small town, safe neighborhood, their dad's office three minutes away, all of us lived under the same roof. And yet I was stressed?

It's about any port in a storm. We are at our wits end to know what to do with Russell and Dorothy during vacations – because Huntingtons have told us point blank they aren't keen about them being there – especially in Russell's case!

Grandma tossed out more ideas for my mom. Music and typing were a constant, then she leapt to this: *Why not inquire in the office, or of your class Dean, whether some other college gives a summer-school, even Cornell or Syracuse, or some others where you could go to take a regular summer school course.*

Were the dorms open?

I would like to get you and Dorothy started on Spanish. If you ever want to take a trip down here you should be able to speak Spanish well, before you attempt the trip alone.

The three little sponges missed out on what could have been a rich bilingual experience in their early childhood. English dominated Campamento *Americano* at the time they learned to talk.

Auntie Alta wrote something about feeling she should invite you there [Missoula] also, if Dorothy returned.

My lucky aunt spent summer 1937 in Montana. My mother fell dutifully in line "at home" with Auntie Rhea and Uncle Frank. Where was Skeeter?

So let's see if we can arrange something else for you this year. Don't you think so? Then you go to Missoula some other summer by yourself.

Dorothy gets to go back to Montana, this summer, too? Not fair.

After Dorothy gets in college and both of you possibly can get into some summer courses I hope we can ease up on Auntie Rhea some. She isn't well at all and we hate to feel we are making her load heavier by having you children there the entire 12 weeks.

Is Auntie Rhea sick?

A summer camp (private) costs as much as most anything any one could think of I guess – most of the private camps are around $300.00 and that's tremendous just for a life of recreation. If one is putting $300.00 into a summer school course it isn't so bad.

What? My mom would be twenty in a matter of months. Are we talking a health resort? Certainly not a fat farm or substance abuse program the likes of which are relegated to conversational holes and corners today.

If Dorothy goes to Missoula again, I want her to go into the University of Montana summer school there. She couldn't enter last summer. They wouldn't accept her because she hadn't finished high school.

Ahead of her time, Grandma embraced the merit of Advanced Placement twenty years before the College Board.

I do so hope you made good in your mid-year exams. Even Auntie Alta wrote recently she did hope you were working, that she didn't want any of her relations to have the name of being kicked out of a college because they flunked their exams. The first and second year in any college is quite serious business, because the colleges all plan on weeding out the poorest students during the first two years. Mostly the first year. So a freshman and sophomore have to attend to business pretty strictly.

Like journal therapy, my grandmother spilled ruminations all over the stationery. Pray she exorcised her distress through the tip of her pen.

Daddy and I ran down to Santiago to get five days out of the altitude recently and then hurried back up to vacate our house to have it painted throughout. They don't use wallpaper here – walls and ceilings all painted. We moved into the house just above us – about 70 steps up – and with no moving vans or trucks you can feature what it means to carry everything by hand. I ran up and down flights of stairs for three days until I was about all in. It will take them at least 15 days to get the house finished and then we will have the same ordeal to get back into our house again.

As much as all the moving was a pain in the ass, I know from experience exercise is the best way to fix a worried mind. But it was a short-lived fix. Grandma acted like a piece of Swiss cheese. She stuffed all her holes with woe: *My school begins the first part of March. I don't know where the summer vacation is going to. But with two jobs to run right this vacation I have been busy. Of course haven't kept the late hours that I have to during the school year, when I have all my school work to do in the evenings, but I've had to put about 1 ½ - 2 hours into the flower work during these months. The yard has to have attention, so all in all I've been pretty occupied. Now I have to give up my 17 or 18 days with eight hours per day staying at the laundry to give the head woman her vacation. That has to be done before my school opens.*

At the age of forty-eight, Lelia was still young enough to physically handle the load, but exceedingly unhappy about towing the line emotionally. Were her personal educational aspirations for her children worth her sanity?

When we have your and Dorothy's college education finished, I hope to be able to let up a little and not be running three jobs. That drives me too much. I don't have a minute for letter writing or anything. And I don't like working until 11:30 every night for the nine-month school year either.

Write your little brother Skeeter once in a while, won't you?

Five weeks later, the shit hit the fan.

L.M. Skinner, Rancagua – Sewell, Chile – March 16, 1938

Dearest Roberta,

It is with sadness that I write this letter. The air mails have been flying back and forth between Miss Corwin and Huntingtons the past three weeks and Daddy and Mother are worried just sick. Miss Corwin says they have given us the most serious warning that Smith College gives – that if your work doesn't come up at least to the C grade they will ask us to remove you from college in June. Here you were writing us you were prepared for anything they sprang at you, before exams. Why do you kid us? Huntingtons – Dixons – and we will be so ashamed we won't know where to hang our heads if you are kicked out.

Like canaries in a coal mine, every living McLatchey clan member was choking.

I have told you all year that <u>all</u> colleges plan on weeding out their poorest students in the freshman and sophomore years. A student needs to buckle down and grind until past their 2nd year... Now here are the facts - we as parents demand that you cut out all social stuff – weekend pleasures and everything until you get up to a C level. Remember that – no parties – dances nor anything else.

Then she launched into the *"when I was in college"* lecture. Referring to her own mother (my great-grandmother, Tryphena "Marie" Baird McLatchey), she wrote: *Grandma would have said you can just come out of college if I hadn't kept my own work up.*

Recall, as a student in 1909 my grandmother had no choice but to mind her Presbyterian lay preacher of a mother Marie McLatchey. For heaven's sake, they lived under the same roof in Philly! Other than suffragette work, I'm not convinced the two women had any social life beyond church on Sunday.

It hurts like the dickens to pay out money for tutoring – but that's your last chance now. You ought to be ashamed with Daddy and Mother working the way we are until nearly 12 o'clock every night to have to see our hard earned money go for a tutor. It just seems you don't appreciate our efforts... Tutors at Columbia charge nearly $5.00 an hour and probably about that much at Smith. Now you stay there at Northampton Easter vacation and work like a dog. We wrote Miss Corwin we'd have you tutored in whatever subjects were necessary. Now if you need tutoring in math, get it. It is evident you'll have to work all summer and then have exams to take in the fall – before college opens, to see whether you can go into sophomore year or not... Get your mind off from boys – dances and everything as well as going places. Why didn't you stay there Xmas vacation and be tutored instead of going off to Placid?

Grandma has lost it! The answer is obvious. Campus was closed. There was nowhere to stay. Besides, no tutor would hang around over the holidays. Though I suppose her cousin Oscar Leroy "Roy" Huntington, son of Rhea and Frank, might have set himself to the task at home in Amsterdam. Dull as *that* would be.

I don't know when you are going to wake up to the fact that there are serious things in life – and not all good times and fun. Now perk up – don't get discouraged, dig in and show everybody that you can make the grade. It needs a stiff upper lip but you've got to do it... Shut that radio off, and don't turn it on again before June!

No way! Music in the background is the magic that keeps me relaxed and on task. Seems it did the same for my mom. Though in my teen years she was quick to shout "turn it down" over the bass rhythm that thumped through my bedroom wall.

Daddy and I seem to be the ones that have to pay the penalties... We need every cent saved up to try to get Daddy up to the States this year. Now he'll probably say he can't go with all this extra expense...Now is no time to consider our vacation – at this point if you don't have tutoring you'll be thrown out and that's a nice disgrace upon us all. It is about time you considered your parents something other than money making machines. Now show whether there's any metal in you or not. I'll try and keep money in Auntie Rhea's hands for this extra expense – keep in touch with her.

Mother

Inflamed words in a shadowboxing bout! Grandma went all out, toe-to-toe... *buckle down and grind, cut out all social stuff, no parties – dances nor anything else, work like a dog, work all summer, get your mind off from boys as well as going places, wake up to the fact that there are serious things in life – and not all good times and fun.*

All of that, peppered with guilt: *worried just sick, so ashamed, you don't appreciate our efforts, no time to consider our vacation.*

My mom countered the family firestorm in short order. Grandma turned her own comeback around like a completely different person.

L.M. Skinner, Rancagua – Sewell, Chile – March 26, 1938

Dearest Roberta,

Your air letter received yesterday – saying you had pulled up your chemistry mark to a B – congratulations! Of course you can do good work when you apply yourself. That's what I wrote Miss Corwin that you had never been among the lowest in your classes and there was no real excuse for it now. But OH! My child, it's much more difficult to <u>pull up low marks</u> than it is to do a good grade of daily work all the time.

Here we go again.

I think you have learned it by now or will have, by your sophomore year, and from now on do good work each day, then college work is not difficult.

Bullshit. Parents forget how difficult college work is. The same way women forget about the pain of childbirth.

Now about summer schools – if you will agree to go to Harvard and attend to your business and not be chasing into Boston Daddy says for you to register there instead of Cornell. We feel you are too young to be in New York by yourself – it's too big a city.

It's a short chase from Harvard Yard to Boston Common. Harking back to Robert McCloskey's *Make Way for Ducklings*, I agree with Grandma. It was a safe place for Mrs. Mallard, her eight ducklings and my mom. But did Grandma not know that Cornell University is in Ithaca, New York? Hardly a big city. Despite the mixed messaging, her preference for Harvard was clear: *Are the classes in the summer school for women at Harvard proper (or at Radcliffe the women's part of Harvard)? Possibly during the summer months these classes are on a co-educational basis. You must get about registering right away and be sure Miss Corwin helps you in selecting your subjects. I doubt whether you will have time for music – but do try and work in typing, if it doesn't take too much time from your studies. As soon as you get a catalogue of Harvard summer school, let us know how much the tuition will be and when it has to be paid.*

Love and luck in your work, Mother

L.M. Skinner, Rancagua – Sewell, Chile – April 2, 1938

Dearest Roberta,

Well about another month has passed. I wonder how your grades stand now. I feel sorry for you with all that stiff work – but after all it was nobody's fault but your own for letting your grades slough off that way. I do hope you have learned your lesson and from now on until you graduate your daily work will be good.

A check to be paid with the filing of her course card for sophomore year at Smith was enclosed with this letter. Then more about summer school at Harvard.

I have no idea how much those big Universities charge for summer school tuition. Daddy thought he paid about $80.00 at Columbia 25 years ago – but that's a long time ago.

Anyone want to compare college tuition costs? Not me. How lucky are we today? Curious minds indulge in *free* courses from the comfort of home through the likes of *edX.org*. Let me recommend this one from Harvard: *Humanitarian Response to Conflict and Disaster*. Laudable curriculum. Let's make it mandatory for elected officials in all fifty states.

I wonder if you got to go to Washington for the weekend? I am afraid Miss Corwin wouldn't approve when you had that work to do.

Hmm. She was supposed to get her mind off from *"going places."* It's Miss Corwin's job to play bad cop. Grandma is wallowing in a half-cup of guilt, with a gallon of self-pity when she writes this: *Am glad you like Smith so well. It's a comfort, when parents can't be with their children, to know they are at least liking their daily life and surroundings. Oh! I am just praying for good health for another three years until one child at least is through college. Hope I won't get to feeling as miserable as Auntie Rhea has the past two years but living in an altitude it wouldn't be any wonder if I felt worse than she. Auntie Alta was so miserable also for about five years – too bad women have to be so afflicted at a time of life when they would like to be enjoying themselves a little bit. The days and nights are feeling like late fall here. I fear an early winter and just dread a long one. I have to get out so early mornings – 8:30 in winter, the stairs are never shoveled off.*

I am just swamped this weekend with the first month's test papers to correct – school report for the Government to make out and bookkeeping to do.

Love and hugs, Mother

Before you turn the page, I need to woman-up for a moment and do the menopause math. My great aunts were "afflicted" with that (naturally) unmentionable biological process.

Auntie Rhea, born in 1884, suffered "the change of life" at age 51. Still today, that is the average age of onset. Auntie Alta's womanly affliction lasted for five years; beginning, by my calculation, around 1930 at age 52. All normal. Personally, I think Alta, as the oldest, milked it for all it was worth. Sisters do that sometimes.

If the associated risk factors for heart disease and osteoporosis were within their scope of knowledge in the 1930s, they'd bury themselves fretting over that, too.

The symptoms haven't changed: Hot flashes with flushed skin, trouble sleeping due to night sweats, mood swings, vaginal dryness, sagging skin and lagging memory. Except that today a woman is permitted to openly fan through a flash, wear performance sportswear in place of pajamas to wick away night sweats and sample a myriad of wrinkle and bleaching creams an aging beauty can "trust."

One easy solution; go with whatever Oprah knows for sure.

Building Castles in the Air

Chapter Twelve

The distinctly rich scent and full grain genuine leather feel of my mom's "Five Year Diary," embossed in shiny gold leaf, resembles a pocket Bible, five and one-half inches tall, four and one-quarter inches wide. At one time the sturdy gold lock kept out prying eyes.

The latch, a solid seventy-five years old, invited me in with a solid, tidy click.

No time wasted trying to pick the lock. An inscription inside left no doubt: "This Book Belongs To" <u>Roberta Skinner</u> "Date" <u>September 23, 1938</u>. A gold metallic ribbon bookmarked a moment in time. The ruled pages document half a decade of her coming of age. Structured as a comparative record of events, my mom could revisit any given day looking back to the year (or years) before.

And more than three quarters of a century later, so could I.

It took personal diligence and sheer nosiness to grasp her tiny enlightening entries scripted in now faded pencil, juxtaposed with still vibrant fountain pen. This little black book became my DeLorean time machine. Like Marty in *Back to the Future* I dug deeply into the circumstances preceding and surrounding the meeting of my parents. My folks told me their fairy tale version, but what kid listens attentively (let alone retains) the reminiscent speak of their parents' courtship? Squirming through the wormhole I uncovered, I hovered over a credit card magnifier to bring the essence of my mom's being into focus. Forensically speaking, I'm darn lucky that my own story exists. One of many reasons I am spurred on to tell theirs.

Mom covered a lot of territory between the ages of eighteen and twenty-one. What girl doesn't? Look over your shoulder and recount your own coming of age. Her penned entries began with sophomore year at Smith. The academic crisis had calmed but was far from over. My aunt Dorothy joined the fray as a freshman that year, in the class of "Cute '42s." The young men coming and going in their lives were like hummingbirds to a feeder. Some wing whistled in for a quick snack, others displayed big attitude defending their sweet claim. If my mom held up a mirror I swear there would be one guy or another hovering behind her nearly every waking moment. Ditto for my double-dating aunt.

Let me remind you, however, that one of my dad's hobbies was girls. Recall he predicted his date, Mary Jean, was expected to be "going around plenty." Well, my mom was going around good and plenty.

Like an amateur anthropologist visiting the tribal village of Smith to study its inhabitants, I've deconstructed a few fundamentals of my mother's pre-marital existence. You've picked up on "letters flying" and "the most serious warning that Smith College gives," which was the looming threat of removal from school at the end of her freshman year. In my mind's eye, Miss Virginia Corwin took on the image of Cloris Leachman in her role as Frau Blucher in Mel Brooke's *Young Frankenstein*. Did you hear the horse whinny? At my grandmother's suggestion my mom had a talk with Miss Corwin, several talks in fact, to point out weak points. Corwin told her B's were expected and *"The price of peace is eternal care."* Smith-speak to say, "Get your shit together, young lady!"

Meteorologists could not predict the biblical size and fury of the Great New England Hurricane of 1938 before it slammed into campus on September 21. At registration the day before, class schedules were revealed. Then the semester began like a flashlight adventure. Slashing winds uprooted trees. Power knocked out for two days led to further escapades such as hair-washing by candlelight. My mom and her new roommate, Lolly, bonded over shopping for white curtains with blue braids, now backlit by flickering hurricane lamp light in the windows of Wesley House. Dates canceled because *"hoodlums are loose."* The 1938 hurricane rates its own special disaster story on the History Channel—and my mom and aunt were there.

Was weather cosmically intended to bookend my mom's adult life? I found myself stranded in Denville, New Jersey, when Hurricane Irene barreled up the eastern seaboard and blasted North Jersey on August 28, 2011, ten weeks before she died. As my parents aged into their nineties, I'd occupied a guest room in the Franciscan Oaks Retirement Community with increasing frequency. That summer, my mom had taken up residence in the "health center" building. It was a permanent move for her at age ninety-two, due to a summer of unfortunate events: a fractured ischium ("sitz bone") in June, surgery for an emergency pacemaker in July, a broken humerus (upper arm) in August. There's more, but that's another story. After breakfast with my dad, my quest that morning of August 28 was to get from the independent living building to the health center to see Mom. Due to surrounding flood waters, buildings were on lockdown. No one was going anywhere. Except me.

Evading security, I snuck out an unalarmed basement door. I waded up to my crotch hugging the parking lot perimeter. Unidentifiable bits and pieces of floating debris surrounded me. All kinds of weird shit (figuratively speaking, but I didn't know it for a fact) bobbed in the muddy water. Sediment carried for miles in the upstream flood clung to my naked downstream legs. I emerged unscathed only to be berated by a self-important badge-wearing Jersey-tough dude with an attitude like The Fonz in *Happy Days*. As if an offense directed at him personally, I subjected myself to death by electrocution under his watch. Another overly concerned elderly woman nodded her head in agreement, warning me of snakes on the loose, too.

At the health center, I made my way upstairs where I found my mom all in for the excitement. The sheeting rains had subsided. I wheeled her out the door to the fourth-floor balcony, pulled up a chair and held her hand while we surveyed the disaster scene. Her wavy auburn hair (trending red tones, never gray) blew wildly in concert with convective wind gusts. We watched a kayaker paddle purposefully across what, the day before, was a field in a (now obvious) flood plain. Water coursing, the neighboring Rockaway River exploded well beyond its banks submerging Pocono Road and the parking lot below. Except for pedestrian crosswalk lights that stood like sentries on their posts it was impossible to tell where the road was exactly. Nurses on graveyard duty, in a precautionary measure, moved their cars from the staff lot to higher elevation in the calm before the storm. Powers that be "permitted" parking on higher ground in the otherwise restricted visitor lot. By morning, flood waters crept right up to their windshields.

Like the 1938 storm, trees snapped and uprooted. Branches, ripped from stately oaks, and took down power lines. The entire grid blew. We were thankfully in a safe harbor of backup generators. Burning candles in an elder care environment might fire up their own headlines.

It took the National Guard, maneuvering monster troop transport trucks, to ferry in fresh staff for the long overdue shift change. By then approaching seventy-two hours, the evacuated workers loaded and waved a weary goodbye, already anticipating their own personal disasters ahead at home.

If my mom silently reminisced the Great New England Hurricane of 1938 while living through those balcony moments near the end of her life, she didn't utter a word about it. I love her all the more for never growing too old for thrill-seeking. The prattling amongst the residents went on for days, but for my mom, it was simply another splendid adventure.

Far from a disaster story, I judge my mom's college experience (based on me nosing around in her diary) as one of intellectual excellence given the caliber of the institution. And it is clear to me that the role of faith was central to cultivating moral integrity. I had to open my heart and mind to untangle a few thematic strings transcribed in her little black book; morning chapel and evening vespers, dating, favorite hangouts, school clubs, and sports. She weathered the storms of life bobbing and weaving like a surf champ.

For example, let me synopsize the curious content of Chapel at Smith College in 1938. Here, the girls tuned into a mosaic of current events and persuasive essays delivered by college presidents, faculty, and esteemed visiting dignitaries. Moral, political, and religious issues were all fair game. Here is a sampler of spliced content; what my mom noted: *"Went to chapel - European situation was reviewed. Praise was given for Czechs for a peaceful settlement."*

This entry was October 3, 1938, six days after FDR wrote to Hitler seeking a peaceful resolution to the threat of war in Europe starting with the invasion of Czechoslovakia. That "peace" lasted for five months after which Hitler's troops invaded and occupied Czechoslovakia anyway. The rest, as they say, is history.

On Sunday, October 30, 1938, my mom completely missed Orson Welles' *War of the Worlds* radio broadcast. Here is what her day looked like: *"Got up at 9:30. Telegram from Jack. Breakfast with Bill. Walked for a while then put him on bus. Thank God! He is so uninteresting – grrr. Mr. Niebuhr spoke in Vespers about our faith in the Christ and un-Christ factors in world today – our sleep and drunkenness – in force of triumph of evil factors in Europe today. Went out with Bob and Louis and Dottie – Bob gave me back my ring – Homesteader."*

So rather than get caught up in an alien invasion, my mom was caught up in Mr. Niebuhr's Christian perspective on political thought. All while being entangled in one form or another with Jack, Bill, Bob, and Louis, my aunt "Dottie" sparkling by her side.

"Mr. Niebuhr," (the noted theologian Reverend Reinhold Niebuhr, Doctor of Divinity, Union Theological Seminary in New York) was the type of thinker to challenge these young women in a stirring sermon along these lines: "Seek the ultimate meaning of life; trust in divine providence."

His Old Testament insight went far beyond the "Jesus loves me" lessons I learned in Sunday School. His text that day was Psalm 73, a litmus test for faith in God and purity of heart: "For I envied the arrogant, when I saw the prosperity of the wicked…"

Hitler's un-Christ and arrogant Aryan "master race" and indoctrinated underling "Hitlerjungen" called forth fervent patriotism teamed with racist ideology. The power of these twin Nazi ideals became "enviable" evil factors in Europe, as preached by Reverend Niebuhr that day. Psalm 73 continues in part:

"They have no struggles; their bodies are healthy and strong.

They are free from common human burdens; they are not plagued by human ills.

Therefore pride is their necklace; they clothe themselves with violence.

From their callous hearts comes iniquity; their evil imaginations have no limits.

They scoff, and speak with malice; with arrogance they threaten oppression…."

The truth is, Welles' *War of the Worlds* foreshadowed the tactics and strategy of what Hitler would plan and deliver in the form of the London Blitzkrieg. Both events demonstrated the powerful, instinctive human emotion of fear that underscores today's world, and remains a global constant. Unless a person lives underground in a remote region like the Australian outback, the politically alarming madmen that currently exist in our all-to-often misaligned world are far more unnerving than any alien, human or otherwise.

In her October 1938 *monthly memoranda* diary section, my mom wrote of Dean Marjorie Hope Nicolson. A professor of English Literature at Smith, Dean Nicolson brilliantly unveiled relevant facts regarding the importance of a liberal arts education in occasional Chapel talks. Her delivery carried a lofty, scholarly message. It imprinted on my mom as if she were a baby duck: *"Liberal arts gives us a chance to become acquainted with the past in an understanding of the present…." "Learn ye the truth, for the truth shall make you free" "…chance to glorify the gifts of reason." "I Will! Keep building castles in the air – Keep building castles in the air."*

Let me take a crack at my own interpretation of Dean Nicolson's Chapel talk. After all, her words ultimately impacted me personally as a teen on the hunt for an institution of higher learning.

Around the dinner table at the Crane Road house, my dad repeatedly lectured on the importance of a liberal arts education. And my mom stood by him on that point. The words *"You must be able to think for yourself,"* were accompanied by his fore and middle fingers tapping the table like a metronome in quarter time. They punctuated the profound effect that he believed a liberal arts school would have on my success. It was his preface to my perusing the College Board's *College Handbook*. In the early 1970s that was the go-to resource for comparison shopping. I poured over institutional descriptions, state by state. I determined whether my rather mediocre SAT score met the threshold, and then read about such things as "student life." It began as a process of self-selection that became heavily weighted by parental influence. I expect most college-bound Boomers felt the same way.

Just the mention of "liberal arts" manifests bullet points in my brain like coded data. To name a few: cultivating the mind, logical analysis, problem solving, critical thinking, effective communication, sincerity, integrity, connecting the dots. In the end it all adds up to intellectual ability to ensure social responsibility. That outcome meant a lot to my parents, and my grandparents, and as far as I can tell, the forebears in the whole family tree.

Though I knew nothing about the family tree at the time.

So without much wiggle room, like my siblings before me, I followed the liberal arts college track. My brother Bob (Princeton '64) and my sister Dianne (Skidmore '70) were resigned to that predictable route, as the first and second born, at a time when my parents could afford it. My near-Irish twin Dorothy (Princeton '78) was so primed and prepped that she wrote a letter of interest to that all-male institution at the age of twelve, acting on the news that University President Robert F. Goheen believed co-education was just a matter of time. The admissions office kindly replied with a letter asking her to re-apply when she was a little older. The first women under-graduates were admitted in 1969. In 1974 an unflappable Dorothy arrived to build her own castles on the gender imbalanced campus.

I restlessly landed at Skidmore, as if required to complete a choral refrain repeat in the family sing-along.

Reflecting further on Dean Nicolson's Chapel talk, *"the truth will set you free"* was a common saying in academia. It's what Jesus said in *John 8:32* and it's gained traction in many applications since. Notably, Gloria Steinem nailed it with the grit of an activist: "The truth will set you free, but first it will piss you off."

As for Dean Nicolson's Chapel talk reference to *"building castles in the air"*? Coincidentally, it was the theme of Aaron Burr's commencement oration when he graduated from Princeton at the age of 16. Burr dreamed about success in 1772. So did the Smith girls in 1939. Though in '39 a success-ful husband might do equally well. As a known advocate of higher educa-tion for women, I hoped this was not the message Dean Nicolson was trying to convey. Matching her words of inspiration, picture this chapel scene: young women melded like an untamable force singing with raised voices in harmonized parts. My mom loved to sing, an alto crossing into tenor, as needed in the absence of male voices. Were the songs more prayerful during exam week? Something along the lines of *Be Still My Soul?*

With respect to my Skinner grandparents, guilty in absentia, they wanted "their girls" to attend schools where the student population was "relatable." An assignment to a dorm room, conscripted to share living quarters, adds to the drama of uncertainty for all college-bound kids. As my mom adored her roommate, Lolly, it happened, I adored my "roomy," Pam, too—though shopping for curtains never dawned on our to-do list. She, a P.E. major, introduced me to the delicacies of cheese blintzes and baklava. Her care packages were over-shared with me. The adage "one minute on the lips, forever on the hips" led to a fast "freshman 10." But, damn, we had our step, tap, turn, slides totally down in choreographed line dancing to the funk sound of Stevie Wonder's *Higher Ground*. We completely agreed on our dislike for disco, simply refusing to *Do the Hustle*.

Even so, I only lasted one school year at Skidmore College. There the young men from Williams, Colgate, Cornell and Rensselaer Polytechnic Institute (that's RPI, east coast competitor to MIT and other nationwide poly rivals) extended their learning well beyond the classroom at the "mixers" on our predominantly female campus. The parallels between my mom at Smith and me at Skidmore ended there. You will come to better understand that the student population at Smith was relatable for her— Skidmore not so much for me. I was not a daddy's girl spending daddy's money. Nope. Not looking for a ring, nor the MRS degree that went along with it.

With transferring on my mind early in the academic year, I hunkered down on my studies taking the classes I knew would carry transfer credit. It was a 4:1:4 academic calendar, meaning that the month of January we picked one focus class. While others traveled abroad building castles in the air, I stayed on campus and took *"Library Research Techniques."* How dull is that? In my unique and intuitive way of finding my own truth, I set myself free and transferred to the University of Utah as a sophomore.

Enough of my 1970s reminiscence. What were the takeaway action points in a 1939 marriage forum? Those over-the-moon qualities of a prospective wife? *"Emotional stability, maturity and a good disposition,"* so noted my mom in her diary. Respectable, Pollyannaish qualities over the long haul. I laugh, visualizing a black cast iron enameled metal trivet set over the fireplace in the basement of the Crane Road house inscribed with: "Beyond every successful man stands a woman telling him what to do." True that.

At Chapel in March of 1939, my mom took note of *"A line for '5 nights' drawn."* Curfew! She repeatedly confessed her tardiness returning from one date, then another. A definite pattern. Five nights was the new limit. The law laid down in no uncertain terms. Glad she paid attention enough to write it down. As far as I can tell it didn't change her behavior.

Let me add to that her Chapel note *"$100 added to tuition = $1,100."* A 10% increase reported like the "business" portion of a church worship bulletin, talking about a blood drive, poking at another vein for the cost of college.

Based on the content of my mother's diary I was inspired to turn to the Smith College website. At the end of her sophomore year, here's what she wrote on May 3, 1939: *"At chapel this morning President Nielson talked about our motives in social contacts – belonging to best set, etc."* Those were parting words of this esteemed president's tenure. It made sense, of all the available clubs on campus, the *savoir-faire* of "Cosmopolitan Club" was a natural match for my mom. If the cosmopolitan quest was to unite a community, morally and socio-politically in some manner or another, she appeared to be in lock-step with President Nielson. Her life experience was worldly enough. The direct result of an early childhood in Rancagua, Chile, and formative years on the West Coast in California. Blend that with the teachings of her preacher grandmother, Marie McLatchey, and watch out. As a free-thinking, modern young woman, she was well suited to serve on the admissions committee of Cosmopolitan Club. Making it her business to recruit, she'd convinced Lolly to join, too.

Here is how the Smith College website remembers President Nielson:

William Allan Neilson, 1917-1939

President William Allan Neilson transformed the college from a high-minded but provincial community in the hinterland of Massachusetts into a cosmopolitan center constantly animated by ideas from abroad.

Following Nielson's departure, Mrs. Dwight Morrow (better known as Elizabeth Cutter Morrow) became the first woman to lead the college as acting president from 1939 – 1940. *"Awfully sweet and nice,"* according to my mom at the beginning of the year. But at Chapel four months later she wrote, *"Mrs. Dwight Morrow spoke and said, 'Onward Valiant Girls'."* A fired-up message, spoken with gusto, and what I would expect of the mother of Anne Morrow Lindbergh – herself a graduate of Smith in the class of 1928.

In retrospect, my mom was an *onward valiant girl* kind of mother to my sisters and me.

Like a fly, my eyes compounded, revisiting the subjective college experience she shared through her own words. It gets to the heart, the essence, of the way in which my mom operated in her world, then, and more importantly, for a lifetime.

At first I felt a bit tripped up sorting out her use of honorifics (Mr. ... Miss...Mrs.) in her diary entries about Chapel. Growing up in Mountain Lakes, I was expected to use the courteous formality of Mr. and Mrs. with the parents of my friends. Although my folks were cool with Mr. and Mrs. "B." It occurred to me that once I left high school, I rarely "properly" addressed most teachers that way again. Even though "Ms." had made its mark as an acceptable calling card with the feminist movement, I was on first name basis with more than one Skidmore college professor. Maybe the script-writers behind the disingenuous Eddie Haskell, addressing Mrs. Cleaver like such a suck up on *Leave it to Beaver*, had a hand in the demise of that propriety. Here's my theory. The East Coast ends in the fictitious town of Mayfield, Ohio, where Eddie displayed the Ohio State pennant on his bedroom wall. The Mid-West begins the next state over. In a fact-check on this point, my respectfully polite and friendly confidants from the heartland tell me they kept up with the honorific formalities through college. Proof of our regional differences.

As for my dad's nickname "Buz," it got a lot of mileage in its homonym form among my friends: "get a buzz on" or "catch a buzz." Forgive me a fast flashback to Firesign Theatre's, *Don't Crush That Dwarf: Hand Me the Pliers.* Hello, dear friends, if you by-passed (or missed out due to your birth year) this troupe of four, look them up and live a piece of epic comedic history. Inane humor, along the lines of Cheech and Chong, served up on 1970s LP vinyl generally shared a smoke-filled room with a bong.

Respectful as they were in the late '30s, my mom wrote that Mr. Kochnick (possibly a political science prof) lectured on *"the value of true learning in present day world – here and in the totalitarian states in the future."* Kochnick also predicted *"this war will last longer than last,"* now validated by historical fact, with WWII lasting two years longer than The Great War, "the war to end all wars," a.k.a. WWI. And Mr. Ranshar, presumably a professor of philosophy, inspired his audience with these words: *"Know thyself – rational action. Value of true love and true loyalty. Desire to fight for what we believe in."* One of so many brilliant thought provoking memes, "Know Thyself," brought to us by Socrates, a personal hero of mine.

I cringe when I call to mind a 1970s memory of my mom tuned in and taking notes on index cards sitting in front of televangelist Dr. Robert Schuller's *Hour of Power* program. Schuller had her dialed in to *his* Chapel thirty years after she left Smith. My recall of his silver hair, aviator glasses, pointy nose, and clerical robes preaching to the world on TV from the Garden Grove Community Church (later the Crystal Cathedral) remain clear cut. While I bemoaned the '70s economic squeeze, she sent money to support a television empire that espoused "possibility thinking."

In retrospect, Schuller was a step above evangelists Jim and Tammy Faye "bleeding mascara" Bakker. Let's get serious about TV church for about two seconds so I can confess this. The one and only religious figurehead that would have me bellowing *How Great Thou Art* (through tears of hilarity) is the Church Lady. Thank you, Dana Carvey and *Saturday Night Live.*

Cliff Note Beaus

Chapter Thirteen

Just before Thanksgiving 1938, my grandmother Skinner wrote to my mom with a hint of possibility thinking—a proposed trip west the following summer. Robin had grown into a disbelieving cynic. Her candid diary reaction? *"Haw Haw."* The consequence of too many hollow parental promises. The importance of a mother's companionship had been declared by Lelia in her letters. For years now, it amounted to all words and no action.

In back to back summers, Dottie had traveled west to Montana. An attractive, albeit wild child, she adapted well to summertime fun in and around Missoula, where Auntie Alta and Uncle Frank Dixon extended a hearty Western welcome. My mom, on the other hand, dutifully accepted her dull domestic assignment with Auntie Rhea and Uncle Frank Huntington in Amsterdam, New York. Their son (Robin's cousin) Leroy, eight years older than my mom, lived at home at the time.

A surrogate of an older brother, "Roy" stood five-feet eight inches; brown hair and eyes, a ruddy complexion. He'd graduated from Union College in the spring of 1933. Poor bastard. It's sobering to think how Prohibition stifled the social aspects of his college experience. Ratification of the Twenty-First Amendment came six months post-graduation. Then, tangled in one of the *worst* years of the Great Depression, Roy moved back into his parents' home in Amsterdam. He stayed put for years.

Union's *Garnet Yearbook* (named for the mining of industrial garnet in the region) fell short of a five-year diary like my moms, but it held clues to Roy's collegiate extracurriculars: The Lamda Chi Alpha brotherhood and Spanish Club. Perhaps he aspired to visit Campamento Americano one day. His membership in the "Mountebanks," (a cleverly baptized student drama group) and "The Philomathean Society" (a grand tag for the school's literary club) revealed personal interests. I considered his resume in a non-judgmental way, with an open mind. It's possible Roy was gay. If that were the case, he would not be the odd one out to stand alone in the family tree, like the cheese in the children's song *Farmer in the Dell.*

Moving off themes of Chapel-talk and sexual orientation, let's roll with the backstory on Robin's "going around plenty." A Cliff Note version. A sampling of choice cuts, so to speak. Thank goodness there were no online dating sites to swipe left or right.

I weighed the (one-sided) substance of eligible men prior to the time she met my dad. Had Buster not won her over, I'd be non-existent. Or, at best, genetically half the person I am. Their generational run-around was born of societal pressure to find a suitable mate. As her now grown, middle-aged daughter I appreciate why our dating rituals, divided by a generation, were very, very different.

Louis "Louie" Benton was a "townie." The one non-ivy leaguer of her lot, he came across with candid honesty. Even better, my mother thought enough about what he said to write it in her diary! Taking the long view of her short four years at Smith, Louie's abiding, unconsummated relationship with my mother struck me like the gift of an unveiled storyboard.

Initially, in her words he was *"nifty."* In turn, she believed he was *'fallin' tender."* Like Elvis the King crooning *"Love me tender, Love me sweet,"* had she made his life complete? Then he called her out. *Louie said I'm greedy about men - also that I have some bad habits – won't tell me 'em. But then he did! I've got a position to maintain – not a waitress one either. Doesn't like my picking up strange men à la college girl type – they're vultures! Aren't out for anybody's good. People don't talk about it – but jump to conclusions very rapidly.*

He had a point. My grandmother would ditto that sentiment. As her daughter without any say at all, I agree.

Louie admitted, *"I'm a regular guy."* *Likes me when I kiss him – I'm lovely – Ought to commercialize my face.*

Exploit her looks for profit? If he was a "regular guy," any relationship with a model the likes of those blooming from the Powers' Modeling Agency was unlikely.

At the end of sophomore year... *Great discussion about our possible marriage problems. Wonders whether I have any scruples or know difference of right or wrong. Decided to wait two more years before getting married. Guess he needs me.*

In what way did he *need* her? Woo! Waiting two more years before getting married coincided with my mom's graduation – a serious indicator of what the future might hold.

Thanksgiving of 1939 was spent at the home of Louie's parents. Later, *Louie said his mother liked me. I'm sure he likes me now. Got hold of a rumor about our engagement.*

The following spring played like ping-pong. He scolded her! *I'm not honest with myself or other people – just rationalize - too selfish. Should grab somebody now. Don't wait till after college. Too hard to make friends then.*

More on Louie to come.

Moving to door number two, Jack was a Dartmouth man who, as far as I can tell, steadily dated my mom through 1939. There was some definite undertow between Jack and Louie. As it happened, Jack turned my Aunt Dottie's head. Or maybe Dottie turned his, *not so coincidentally about the time Robin met Buster.* It's possible my mom was an enabler, a matchmaker that sparked the fire between Dottie and Jack in January of 1940. But then Dottie and Jack's relationship fell apart five months later, on June 1, 1940, when Jack found out about her long-distance romance with Bud, my uncle to be. Her man from Montana.

Poor Jack with that shape of an "L" on his forehead. Are you keeping up with me here?

To fully convey the pre-WWII Smith dating scene, I picked apart a few other young men on my mother's college dance card. Rewind to December 1939, when my mom called out Glenn Miller's *In the Mood*, as *"a pagan love song."* For me, a reliably solid 1970s Crosby, Stills, Nash and Young, *Change Partners*, better described it.

Next was Ossie, a Williams man. He impressed the bobby socks off my mom in April 1939. This was serious. By the end of May, she'd given him her Emma Willard prep school ring. The ring, according to school tradition, symbolically binds Emma girls together. For that summer of '39, it was most certainly a sign of affection binding her to him. Sort of. In a reciprocal move at the beginning of June, he gave my mom his fraternity pin, her very first. Need I point out this was at the same time she and Louie were talking marriage?

Now you know what Louie was ranting about.

Mom eventually found out what the scene was with Ossie in November of '39; *"another girl! Eleanor."* Ossie's summer love? It's a relevant, raise your hand, coming of age theme that's crossed generations.

Then there was Bob Pearmain, a Cornell man. The flower-sending type, with a beautiful voice on the phone. And his mother was *"sooo sweet."* Bob arrived on the scene in October 1938 and stayed a player until February of 1940. So by my calculation, Jack, Louie, and Ossie were all in the mix along with Bob.

But wait...there's more.

Greg was another young man from Williams. He entered the fray in April of 1939. When my mom tied the lyrics of Benny Goodman's number one hit *"And the Angels Sing,"* to Greg, he became a noteworthy entry in her black book. *"We meet, and the angels sing..."* she wrote like a woman in love. *"The angels sing the sweetest song I ever heard... You speak, and the angels sing...."* yadda, yadda, yadda. Then it took a turn: *"Greg came down tonight. Had good time at Toto's. He's too attentive."*

Attentive is not a bad quality. They played tennis and attended movies with variety: *The Saint Strikes Back*, the second of nine films in *The Saint* series, and *The Little Princess*, starring child star, Shirley Temple, filmed in Technicolor. (To this day, curled up on the couch with a bowl of popcorn, I am a huge TV re-run fan of that cunning Simon Templar, played by Roger

Moore in the 1960s TV series *The Saint*.) Their personal parties often left my mom with a headache: *"Went out with Greg and tied one on at Tavern, Joe's, and Toto's. Too strenuous for little Robin."* Then this: *"Greg came down from Williams tonight – was very bored at Wayside– three Tom Collins – Too much."*

The show with Greg came to a screeching halt with a "Dear Jane letter," following the Williams Winter Carnival. My mom's diary read like a good time in a 1940s movie; jazz pianist Teddy Wilson's orchestra at the dance, *"Not the usual rush-rush."* In other words, sophisticated and elegant? *"Intermission in Greg's Room for scotch."* Only my mom knows what happened there, but February 5, 1940, came to this: *"Letter from Greg stating we were through. Wrote him a thank-you note. It was rather an unhappy weekend."*

Did she get too loose in Greg's room, or he too forward? Or did she humiliate him by landing in someone else's arms on the dance floor? A note of thanks gave her the last word. Clever girl. No matter how bad the behavior, she remembered her good manners.

Bruce was the third young man from Williams. Bruce played tennis, skied, had a nice family, talked eastern picket fences and always showed my mom a good time. September 17, 1939, had this to offer: *"Dinner at Louis Sherry's on Park Avenue. Saw finals of Forest Hills tournament. Bobby Riggs beat Van Horn three straight sets. Alice Marble beat Helen Jacobs in three sets 6-0, 6-8, 6-4."*

No small tournament. In 1939, it was The U.S. National Championships where players competed on grass courts. We know it today as the U.S. Open for tennis.

"Bruce left immediately. Louie came for evening. Left at 1:00."

Yep, there's Louie again.

But then, on January 23, 1940, she wrote, *"Went skiing over in Greenfield with Bruce all afternoon – Dinner at Weldon – Home with our usual wrestling!"* After which Bruce was summarily dismissed from any further diary entries.

Another in this cast of characters, nicknamed Wendy, came swinging into the scene on New Year's Eve, ringing in 1939. For good reason, Wendy (short for Wendell, clearly a man secure with his masculinity) quickly ranked among the "man score" top five. Telegrams and letter-writing connected the two between New York and Northampton.

By all accounts, Wendy brought the Big Apple to life for my mom; Radio City Music Hall, Greenwich Village, Longchamp's Restaurant on Madison Avenue where they savored saucy continental cuisine amidst fashionable art deco, with red, black, yellow and gold color palate mirrored into infinity. According to Mom's diary, following drinks at The New Yorker Wendy escorted her to The Savoy Ballroom, a hotspot on Lenox Avenue. Known for its anti-discrimination policies, The Savoy served a connected Black community where folks cared more about avant-garde dance dynamics than skin color. The huge space with pink walls, mirrors and a bandstand at each end of the ballroom accommodated a crowd of 4,000. How? It spanned a full city block between 140th and 141st Street. There, Wendy took my mom's hand and led her out with his best Lindy-hop dance moves in a Harlem light years different from the one I knew in the 1970s. On another date he took her to Hickory House on 52nd Street in Manhattan, an internationally famous restaurant that specialized in sizzling steaks and cool music. There they saw Louis Prima and "The King of Swing" Orchestra. All *"Loads of fun!!"* she wrote.

Devilishly understated by my mom, Wendy was a good dancer, skier, and movie aficionado. Together they saw *In Name Only* starring Carole Lombard and Cary Grant; *The Rains Came*, starring Myrna Loy and Tyrone Power; *The Real Glory* with Gary Cooper and David Niven. Historically, 1939 is one of the most remarkable years in Hollywood history for releasing quality, iconic movies. My mom, a great fan of cinema, was counted among the throngs boosting ticket sales for first-run classics.

At this point, it's important for you to understand the method my mom invented to keep track of how the men in her life stacked up. Her entry on February 18, 1939, went like this: *"Brown boys arrived at 5:10. Was at fencing matches with Yale. Met Bob Johnson about 7:00. Quite nice. Dinner and danced at Toto's. Wonderful fun! Told Dottie about 'scoring situation' – thinks it's a good idea."*

I didn't quite understand what "scoring situation" meant here. In 1970s speak the definition of "score" was to have sex with a girl. My aunt Dottie thought it was a good idea. Not me. We're talking about my mom, after all.

But then the "scoring situation" was revealed in her June 1939, memoranda:

Man score in order to date – Ossie, Bruce, Jack, Louie, Bill Hoblitt, Wendy.

And then again in August!

Man score: 1. Bill Hoblitt; 2. Ossie; 3. George; 4. Louie; 5. Wendy; 6. Bruce

That's some very telling diary dialogue right there.

When my parents advised me to "play the field" during my teen years I was shocked and quite frankly disgusted at their slutty suggestion. Did they secretly hope I'd fall for someone authentically Ivy bound in exchange for the long-haired free-thinking beaus I chose? Of course they did.

Therein lies proof of a perfect trifecta of gaps: communication, culture, generation, all the ingredients for a reactionary ethos under the roof at Crane Road. It gave me even more reason to filter my world through the ridiculousness of Firesign Theatre in a smoke-filled room.

By definition my mom and dad both "played the field." According to the rules of 1940, evidenced by the man score and all those diary drop-ins who never "ranked," my mom dated multiple guys at the same time. (Undoubtedly my dad got around, too, but I just can't substantiate the allegation because he didn't commit his antics to paper—beyond what he wrote his parents.) True, a more conservative culture governed their day with far stricter rules of etiquette and reasonable moral code. Good manners mattered. Think proper introductions, firm handshakes, "how do-you-do's," and dating in public places. (Was "parking" even a thing yet? A young man would need a car for that.) Part of the code included keeping their clothes on until the relationship was committed and exclusive. Often (swear to God, no crosses count) until their wedding night.

With my coming of age in the 1970s it's no secret the culture of "free-love" made dating more about sex. At the time we were clueless as to what was expected on a first date, except that girls were told to have "self-respect." We had to define that line for ourselves. People talked. Especially guys. Looking down long halls at Mountain Lakes High there was plenty of locker love happening. Until the administration adopted rules prohibiting "public display of affection." In anti-establishment backlash, that code of conduct only made corridor courtships all the more exciting. There was some satisfaction if a guy could get to "second base" under a girl's shirt during the three minutes between classes. It's the reason I chose for the most part to have "steady" boyfriends, one at a time, from the sixth grade on.

Starting with that game of spin the bottle in the basement.

Jump Back to the Summer of '39

Chapter Fourteen

O n June 17, my dad graduated with all the pomp and circumstance befitting a young man of intellect, athleticism and social grace in the Princeton Class of 1939. Three weeks prior, on his twenty-first birthday, his mother (my Grammy) gifted him a King James Version of *The Holy Bible*. She inked a heartfelt verse inside the cover, inferring her faith in the plan God had for her son:

> *"Accept this Book the Word of God*
> *And may it be thy faithful chart,*
> *And ever point thy onward road,*
> *And ever guide thy trustful heart."*

The Good Book's tattered condition is a testament to Buster's journey on this planet. Tucked in his duffle, it served him through the Second World War. I know for a fact he and this Bible also survived decades of teaching Sunday school, at the Community Church of Mountain Lakes, in classrooms filled with adolescent shenanigans. Daniel in the lions' den is a relevant lesson. When he instructed my out-of-line peers to stand facing the corner on Sunday, I rolled my eyes in anticipation of the crap I'd take changing classes on Monday.

For my mom the summer of 1939 was one to reunite the family. As the Smith campus was mothballed for summer, she packed her trunk and moved "home" once more to Amsterdam, with Auntie Rhea, Uncle Frank and cousin Roy. There she learned *"bad news of Uncle Frank's condition."*

The summer events documented in my mom's little black book were evidence Lelia stayed true to the words she'd written last November, with respect to a trip west. In a diary entry dated Tuesday, June 20, I learned Robin and Dottie climbed aboard a luxury passenger train: New York Central's *Lake Shore Limited*, Train #19, bound for Chicago. The way I imagine it, they were adorned in new summer dresses, gloved hands, and hats, dressed in their best for travel. That evening, Robin was shocked to meet a *"Mr. in the ladies' room... me in my bare feet"* but she didn't lose sleep over it. In her own words, she confirmed the overnight on the locomotive was *"not so bad."* The girls pulled into Chicago's Union Station in time for a planned reunion lunch with former Emma Willard classmates, then picked up the adventure on the Northern Pacific rail line that afternoon. The girls were tickled to find the *North Coast Limited* offered creature comforts for college girls. Radios for entertainment and a soda fountain. By night they tucked into Pullman-sleepers. By day they sat in a parlor car and scanned the plains along the path of Lewis and Clark. *"Saw Indians – some woman ripped out 'my knittin','"* scrawled my mom. The sisters swept through Bozeman Pass and into Missoula (*"lovely country"*) on Friday, June 23. My mom found Auntie Alta Dixon and Uncle Dix a refreshing departure from East Coast conservatives. Bear hugs were so big on the station platform, hats got knocked off.

A handsome twenty-one-year-old Bud McLeod lit up at the sight of Dottie and greeted my mom in a mannerly way with a short bow and tip of his Stetson. It's possible she returned the gesture, taking the edge of her skirt, pinkies out, in a short curtsy.

"Very sweet people – good food! Talked to folks all evening about Uncle Frank's condition."

The sisters were there just long enough to wash hair, clothes, and unpack – exactly one night – when a wire from my grandmother arrived. *"Come to California."* Robin relished a two-day whistle-stop tour under the big Montana Sky. *"Rode and saw country. Read all evening. Heard 'My Last Goodbye' – Glenn Miller."* Up early the morning of June 25, *"Left at 9:00 a.m. for trip to Seeley Lake with Bud, Dottie, and Bill Hoblitt. Had marvelous dinner.*

Mr. McLeod asked me to come next summer. Whee! Saw Mrs. Grover - characteristics – determined, can be coaxed, won't be led! Harum-scarum – still a child – Fortune – letter – bad news concerning heart – Dark lady – Going to get money – Disappointment in love – Got wish for happy life."

Re-read that ominous warning. Who the heck was Mrs. Grover? I had to know. Here's what I dug up on "Ma Grover."

The Seeley Lake Writers' Club compiled a book titled *Cabin Fever, A Centennial Collection of Stories about the Seeley Lake Area.* Ma was a veteran of World War I, France. Though her photo is published in black and white, it reveals a colorful character top to bottom. Hair tied and tucked up beneath a gypsy bandana, square glasses across her round face, a bit of a pointy chin. A hibiscus print dress cloaked by a hefty plaid flannel lumberjack shirt for warmth, an unforgettable Montana fashion statement. The caption states, *"She was known for her lively personality and "God Bless Ye Dearie" salute to everyone she met."* Is it a practiced psychic sort of reading Ma Grover dropped on my mom? Don't love, relationships, health and money cover the criteria? No mention of "career" in the fortune-telling of a woman in the 1930s, I suppose.

After meeting Ma Grover, my mom (in the company of Bud, Dottie, and Bill) *"Rode to the Lookout. Had wonderful dinner – Paddled canoe and pitched horseshoes."* Simply good times. I knew in my soul the seduction of the West for my mom had just begun.

When the Northern Pacific whistled steam at 3:00 p.m. on Monday, June 26, the two sisters clickity-clacked on the *North Coast Limited* toward Tacoma. Such a roundabout way to get to California seemed impractical to me. But as far back as 1873, when the transcontinental railroad was under construction, the Northern Pacific powers chose the deep-water port of Tacoma as the western terminus of that route. Hence the nick-name "City of Destiny." The sisters wrote letters to pass the time.

Since Tacoma was not *their* destiny, they made the leap between the Northern and Southern Pacific rail lines. It was *The Cascade* that transported my mom and Aunt Dottie south through Portland. This circuitous route gave them an opportunity to nose up to the window and bow to the majesty of Mount Shasta and Mount Hood. Twenty hours out of Portland, they were deposited on the station platform at the Market Street Ferry Building in San Francisco. It was a celebratory Wednesday, June 28, when they re-united with my grandparents. *"She looks even better than five years ago, Daddy looks older but not changed."* A shocking reality check for me. I didn't need any "new" math. Short of anyone dying, who knew the course of action documented in T. Wayne's Last Will and Testament was the intended plan of abandonment. Not for eternity, but five years is a long time by any young person's standards.

By now you've read enough to deduce my mom was like a case study in peer group influence. This apple didn't fall far from the tree. If you're a modern parent, you are aware of how a kid is (or isn't) set up for risky behavior. It boils down to temptation and opportunity, and the way in which the two come together. Resigned to their destiny in Campamento Americano, my grandparents yielded discipline to some combination of Auntie Rhea, a circle of housemothers, Auntie Alta, and the (rather hopeless) personal letters laid out in the chapters that follow.

By comparison, the culture of the 1970s fashioned a perfect personal storm for the likes of me. Do you know that saying "nothing good ever happens between midnight and 5 a.m.?" Heck, I could find trouble in the five daylight hours it took my parents to play eighteen holes of golf. As God is my witness, so is my near-Irish twin. She bailed me out more than a few times, once with a note on a string slinked outside her second story window to appear within reach of my bedroom window one floor below. She'd hatched a brilliant exit strategy for my boyfriend who escaped undetected from the boxed canyon bedroom end of the Crane Road house. With her planned diversionary tactics, Robin and Buz remained blissfully unaware.

I am sure my mom would have been happy to send me off at the age of fifteen (peak of my teenage dysregulation), but I believe she was sad to see me go off to college at seventeen. My grandmother, by comparison, missed out entirely on the most difficult years. "Teenagedom" was absent under her roof. She experienced it only through the voice of letters, never physically within earshot of cranked up music, slamming doors, or foot stomping arguments about bathroom hogs.

My Uncle Russell was a whole different story. The lofty educational goals laid out for him in T. Wayne's Will and Testament (Yale or Harvard) imploded. Left behind at the pre-pubescent age of eleven, he'd make a fine forensic human development case study. The subject? How insecure parent-adolescent attachments can screw a kid up.

Because there was no mention of Russell's presence at San Francisco's Market Street station, I played this moment in my mind's eye without him. Lelia and her daughters enthusiastically hailed each other from a distance on the railroad platform and ran (in theatrically slow motion) toward one other. Then my grandmother, holding my mom and my aunt each at arm's length, assessed them up and down. Silently Lelia's eyes conceded they'd grown into womanhood. She'd missed it. As if in a 1939 movie clip that belonged only to them (and me), they linked elbows and rushed off to find my grandfather. He'd been distracted, doing the manly thing, wrangling baggage off the railway luggage trolley.

This was their summer to make up for time lost and bond over shared experiences.

The troupe spent four days at a *"Fair"* in San Francisco. I was initially baffled when my mom wrote, *"Rode the Elephant Train around grounds."* Over the next several days her entries resonated like a world tour: *"Science Building, Holy Land, and Cavalcade of Golden West...Mormon Temple...Air Transportation Pan American. Beautiful lighting of buildings, Art Building, South American Countries...Spanish in Chile, coffee in Columbia, Marimba in Guatemala and Spaniard that looked like Wendy. (The manly man!) Beautiful 18th Century and contemporary American art – Botticelli – Birth of Venus, Raphael, Madonna of the chair, Titan[sic] Portrait of Pope Paul III, Michael Angelo[sic] ...Mary, Jesus and baby John. Nite – Folies Bergere – Whee! Ate at Argentinian Restaurant. Roller Coaster, Stella, and Birth of Twins – cesarean. Hindu rope trick. Swiss village."*

The "Fair" turned out to be the San Francisco Golden Gate Exhibition. It showcased the 1937 completion of the Golden Gate Bridge and the opening of the Bay Bridge six months before. Mom had little to say about those feats of engineering. But it was in this "June Memoranda" the man score was first revealed. Ossie was number one. He had taken the big step to "pin" my mom in early June before she escaped out West for the summer. For the unenlightened, to be pinned was the precursor to being engaged. Kind of like being engaged to be engaged. Darned if that Billy Hoblitt didn't take a position on the man score just three weeks later, in a matter of 48 hours' whistle-stop time like a Montana magic spell! *Man score in order to date – Ossie, Bruce, Jack, Louie, Bill Hoblitt, Wendy.*

Following the Fair, a *"Very thrilling first air trip"* ensued. *"Beautiful moonlit night started getting light at 3:30. Stopped at Sacramento and Medford and finally arrived at Portland very much asleep on Sunday morning. (Nothing alive!)"* This milk run sounds stomach-churningly awful to me, but clearly an adventure for her. And even though nothing appeared to be alive in Portland, I am glad she was.

Pop into your mind's eye the black and white image of Jimmy Stewart sitting at the controls of a Douglas DC-3. By today's standards that aircraft was bucket-of-bolts noisy. But the "Douglas Sleeper Transport" was considered the height of luxury at that time. The shiny, sleek fixed wing prop plane rolled off the assembly line three years earlier in 1936. With a cruising speed in the neighborhood of 200 mph, and two stops en route, it's no wonder it took half the night to travel the 545 miles from Oakland to Portland. (Flight time in today's world, minus the extra stops, is one hour and seventeen minutes.)

In deconstructing my mom's diary entries, I learned that her seat partner was my grandfather. Like air travel was a game of roulette, Grandpa safely stowed my grandmother and Aunt Dottie onboard the Southern Pacific railroad, back north, en route to Portland. I suppose my grandmother might have suggested that plan, yielding to her husband who, as a mining engineer, would enjoy viewing the earth from clear skies above. Let me take it one thought further. Risk-taking was an accepted part of living and working in a mining camp, where disasters were a given. Pick a poison for the more favorable demise: trapped underground in a tunnel collapse (or a mine car mishap, like poor Mr. Spectzen) versus high velocity air to earth impact.

Marveling at the speed of air travel, my mom reported a side trip with her dad up the Columbia River Gorge. They had time to kill before circling back to the train station in Portland. Bumping along a then-narrow U.S. Highway 30, they followed the path of President Franklin D. and Mrs. Roosevelt who'd visited two years before. Theirs was a rare presidential visit to the Northwest when, on September 28, 1937, FDR dedicated Oregon's Bonneville Dam and Timberline Lodge, two symbolic Works Progress Administration projects. Certainly, the family had seen newsreels!

Workers hired off relief rolls rejoiced with their wage of fifty cents an hour to build the dam that spans the Columbia River between Washington and Oregon. It, by way of environmentally intelligent design, included "fishways;" ladders and locks to facilitate the salmon spawn. It also supported first generation renewable energy, hydropower, utilizing the kinetics of water moving down stream. Imagine if wind and solar energy powered up on the heels of hydro. Would hydraulic fracking have ever been invented?

Just as the presidential entourage proceeded two years before, my mom and grandad tooled along the precarious mountain road and topped out at Timberline Lodge, on the southern flank of a glaciated Mount Hood, Oregon's highest peak.

Like cherries on top, my mom wrote in her diary *"good skiing there still."*

Indeed, she watched with envy. Handsome, fit, well-tanned young men sporting Ray-Ban aviator sunglasses, clunked around in laced leather boots. Casually over one shoulder they carried wooden skis, with bear-trap cable bindings. I imagine my grandad bought her lunch; grilled Columbia River salmon, or possibly Tillamook mac and cheese? The rustic charm of interior décor did not go unnoticed. The Timberline Lodge, unique as a WPA project, put local craftsman and artisans to work. Carved and inlaid wood, tapestries, stained glass, with themes of wildlife, pioneers and Indians hold their place in time within the walls of this national historic landmark.

My own personal experience with the lodge was remarkably different than my mom's. (And, as a film-lover's side note, light years different than the part the Timberline Lodge exterior played as the "Overlook Hotel" in Stanly Kubrick's 1980 film adaptation of Steven King's novel, *The Shining*.)

Let me explain.

"Jogging" became popular in the 1970s and is still Boomer-lit with people like me running to defy age, doing what's needed to fend off (or fuel) middle-age crazies.

The *Hood to Coast Relay* is an over-night long-distance running race dubbed "The Mother of All Relays." This insanity all begins atop Mount Hood, at none other than Timberline Lodge. It ends 196 (give or take) miles later at a huge finish party on the sandy beach of Seaside, Oregon.

I proudly affiliated, as a multi-year participant, with the non-elite team "Leather Lungs and Jog Bras." Our handle played well with ginormous hand-fashioned bras, bejeweled with bling and flashy trim, strapped across the hood of our mini-vans. Seaside or *BUST*, we rolled alongside 1,049 other troupes of twelve. Yes, that is 12,600 runners; rather like a small town of Forrest Gumps moving in wave-like motion, feeling nothing less than irrepressible optimism striding up and over the Cascade Range, to the chilly waters of the Oregon Coast.

It's a sad fact: I did not appreciate Timberline Lodge like I should have. Candidly, I did not know its rich history, but now I do, and so do you. I also understand this: Standing before the women's restroom mirror, moments before the race started, my reflection bounced alongside my mother's seventy years apart. Vicariously she lived and loved the *Hood to Coast* stories I relayed. Had she the wherewithal, she'd be the type to sign up, too. One inconvenient truth: today visibly shrinking snowfields and glaciers mar the mountain experience.

Enough of my glory days, let's get back to my mom's.

The return to Missoula by train from Portland opened chapter two of this iconic 1939 Montana summer. On Monday, July 3, *"Arrived on Northern Pacific with Mom at 3:45. Met Cousin Lois* (twenty-nine-year-old daughter of Auntie Alta and Dix). *Bought slacks and jacket outfit. Bath, dinner, left for airport. Saw Dottie and Dad come in."*

Ah ha! I smell an "even-steven" deal with the Skinner daughters, each taking a turn in the sky with their dad. Doubtful my grandmother was afraid of flying. She had, after all, flown the great distance between North and South America five years before. Was it a family pact to ensure if anyone died in a plane crash it would not be *everyone?* They would not leave their youngest, Russell, alone to fend for himself in the world. In a rather weird way, we humans catastrophize like that.

My mother thrived in the company of the who's who of Missoula over the next several weeks. A bustling summer colony enjoyed the sandy beaches and waterfront fun of lake country. Situated northeast of Missoula, Seeley Lake was hands down the popular hub where the McLeod family built one of the first lakeside summer homes in the mid-1920s. The Thieme family was counted among the homesteaders of Seeley Lake, too. It was Walter Irving "Mick" Thieme who escorted my mom up to the lake that Monday night. *"Danced 'til 1:30. Went to somebody's for ice cream. Drove up to Lookout with bunch."*

On the Fourth of July, *"Came back from wonderful day at Seeley Lake with Dottie, Bud and "Mick". Went gopher hunting, saw Mrs. Grover. Ate lunch, pitched horseshoes with Mr. McLeod."*

Then, *"Mick kinda fell, maybe something like Bruce."* A few weeks later my fickle mama discovered she liked Bill better than Mick. Mick never rated a "man-score," yet George, a tennis player with blonde curls, who *"resembles Ossie greatly when he smiles,"* did. No matter, this summer it's Bill and Bud (thick as thieves, buddies since childhood) who played center stage escorts for my mom and Aunt Dottie.

Had she had to write about what she did on summer vacation it would have looked something like this: *Luncheons, teas, picnics and dinner parties,* horseshoes, horseback riding, tennis, golf, concerts and movies. A lot of dental work. (More on that later.) *A little shopping for newly released records - Glenn Miller's 'Sunrise Serenade.'* She purchased a cowboy hat, a *"ten gallon"* in her words. I imagine my mom disappearing under a bucket like Hoss Cartwright's á la *Bonanza*, when I know full well hers was a very fine felt fur Stetson that only held three quarts. Not that one would ever test the capacity. Picture the hat style worn by the very classy "Queen of the West" cowgirl Dale Evans, wife of Roy Rogers.

My mom confessed to me more than once that my dad didn't like that hat, especially when she wore it. Obviously, it was associated with too many fond memories, ones that didn't include him. So what does a person do with a hat like that? Not so coincidentally it was a partner in crime with the boxes of letters traveling from the back of one closet to another. What is the smell of jealousy? That, of course, is a rhetorical question, but the summer of '39 was a highlight of my mom's youth.

For all her gallivanting around in fresh air adventures, it was the cinema marquees' boast of movie classics that brought her and a gang of mixed company indoors... *Confessions of a Nazi Spy, It Could Happen to You, Man About Town, Grand Jury Secrets, Daughters Courageous, Undercover Doctor, Wife Husband and Friend.* They were not just entertained but felt energized and uplifted by film. A point in history and social place when plopping down on the couch to watch a TV sitcom after dinner was simply not an option.

My grandparents' stay in Montana was hijacked at an abbreviated two weeks. They captured a few rare forever family memories with their girls at Glacier National Park, *"Beautiful mountains, the Going-to-the-Sun Highway and Glacier Park Hotel for dinner. Snow-glaciers – waterfalls – sunset – glorious."* Then, Robin and Dottie were imposed once more on Auntie Alta and Uncle Dix when my grand-folks flew off to Chicago for some unnamed surgery Lelia had scheduled. This proved two things: 1) No fear of flying for Grandma, and 2) She was a model of what it meant to be an "informed patient."

At age fifty, my guess is she headed out for a hysterectomy. Why? Uterine fibroids. How do I know? My mom had the same problem in her mid-40s; except as I recall she was admitted mistakenly for an emergency appendectomy. My sister Dianne shared the same pathogenesis of fibroids. Lucky for her the surgical shift towards minimally invasive techniques over thirty plus years offered a laparoscopic assisted vaginal procedure; no swath of an abdominal scar like my mom's, less down time and cost effective, too. (The latter being health insurance plan dependent, I suppose.) All this establishes the fact that family medical history proves knowledge is power.

Enough discussion of gynecological disorders, let's return to young love.

"Spent wonderful evening riding with Bill on Star Dust and Escobar. Love 'em more n ever. He's so sweet and gentle." I assume my mom was talking about the horse she rode, although it could be she was just as taken with Bill.

"Phil Harris Orchestra was marvelous! So was Bill. Guess he cares a little maybe. Riding date for Monday. Bill and Bud brought roses."

Partnered up with Bud, my aunt Dottie made it a perfectly tidy foursome for fun.

I don't remember (or maybe I forgot) ever receiving flowers on a first date, so the mention of roses at the stoop struck me as sweetly old-fashioned. Call me wistfully sentimental, but today I'd re-define it as a timeless gesture. The double-daters motored for more than a couple hours along U.S. 10 (known today as I-90) to Columbia Gardens, an amusement park in Butte. There the Phil Harris Orchestra stopped off to perform a one-night stand on their summer-long 1939 cross-country tour. Those born in the early 1950s may remember Mr. Harris as the hip-talking beloved house bandleader for Jack Benny's weekly sitcom radio show on NBC. (Boomers of the late '50s will do better manifesting the voice of Baloo the bear in Disney's animated 1967 release of *The Jungle Book*.)

"Went for a memorable Ford ride to Cottonwood Lake with Bill tonight. Sauterne. Wild animals – fawn and two porcupines. Back to liquor store, dance and then home to porch – 'til 3:30."

I wonder exactly what made that Ford ride memorable. Possibly the first big action closed cab half-ton pickup she'd ever bounced around in? Were the seats bucket or bench? Maybe it wasn't the ride itself, but simply being alone with Bill. An eligible young man, two years her elder, and a recent "animal husbandry" graduate of Montana State, apparently without a steady girl.

One bottle of Sauterne? Not to be confused with a 1939 Chateau d'Yquiem Sauternes derived from France. (By then production and supply of wine from the Bordeaux region was disrupted due to the war.) It was simply a California white "Sauterne" (correctly spelled by my mom without the "s" on the end.) I imagine they sipped and stared out across the lake, the wafting of pines scenting the air, cozied up with his arm around her shoulder.

Unlike my mom, I don't consider a fawn and two porcupines to be exactly "wild" animals. I doubt Bill did either. Somewhere in heaven she understands why I would chuckle over that diary note. In Utah, I regularly run into moose, elk, mule deer, and the occasional coyote. I've nearly stepped on a porcupine, slow moving rodents that they are. On one occasion I crossed paths with a cougar. It ran, as they generally do, being rather stealthy and shy creatures. In her later years my mom never failed to ask about my animal encounters every Sunday evening when I phoned.

For Billy and my mom, in their tireless twenties, the liquor store and dance set up a late evening that rolled into a long, long visit on the porch; well into the wee hours. Here's what I see in my mind's eye. Bill, acting with propriety, sits upright. My mom stretched out, knees bent, across the length of a fine, four-foot lodge pole pine swing. They rock gently within the confines of its A-frame stand. Her head in his lap, gazing into his eyes, swinging on a metaphoric star until 3:30 in the morning.

The swing, intended to last for generations, undoubtedly did. But that night, in the "tick" of time, morning arrived all too fast.

"Picnic with Bill and McLeods tonight, nifty fun. Hamburgers and salad and apple pie á la mode – good stories."

Hot, sizzling summer, beam me back to that picnic blanket. Let me eavesdrop, elbows down, ears up on the storytelling. Have a bite of pie? Homemade, no doubt, and they churned the ice cream, too.

"Went riding with Bill. He looked so handsome! Tan checked jacket – tan breeches and a red shirt – Whee!"

Whoa! The jacket – a Pendleton wool cruiser field coat? The breeches – tailored riding trousers flared at the hip, tight fitting at the knee, perhaps tucked neatly into two-tone Tony Lama boots with stacked leather riding heels. The red shirt would set off the rather rosy undertones of Bill's healthy summer tan. It appears my mom sallied forth as his partner in crime, caught up in the rapture of flirtatious mischief.

"Climbed up to the falls on Holland Lake with Bill and went swimming in ice water. Picnic. Saw eagle, four blue heron, a beaver, and a laughin' loon. Heard coyote in evening."

Did they harvest huckleberries to the accompaniment of the bobolinks' bubbling song along the way? Holland Lake, in the Flathead National Forest, is one in a chain of lakes. I found myself humming *Cool Water*, not recorded by the Sons of Pioneers until 1944, but you might know the lyrics... *Cool, clear water*. They were nowhere near a desert, as the song goes. Rather they were between two glacially sculpted mountain ranges. The lake water as cold as hypothermia waiting to happen, and clear enough to see the black spots on the west slope, cutthroat trout lurking below the surface. Water, wildlife and wilderness... for me envisioning the scene now (and her being party to it then) proves the best things in life are free.

"Had another picnic with Bill and McLeods. Sang songs. Beautiful moon."

It may sound cliché, but I mean it sincerely when I say if good times were dollars, my mom and Bill were rolling in dough...maybe the hay, too. Except I don't believe he took liberties.

I fancy that's the truth for this reason: She wrote in a diary entry nine months earlier about her escort to a West Point "Hop." She nicknamed the cadet *"hot lips"* and noted his *"plenty hot latch-on."* The day after, she revealed this: *"lips were still swollen today."*

There was no talk like that with respect to Bill.

Bud's folks, Walter and Olive McLeod, flew about like cupids instrumentally orchestrating wholesome and gay outings to make magic happen for the "kids."

"Rode tonight on Escobar up Bass Creek Canyon with Bill. Saw Mars very close tonight."

Did they ride double... possibly bareback? Bill in control of the reigns up front and my mom clinging hands around his waist from behind? They stargazed with Escobar tethered close by. Jupiter and Venus had moved off behind the canyon wall leaving the red planet to shine brilliantly. It dominated the night sky.

Giving some thought to their stargazing, I should point out my mom was branded with a certain conversational personality type. Newsworthy events rarely evaded her. Perpetually fueled with topics to talk about, she especially liked science. I expect she bantered with Bill on the presence of life on Mars. The camera studies of the renowned Lowell Observatory in Flagstaff revealed keys to such planetary secrets in 1939.

Fifty-five years later, Mars Rover *Opportunity* bumped along, over and through the geologic features on that planet's rocky terrain. I'm glad she lived to see that day. Ironically the Martian map now pinpoints a rock outcropping named "Missoula."

The night of this Bass Creek Canyon escapade with Bill, it happened our planetary neighbor swung close to earth, in the vicinity of thirty-six million miles. When she wrote *"Mars very close tonight,"* she knew it for a fact. Over the course of her life, the little red planet repeated that performance only three more times, a personal cosmic connection when she might have thought of Bill, and he of her.

At the same time in July 1939, Hitler was advised by his own personal staff of "Ma Grovers." They coached him on planetary aspects and history tells us it may have been their astrologic advice that unraveled *der Reichsfuerher* enough to convince him the time to strike out at the world was weeks away. Imagine that, as my mom wrote this: *"The beginning of a beautiful weekend at Seeley Lake. Drove up with McLeods. Full moon. Hit Parade and Bill. 1. Stairway to the Stars. 7. Beer Barrel Polka. 2. White Sails. 3. Moon Love. Gathered porky quills. Bill told me he loves me for first time tonight. Gee, but I do love him! 1. So ornery. 2. Love him. 3. Swell personality."*

Ornery? Did he tease her about the songs she liked on the Hit Parade? Compared to his East Coast counterparts, those competing for the top spot on the man score, perhaps she found Bill slightly rough around the edges, or even tough as nails. He strikes me as a proper cowboy, rather gentlemanly, with a big laugh and great sense of humor. He likely learned leadership and citizenship through a local 4-H club. I'm convinced he was a young man who would innocently melt a girl's heart. I'll be darned if he didn't dissolve hers.

"Had wonderful ride in full moon with Bill - Creek, barb-wire fences – horses and sittin' on stumps."

Hey Mom, how about being a little more descriptive in the diary detail? Did you cross a creek along the ride? I've ridden horses that refused creek crossings. They could not be spurred on to even dip a hoof. On the other hand, I once sat in the saddle atop "Felix," an overly stubborn mule, when he trotted into a lake taking me straight to the middle. During an endurance race no less! That dumb ass ruined my shoes. What about the barb-wire fences? Did Escobar rub up against the barbs tearing your britches in a subtly revealing way? No matter. Sittin' on stumps strikes me as a simple pleasure to be cherished alongside Bill. He patiently shared his western ways, a marker of a man in love.

"Off with Bill to see Mrs. Grover. Saw three-week-old colt. Swam for three hours. Went for motorboard ride on lake. Beautiful sunset."

Glory be, pray tell what future Ma Grover saw as she watched them gush over the long-legged foal. I imagine Bill worked his animal husbandry magic, assuring all within ear shot that this colt was nursing well and destined to be a fine, strong ranch horse one day. Then, hand in hand, the star-struck couple set off to play on the lake. Summer love grew faster than hothouse blooms for those two.

As written in her July memoranda: *"An extremely happy and merry month gone I don't know where – I love the west now – due to Bill. To date – Mom's operation successful! "I love you" from Bill. Phil Harris and much dental work. Four weekends at Seeley Lake. Two picnics, many luncheons. Glacier Park Trip. Uncle Frank home and healthier."*

Already enamored with the hospitable frontier culture of the west, Bill played the biggest part when he lassoed my mom's heart. He embodied the genuine all-American cowboy to her then, and me today. I've downright incarnated my own personal folk hero.

With hopes on fire, my mom packed all day for her first visit to the Hoblitt ranch. Time to meet Bill's parents!

"Drove out to Ranch in Jitterbug – Bed at 12:30."

Although this so-called "jitterbug" has absolutely nothing to do with the animated, high-energy dance of their day (or the new-age branded smartphone targeting the seniors of today) the ride might have felt that way. A motorized contraption, it was built from the chassis of some unknown vehicle – possibly even a tractor - using a bunch of cast-off spare parts one might find harbored in the back of a barn. The kind of jalopy an innovative person like Bill might have stolen ideas for from the *Handy Man's Home Manual*. A project over which he possibly bonded with his brother and dad, putting their family tinker-genes to work.

The Hoblitt's resided in the small town of Florence, Montana, about twenty miles south of Missoula. Stevensville, home of the first permanent settlement in the Bitterroot Valley of Montana, is another ten miles yonder.

There my mom and Bill attended what I deduced was the county fair rodeo. *"Bucking horse – bareback – calf and steer riding – calf ropin' – stack races. Awful cold, but fun!"*

Thank goodness she had a respectable Stetson to wear, enthusiastically playing the part of a darn cute cowgirl. The Montana chill supported her position in the stands with Bill's arm warmly wrapped around her shoulder. She cuddled close, nuzzling to fill her cold nose with the manly scent she would long remember, Aqua Velva.

Reflecting upon my own life in the West, I never considered myself a real cowgirl. (Though I do fess up to owning the requisite hats and boots, even a leather belt with a silver buckle, my name leather punched on the back.) That image just didn't partner well with hippie-dom when I first arrived in Utah in the mid '70s. That said, in the days when Park City was a no-traffic-light town, home to both peace and love types, real miners of Motherlode, and a small cowboy culture (light years before 2002 Winter Olympic celebrity and the branding of "world class resort") I won a blue ribbon competing in Ernie's Bar Wars Rodeo. Funky stuff like that was part of the social scene. Ernie, by day, made a living as the Wonder Bread deliveryman. Like Santa in his sleigh, "Ernie the Breadman" waved to all about town as he motored grocery store to gas station in his white Wonder-dotted truck, *Hostess CupCakes* emblazoned above the windshield. On summer evenings, "Ernie and the Nightriders" constituted the cowboy way of life, trail riding under the stars on the outskirts of town; the joyful experience my mom shared firsthand alongside Bill.

And rather like Bill, Ernie embraced fun and traditional celebration.

Mind you, I did not actually sign up to compete in the Bar Wars rodeo, but the Chamber of Commerce (where I worked at the time) sponsored a team. Our calf rider was a no-show. As a loyal employee and team player to a fault, I climbed hurriedly down out of the stands, and yanked a pair of surgical scrubs over my shorts. The local vet provided the scrubs, and another generous soul handed me a double shot of Jack Daniels. I scaled the rail over the portable pen and dropped into the chute atop a "calf."

Assessing the warmth of the beast pressed against my crotch, I factored its long, matted hair, curved horns nearly the length of my arm, and my own legs not long enough to hang past its belly. Frankly, if you saw the look on either of our faces, you'd know neither the calf nor I knew what we were doing there. When some cowboy pulled the bucking strap, and another opened the gate, I held on for a whooping eight seconds.

I am glad my folks missed that show. Much to the amazement of onlookers, I slipped completely sideways three or four seconds into the ride. I never thought to let go, since the point was to win. I hung on riding horizontally, parallel to the ground. As far as I know, the only thing visible to the crowd in the stands was the sole of one teal Nike trainer across the back of that wooly beast. I'm lucky I didn't get kicked in the head. After a double bounce on all fours, into a cloud of poofy dirt, a rodeo clown swept me safely out of the arena. A cash prize of fifty smackers accompanied a big, blue Bar Wars first-place ribbon.

Magically cloaked in the invincibility of youth, and a sign of the times well before the Affordable Care Act, my void in health insurance never crossed my mind.

How my parents reacted to the tale of my personal rodeo experience on the Crane Road end of the phone doesn't really matter, though they got a chuckle out of my new nickname: Bronco Bonnie. What's important is that it gave my mom a reason to fondle that fine Stetson shelved at the back of her closet.

Enough of that nostalgic digression.

The day after my mom and Bill attended the county fair rodeo in the Bitterroot Valley, she wrote: *"Up bright and early for Stevensville picnic. Saw parade and all concessions. Wrestling match, Ferris wheel, weight guesser – popcorn, etc. Drove the Hoblitts home. Went for drive with Bill up the road and home early. Got scared off rail fence by an old sow after a little pig."*

What a spectacle. I imagine gut-busting laughter followed that scene. A fast and agile squealing piglet darting on four trotters, dodging its enormous teat swinging mother. In the moment, Billy amused Robin with pig facts. How the piglet's tail laid straight, then curled up in the excitement of the chase. In a sweet and happy heart flipping moment, they leapt from the rail fence together.

My mom's Montana summer love adventure wound down on August 12: *"Drove out to see Mrs. Grover with Bill to say goodbye. Went swimming and to "Basket Social. Had to pay $3.25 for basket – Mrs. McLeod's cover was sweet."* A basket social! Good golly, is there anything more special than that? Men would bid auction style for a basket of food to earn the privilege of eating and dancing with the woman who prepared the basket. I speculate Mrs. McLeod made the basket and then bought it back so that Bill could picnic and dance with Robin.

My mom wrote this little ditty in her diary....

"The Sheik of the Bitterroot soon will be sobbin'
When he bids goodbye to an Eastern Robin
Eat well! Oh Sheik and drown your sorrow
Make hay while the sun shines and
Forget the morrow."

"Home to bed about 5:30 - dawn had broken."

Neither wanted "the morrow" to arrive. They savored the luminous pink of alpenglow that topped the mountains just before sunrise. Beyond the pledge to write often, no one knows what promises for the future were made. With a heavy call of duty, my mom pulled herself away. There was no excuse in the world to derail family expectations for her graduation from Smith. I expect Bill understood and respected that, too.

Later that Sunday morning of August 13, my mom gently nested her "ten-gallon hat" in a STETSON branded hatbox. Images of range riders circled the box perimeter. Respecting cowboy superstition, Bill had surely explained the hat must rest brim up to "catch luck." Neatly folding her garments in quiet contemplation, she might have hummed *Sunrise Serenade*. That night she confessed the painful gut truth she couldn't shake while packing, *"Everything seemed so sad."*

Shortly after she'd latched her satchel, Bill chivalrously heaved bags into the jitterbug. My mom sat beside her cowboy for a final, rather joyless ride to Auntie Alta's. Dottie and Bud bounced along in the back, a seat they would share again in the future. After a fine farewell luncheon, the girls boarded the train at 3:30 – *"Cried pretty hard leavin' Bill – last thing he said, 'I love you.' So hard to leave him."*

It occurs to me now, in a weird sort of way, the cowboys on the Stetson box were like Bill checking up on my mom from time to time. As for the songs from the 1939 Hit Parade? They, too, manifested snapshot memories of that summer in Montana whenever, and wherever, they played.

For me? I invoke the bittersweet lyrics to the song *Cherish*, a 1966 U.S. Billboard Hot 100 summertime hit crooned by The Association. Love had conquered hearts, yet they both moved on. Possibly the right girl, the right guy, but the wrong time. Mrs. Grover was truly psychic after all: *"Bad news concerning heart - disappointment in love."*

I expect they crossed paths again, but only once that I can puzzle out with some certainty. It happened many years later, due to Bill's lifelong association with the McLeod family. I can also tell you my mom kept a black and white photo of Bill among her possessions; handsome and dressed smartly in what I know to be an olive drab gabardine shirt, with khaki tie peeking beneath the lapel of his Army field jacket. A portrait snapped as he prepared for war? For the record, Bill served five overseas tours from 1942 to 1945; and was decorated with the American Theater Service Medal, European African Middle Eastern Theater Service Medal and Asiatic Pacific Theater Service Medal. The framed 5 x 7 in her dresser drawer was there for safe-keeping, through the war and then some: forever. From time to time over many years I stared into Bill's dimpled face and broad smile, as did my sisters. Like Butch Cassidy repeatedly asking the Sundance Kid, *"Who are those guys?"* my siblings and I did the same, except we just wanted to know who the one guy was. Like a personal puzzle my mom left behind, I've finally solved the mystery. Bill was her once-in-a-lifetime cowboy love from Montana.

A man of mystery

It's worth a side mention here that I rode in Ernie's rodeo shortly after I finished graduate school, 1980, or thereabouts. It wasn't long after, on a Sunday evening call to the Crane Road house, my mom asked me point blank: "What are your plans for coming back home?" I clearly remember her question caught me by surprise. While my words were certain, my voice was weak: "I'm not really planning to."

"Ahh," came her sigh on the exhale, followed by a silence as long as the Grand Canyon is wide. Then she softly asked, "You love the West, don't you?" Her inflection not so much a question; more an empathetic statement of hard and fast fact.

Only now, in retrospect, do I fully grasp her complete lack of argument. And why, more than anything during her retirement years, she lived in anticipation of boarding a flight from EWR (Newark) to SLC. When she glimpsed the drawers of her mind (and her underwear) she thought of Billy Hoblitt. Maybe what her life with him might have been? She envied my life in the West. As much as I've never had a regret about my own move, I am especially grateful to have shared it with her.

Marco Polo

Chapter Fifteen

From Missoula the girls steamed eastward through St. Paul station and arrived in Chicago two days later. My grandfather met the train and escorted them to The Palmer House, the legendary historic hotel of Chicago's city center. Known as the home away from home for notable dignitaries, it also boasted a glittering roster of entertainers: Louis Armstrong, Ella Fitzgerald, Judy Garland, Benny Goodman, to name a few my mom would especially appreciate. Some of the most quotable characters in history, Mark Twain, Charles Dickens and Oscar Wilde signed that guestbook, too.

As the nation's oldest operating hotel, the Palmer suffered a few ups and downs over the years. Literally. The original Palmer House opened its doors in 1871 but burned just thirteen days later, in the Great Chicago Fire. It re-opened in 1875.

Fifty years later, the hotel was strategically rebuilt on the same site, in stages, between 1924 and 1927. The new structure stood twenty-five stories tall, with twenty-three guest floors. Pardon their dust but, in a tricky marketing maneuver, the Palmer preserved its claim to fame as the longest continuously operating hotel in the country by serving their clientele throughout construction.

As for my mom and Aunt Dottie, feeling the effects of forty-eight emotionally exhausting hours on the train from Missoula, the sisters appeared dusty themselves. They trailed behind my baggage-dragging grandfather. As they reached the magnificent Tiffany-designed brass

"Peacock Doors" fronting Monroe Street, the girls stepped over several thresholds straight into heaven. The gilded lobby and grand staircase oozed exquisite beauty. The troupe of four checked into their elegant accommodations, room 1309 to be exact.

The beds at Palmer House in 1939 were made up with buttery linen sheets; airy, cool, and smooth, a symbol of prestige. I had to know more about room 1309. What was the room configuration? Is it actually on the thirteenth floor? It's a fact many hotels omit the thirteenth floor altogether or make up a name to avoid using the number. The reason is triskaideka-phobia: the dark suspicion that surrounds unlucky number thirteen. Why risk losing heads in beds to a superstitious clientele? I suppose bad luck manifested when the hotel burned in the Great Chicago Fire, but that did not keep them from rebuilding with a thirteenth floor.

I dialed the Chicago 312 area code and got the recorded Palmer House chatter "Where history meets cutting edge every day." (The cutting edge? That would be me baffling the family tree by using my smart phone as an electronic door key.) Curiously, the desk staff I spoke with could not locate room 1309. Yes, there is a thirteenth floor. But today, as I understand it, floors have named wings with room numbers. There is no 1309.

The family whirlwind of 1939 picked up the next morning in the Windy City. Shopping downtown Chicago, my mom snatched up two skirts and a velvet jacket. To escape the summer heat, they wandered into the Art Institute where they studied the water colors of Thomas Rowlandson, then explored the Adler Planetarium. In the opulent Victorian Room at the Palmer, Lelia celebrated her fiftieth birthday in the company of those she loved most in the world. In the same three days the family packed in three movies with popcorn: *Goodbye Mr. Chips*, *Lady of the Tropics*, and *Naughty But Nice*.

They departed Chicago's Union Station on an evening train, and rolled into Syracuse, New York, the following day. There they made a plan to see my uncle Russell, nicknamed "Skeeter" for what reason I can only imagine. Possibly he was a pest, though they hardly knew him. *Stanley and Livingstone* was the movie of that day, followed by the new Technicolor spectacle, *The Wizard of Oz*.

It struck me as just plain sad that even though Skeeter (finally) joined the family on this trip, he did not reunite with them in time to see *The Wizard of Oz*. Of course, my grandparents had no way of knowing it would be lauded by critics and ranked on the best-movies-all-time list. A pigtailed Dorothy, played by Judy Garland, might have propped up a sense of fun-poking normalcy in Skeeter's distanced relationship with his older sisters.

The way I feel about it, Skeeter played Marco with his feet stuck in shoes filled with cement, while the rest of the family Polo-ed about atop the crest of a great American wave: sightseeing coast to coast in planes, trains and automobiles. A jitterbug, too!

It turns out a place nicknamed "Republic" was Skeeter's default home away from home, selected exclusively by my grandparents. The school's official name was George Junior Republic, located in Freeville, New York. As a nationally known institution for juvenile self-government, he lived amongst other kids in a small society where citizenship was vested in the students, and everyone was expected to work.

I guess the school's academic calendar didn't leave room for an entire summer off. The lessons in what it meant to be a responsible citizen taught self-reliance, self-control and morality. The work of the "citizens" kept them on task and out of trouble. If everyone left the grounds in June and didn't return until September, the place would fall apart.

The family traveled out to Freeville on Saturday, August 19, to see Skeeter, but first they had a sit-down with Donald Urquhart, the head of Republic. As a published author, Donald G. Urquhart wrote *Crime Prevention through Citizenship Training at The George Junior Republic*. At first this led me to believe Skeeter was a delinquent needing the brains, the heart and the courage that only the Wizard could deliver. After all, Republic was a model dedicated to helping "at-risk" youth.

Rising up as the defender of the baby in the family (he was number three of three and I number four of four), let's do a fact-check. As an infant, I doubt anyone gushed over his cuteness as the third child living in

Campamento Americano. On the other hand, he was a boy. That must have made the men in the family tree happy. He should have stood proudly in his place as a man.

The problem circled back to this point. If my mom had not seen her mother since the age of fifteen, Skeeter hadn't seen her since he'd barely turned eleven. Do birth order outcomes apply when a family unit is way, way out of whack? Do the words "There's no place like home" ring true?

We already know the Huntingtons did not want Russell hanging around their home in Amsterdam during school breaks. There had to be a reason for that. He had not endeared himself to Auntie Rhea and Uncle Frank enough for them to call him "Skeeter," even though he appeared to be a pest to them. For whatever reason, Dorothy was not welcome either. My mom had the blessing of being the first born, with positive attributes heaped on like salad bar toppings.

When my grandparents sat in the office of Donald Urquhart at Republic, they made a convincing enough argument to have Skeeter, now sixteen, join the family entourage. As much as I imagined an illuminating and joyful reunion, it might have been equally dim with an awfully awkward vibe. He was a full-fledged teenager, after all. The last time they had spoken to him, he had the voice of a soprano. Puberty changed that, and his stature, too. They turned to film to break the ice and buffer the transition: *Charge of the Light Brigade* and *Texas Rangers*. Whoa! These were movies made in 1936. Re-runs screened near Republic with male gender appeal.

Nonplussed by the inclusion of this total stranger, who doubled as her younger brother, my mom made out her clothes list and washed her hair.

A day's train ride from Freeville, my grandparents, with their whole nuclear family intact, arrived and moved into temporary residence at the Hotel McAlpin on Herald Square, the corner of Broadway and 34th Street, Manhattan.

With her arrival in the Big Apple, my mom was no worse for Western wear. On Tuesday, August 22, while Hitler informed his military commanders of his war plans, and the Dutch border guards took position against a German invasion, the Skinner family unit was on the subway to the 1939

World's Fair in Flushing Meadow, New York. At the end of the line for their coast-to-coast summer tour they walked into "The World of Tomorrow."

The Fair was broken into different zones... the Communication Zone included the telephone, the radio and (new!) the television. At the time AT&T (the Bell system) was big. At the American Telephone Exhibit my mom lost out on a lucky number. She wrote with disappointment in her diary. Apparently, winners of the lottery could make a call while visitors to the exhibit looked on. She might have called Bill! The marketing message was to make the wonder of long-distance phone calls come alive for an average American person. When I think of my parents not understanding my unlimited friends-and-family cell phone plan, it is now obvious to me why they couldn't grasp it. What we all take for granted seemed impossible to them.

Eastman Kodak and General Motors both took part in The World of Tomorrow. And according to my mother, *The most wonderful thing ever – Aquacade – oh so lovely."* The synchronized swimming and high dive, choreographed by Billy Rose, was considered the hit attraction. And I would have to agree, because now it's available on YouTube. How surreal is that? I've watched it. Of course, by today's standards, it's downright corny. As more of a "girlie show" with all those women in swimsuits, I'd wager it was Olympic gold medal swimmer Johnny Weismuller who impressed my mom. Remember Johnny, the star of multiple *Tarzan* films? If not, just think in black and white and recall his iconic Tarzan jungle cry. I'm disappointed he didn't rate a mention in the diary.

Some of the World's Fair exhibits that did make the diary cut? The Sun Valley Lodge featured figure skating on real ice, a brief respite from August's heat and humidity; The Florida building pitched the Sunshine State as the tourist capital of the nation. Undoubtedly the Fountain of Youth figured into that theme. After traveling coast to coast in 1939 (something few people did back then), it made perfect sense to me that Florida was soon top-billed on my mom's bucket list. The beautiful fountains, fire, fireworks, and water features all came together in Robin's utopian memories. It's true the 1939 World's Fair was a wondrous Futurama.

Except for the specter of war hanging around the Russian Pavilion.

The Soviet exhibit, epic in scale, was the last to be finished before the Fair opened in April of 1939. Deservedly, Germany and the Third Reich, had no presence at all. By early December 1939 the Russians quit the Fair, packed up their pavilion and shipped "Joe the Worker" (a symbolic entry statue the size of Gulliver in the land of Lilliput) back to the Motherland. With events in Europe leading up to the war, "The World of Tomorrow" seemed an incongruous theme at best. When the Fair re-opened in 1940 it was re-themed "For Peace and Freedom."

Beyond the boundary of the Flushing Meadow fairgrounds, New York brought about reunions for my mom with Wendy and Louis. She also had the chance to spend more time with my grandparents, Aunt Dottie, and Skeeter, as evidenced by this diary entry: *"Wonderful dinner at Keene's Chop House with family. Saw Planetarium and End of the World." Tried to get tickets to Broadway Hellzapoppin. Saw Hotel for Women instead – good stage show. Went to movie – The Mad Miss Manton, and Imperial Hotel."*

The late summer New York City weather behaved in a way to be expected when a torrential thundershower cut loose. Over all these years, steam rising off the hot August asphalt hasn't changed its behavior, but in 1939 I am pretty sure vendors peddling compact umbrellas did not magically appear as fast as raindrops falling, like they do today.

August memoranda: *"Outstanding events* [of my mother's entire summer]: *Week spent with Bill – 'Life on a Ranch.' Basket Social and poem. Stay at Palmer House. Life in Hotels for two weeks. Dentist ordeal. Life with whole family."*

Darn the *"Dentist ordeal."* Let's talk about that since we've all had them, and nobody likes them. Not then, not now. Toothsome tales reach back many millennia. Mythology of the parasitic "toothworm" gave way to the kinder, gentler "doodlebug" by the time I was a kid. Nothing stops these imaginary nematodes from boring little round holes straight through enamel with evil intent to reach the root.

The brushing habit fired up in the 1920s. Even so, in my parents' youth, dentists focused on fixing, rather than preventing tooth decay. An ad campaign for *Pepsodent*, "The Special Film Removing Dentifrice," promoted whiteness and brightness. Ad agencies lacked the graphics capability of a twinkle effect, but tooth film (and the need to remove it) got the point across well enough. Good God, no one wanted *that*.

The 1939 dentist ordeal for my mom entailed seven dental visits in twelve days' time while in Montana. Imagine, no nitrile exam gloves on the hands of her examiner. Fat hairy fingers poked around inside her mouth. Neither hygienics nor patient comfort were part of the protocol. A front tooth filling was only the beginning. The reclining dental chair didn't come along until the 1950s, so her visits went from bad to worse as she amassed seventeen upright neck cranking hours, jaw locked in the "ahhhh" position. On the last day she wrote: *"Filled last tooth and pulled two."* Wisdom teeth, I presume. She bucked up in the endorphin charged company of Billy Hoblitt; complaints were confined to her diary. Anacin and Anbesol were in the realm of pain relief in 1939. She made no mention of either.

As my mother's daughter, I was far from a 1960s Crest toothpaste poster child with a perfect smile. ("Look mom, no cavities!") That kid made me look bad. Luckily, my dad attributed my rotten dental record to "Skinner teeth." It's true, the structure of tooth enamel *is* genetic. My mouth mirrored my mom's, except her fillings were gold; the kind that made gruesome history in the Auschwitz concentration camps.

But to revisit Robin's August memoranda entry, that last line about *"Life with whole family?"* It cast a huge shadow backwards over the sunny summer she described. Like a scattered tribe, her "whole family" had little time to bond, let alone create happy memories. Possibly one explanation for the Hotel McAlpin coat hanger she nicked. A sturdy "broad shouldered" wooden specimen that might, symbolically, hold her up. A skeleton that eventually made its way to the closet at Crane Road.

For the rest of their lives, Skinner family connections became a game of Marco Polo. I have no evidence they ever congregated in one place, all together again. Read on and settle the question for yourself.

It may very well be the reason why my mom's silence was so very long the day I told her I had no plans to return "home" to New Jersey.

Hello Buster

Chapter Sixteen

The literal translation of *Beau Geste* is "beautiful gesture." Ironically, as Robin watched the film *Beau Geste* on Friday, September 1, 1939, German forces invaded Poland strategically across all frontiers. Innocent civilians were bombarded and died violently at the hand of Hitler's ungodly plan. Though the captives in *Beau Geste* were guilty, Gary Cooper refused to shoot. As a point of honor, a person does not shoot an unarmed man. The noncombatants of Poland were not so lucky.

Two days later, on September 3, Britain and France declared war on Germany, honoring their promise to stand by Poland. Flat-capped newsies bantered "read all about it" in real time, as if in their own hit musical, while my mom, her parents and siblings made haste through Rockefeller Center to Radio City Music Hall. That night Ginger Rogers stirred things up shining like a diamond in the film *5th Avenue Girl*. The headlines of the "EXTRA's" screamed *WAR DECLARED*, while FDR pledged his fight for neutrality.

That night, Skeeter returned to the campus of George Junior Republic. My grandmother was (as recorded by the script of my mom) *"very sad."* An enormously understated truth. A two-week vacation made little difference in the scheme of his upbringing, and Lelia knew it. I wish circumstances could have been different for them. And the world. On so many levels.

Each of us has a list of failures all our own. Had I walked in my grandmother's shoes, I'd feel ashamedly short of the *Family Circle* brand of parenting. Boomers like me fought the opposite tug-of-war trying to avoid the "helicopter" label. Every decent parent, generation to generation, is faced with trying to be perfect. "Perfect Parent" should be added to somebody's list of mythical creatures, mixed in with multiple generations of Pokémon and unicorns, too.

One afternoon, for no obvious reason, I (apparently) crossed the over-mothering line. My eldest son told me this: "I'm rather like a succulent. I don't need a lot of tending." In an uncomfortably weird sort of way I congratulated myself. Here's my advice: Hug the people you love often, even though they can be a little prickly.

Turning back to the 1939 New York scene, it would have done Skeeter a world of good had he been granted permission to stay with his family just a few days longer. During the pre-TV era, large cities like New York had theatres *dedicated* to newsreels. Because motion pictures were so hugely popular, visual news clips in the form of newsreel shorts were easily digested by the masses. They complemented print and radio as an important source of reporting on current world events, politics, fashion and sports. Even in smaller population centers, where there were no dedicated theatres, newsreel screenings preceded whatever movie folks were there to see.

Because the family was in New York and interested in international affairs, it came as no surprise to me that Robin noted her attendance at newsreel theatres over the next several days. Lessons taught outside the gates of George Junior Republic at that moment in history would have been on point for Skeeter. On September 4, 1939, Universal Newsreel issued a "Special Release": *Allies Declare War on Nazis*. It included Roosevelt's neutrality speech. The young men enrolled at Republic, approaching the age of draft-eligibility, deserved to know the dope.

Juxtaposed with newsreels, side-splitting laughter brightened an otherwise shell-shocked audience. *"Marvelous"* live theatre. At the legendary Ethel Barrymore Theatre, the view of the stage from Row K – twelfth row in the orchestra section – was *"splendid."* There, Katharine Cornell and Laurence Olivier performed in *No Time for Comedy*. Lighting cigarettes with panache onstage, the "sophisticated" habit of smoking was modeled for the masses. Philip Morris advertised in *Playbill*; America's finest cigarette, fifteen cents a pack. This historic mid-town Manhattan venue has stood for generations in both structure and caliber of entertainment. It was Barrymore and Helen Hayes that fought over the sobriquet "First Lady of American Theatre."

Though tethered to the family and their planned New York itinerary, Robin did not hesitate to thrust herself into the metro social scene. She reunited with the eligible bachelors who suddenly ranked below Billy Hoblitt on the man score: Louie (wanting to marry her), Ossie (who had "pinned" her in April) and Wendy (Lindy-hop superman of fun in NYC).

On September 20, the Smith campus called her back for junior year. My mom packed her new leather Hartmann suitcase (the bee's knees of leather luggage at that time, carried by the likes of Babe Ruth, Bogart and Bacall) and left on the train for Albany. She reflected on the goodbyes of her parents, then confessed to her diary: *"was pretty hard to leave 'em."* A farewell telegram care of the Grace Line was delivered the next day. I imagine T. Wayne read it and Lelia wept. That Western Union message haunted their cabin all the way to the port of Valparaiso.

Later, in the innocence of childhood, it made me sad that my mom only saw her parents two weeks out of the year. In the late 1950s, when T. Wayne and Lelia retired back to the States, they re-located "way out west" in Arizona. The hot, dry desert climate was an arthritis driven decision. When my mom prepared to leave the Crane Road house to go visit them each summer, I'd sad-eye her like a puppy while she packed her Samsonite. She'd distract my ruminations by telling stories. In Tucson a person could fry an egg on the sidewalk! I visualized my grandmother standing outside their modest home on East Silver Street wearing an apron, spatula in hand, minding the eggs.

Upon her return to campus, Robin moved up on the hill into a new room with flawless furniture. *"Talked with girls all evening after getting partly unpacked."* At Chapel with Mrs. Dwight Morrow the next morning, my mom received her course card; twenty-three hours per week and *"still on the Registrar's List. Gee! But I'm gonna get off this year or bust."* Robin prepared for combat with the subject matter; sociology, chemistry, zoology, bacteriology, *"lots of worms, etc. under the microscope."* She confessed to her diary: *"Spent about $15 for books...bought a new pen – $8.75 – extravagant!"* The pen, a psychological boost? Symbolic of a fresh start? Purchased to perform like a magic bullet offering better grades and letter writing, too. The Parker "Duovac" fountain pen, came in three colors: blue, maroon and green, with gold trim and a fine nib. It wrote smoothly with a wet line. Her size, "Ingénue," measured four-and-five-eighths inches when capped. The price tag on a matching pencil? Four-dollars.

In her capacity as acting president, Mrs. Dwight Morrow heaved thick ropes the morning of Tuesday, October 10. Campus stirred like a hornets' nest when college bells unexpectedly rang out, as if buildings were under siege. The chimes announced, "Mountain Day," an unexpected break from classes on a beautiful fall morning. A day dictated by Smith tradition (but never marked on the academic calendar) chosen to "make hay while the sun shines" in New England's famous fiery fall foliage.

It was a tune changer. Mom's often pessimistic diary entries took a holiday from the typical *"worked hard all day,"* mid-semester grades *"bad,"* chem problems *"plenty tough to take,"* chem and zoo notebooks handed in (sometimes not), handed back, and corrected to hand in again.

She didn't stay on campus to study that day. *"Censored pictures of Mountain Day"* were revealed at a Halloween party three weeks later. She had run off with Lolly and friends to swim (goodness, skinny dip?), picnic, and sun like turtles lazing about on warm rocks. That's the truth I believe.

Overall Robin's diary revealed cheery entries of free-wheeling excursions. She spent many evenings at Rahar's Inn (an iconic off-campus institution crammed full of college kids) for a beer and talk, or lobster with wine, and at Toto's Restaurant, where drinking, dining, and dancing made it a chart-topping date destination. There Johnny Walker Scotch and sodas went down easy. Her college experience was academically and socially *well-rounded*.

Then came Christmas break. The afternoon of Saturday, December 16, satchels packed, Robin joined Dottie Davies on the 1:15 p.m. train, headed south. Dottie was one of the "Cute '42's" on the Smith campus, just like my Aunt Dottie. (Confusing, I know, to introduce another "Dottie" character, but it was a common name back then.) They overnighted in New York at the Biltmore, above Grand Central Station, and delighted in the original comedy play *Skylark* that starred Gertrude Lawrence at the (now demolished) Morosco Theatre. Following a blue-plate special at Penn Station the next morning, the two "Smithies" boarded the legendary *Orange Blossom Special*. Like a dream come true, this luxury passenger train bound for the Sunshine State would deliver her to the place she'd fantasized since the World's Fair exhibit, four months earlier. In Florida, Robin was destined to celebrate the season in style, with a gang of impeccably pedigreed revelers, not a dolt in the lot. The *Orange Blossom Special* was an electric train that moved slowly by today's standards. It was a long day and night of travel between NYC and St. Petersburg. They played Bridge most all the way.

I remember my parents telling me they were introduced to one another by Dottie Davies, though I don't remember ever meeting her. If beggars can't be choosers, I can't imagine my mom landing anywhere better than in the company of the Davies family and friends for Christmas vacation in 1939. Her mini-manifest destiny took her to St. Pete.

On their arrival, my mom *"took a bath."* A step above using a pitcher and a basin to sponge off, but I'd have jumped in the shower to remove the railroad grime. Except that showers were not commonplace at the time; one innovation Boomers and beyond take for granted. From the day my sister Dianne schooled me on body odor and dirty hair I adopted the daily shower ritual. In the '70s I was a silky, chestnut colored "Breck Shampoo Girl," with a wish to swing locks like Jaclyn Smith of *Charlie's Angels* fame. Changing classes through the hallowed halls of Mountain Lakes High School, cloaked in my dad's 1940s army shirt, I counted on the feminal bouquet of "Gold Formula Breck" to neutralize Buster's 1940 "man smell."

That first evening in St. Pete my mom *"went to see Joan Davies – Met Peg Laughner. Mrs. Davies awful cute! Grandma's sweet."* Like lightning, six degrees of separation struck. Peggy Laughner was my dad's high school friend from St. Pete, a girl who penned letters delivered to his Princeton address. Not that I was privy to them, but recall my dad wrote his parents that Peggy had written.

So it was to be, on this Christmas vacation in 1939 that life's intricately rich pageantry was invited in to intertwine with destiny.

My mom's diary revealed how this vacation played out. The operative word "play" was as it should be on Christmas break. I don't know who the *"Bob Robert's Society Band"* is that Jimmy Buffett sings about, but just like that song *"it's the magic of the music that still draws a crowd."* Imagine *"young folks, old folks, 'bout to cut a rug. Fox Trot, Bunny Hop, do the Jitterbug."* There is history to take away from Robin's abbreviated notes.

For example, the Pass-A-Grille Yacht Club was fairly new at the time. It was chartered six years before, in 1934. The same year the Bedford father-son duo docked with their haul of Kingfish. The barrier island community of St. Pete, on Florida's Pinellas peninsula, is known for panoramic Gulf coast sunsets. Soft, sugar-white sandy beaches stretch south to Pass-A-Grille. Wind carved sand dunes form endless mounds, covered in hearty shrubs, wildflowers, and deep-rooted sea oats with waving tops. An exciting place for kids young and old to play hide and seek. A place better reserved for nesting turtles and shore birds. Today a section of Pass-A-Grille is a National Historic District with a colorfully interesting past. Here's what my mom said about escapades in paradise, where she celebrated the last two weeks of 1939:

December 19 - *"Went to beach today. Swimmin' and playin' Bridge on sand. Collected shells."*

December 20 - *"Bought red dress for party – $19.75 looks pretty nice. Went for ride with George – out with him in evening to Yacht Club – Egan's and Cotton Club."*

December 22 - "Went to Smith Alumnae luncheon then to my Open House – 150 people all very nifty – got lots of bids [offers] to things – dances, etc. Made quite an impression. Got dates with Charlie Barclay and George mixed up. Went out with Charlie – to Chatterbox, movies "Secret of Dr. Kildare" – saw Happy Felton's band – out to Egan's – Pass-A-Grille, Treasure Island and home for breakfast pretty late."

December 23 - "Got up late! Charlie called. Went to Byrnes dinner party then Everly dance. Had a wonderful time. Nifty people there – met Skip thru Barton – Could go for him in a big way."

December 24 - "Played blackjack all Xmas Eve... went for drive with Skip – learned a lot about Florida and the land boom. He's planning on riding from Washington to N.Y.C. with me. Smoothest boy I ever saw. He ate dinner at the house and then took me to see his mother and boat."

While local boys slept in the fish house on idle nets, my mom spent the evening of Christmas Day with a polished lot at a "Beta dance." This reference? The Beta Theta Phi fraternity, founded on the University of Florida campus in 1930. I flashed on Siamese fighting fish swimming in brandy snifters. Do you understand the analogy between this fish species and a fraternity? If placed in the same tank two male bettas will fight. *Voilà*, Beta meet Betta. In my experience, the "Greek system" is remembered with a headshake due to brothers or sisters who made choices so poor they landed in the national news.

When I moved west to attend the University of Utah, my parents encouraged me to join a sorority. I was the first of my siblings to have that so called "opportunity." But I didn't. Hippie-types did not DO sororities in the 1970s. Sorority girls had families with discretionary income. That did not describe my state of material welfare. I did not have the desire to subject myself to the "best set" by my parents' standards.

But in a matter of affiliating with a social set at all, I chose the Hedonist Society, a loosely knit group of non-Mormons (few, if any, had Utah roots in the bunch). In social moments, we forged friendships on the ski slopes, around kegs of beer and the occasional 50-gallon trash can of Everclear (190 proof grain alcohol) fruit punch. Adult beverages aside, it bears mentioning no one in this group dialed into President Nixon when he declared the war on drugs in 1971. Peyote buttons and magic mushrooms naturally paved the way to personal enlightenment. In a far-out twist of fate, my friend Joan, the ringleader of the Hedonists, came to be my eldest son's high school guidance counselor. We all turned out to be respectable citizens.

My mom recorded the details of her Christmas day in 1939 like this: *"Spent Xmas night with Oliver Sumard at Beta dance – Afterwards to Chatterbox – out to beach – long talk with him – he's awful sweet. For Xmas got ski mittens, scarf, goggles, ring, book, bed socks. Had stocking with everything in it – even a green peach."*

"Chatterbox" struck me as a clever name for a hangout. In a surreal way, I twisted over its address at One Beach Drive, one I recognized. Its doors opened in 1936, a hot nightclub scene for music and dancing. It later became a restaurant and grew in reputation as one of St. Pete's most historic meeting spots, shaded by banyan trees dripping with Spanish moss. Today the Bayfront Towers, a condominium apartment building, sits atop the former footprint of the Chatterbox. Nearly eighty years later, my brother Bob and his wife coincidentally spend winters in their Bayfront Towers condo, *at One Beach Drive.*

How's that for serendipity?

The green peach in my mom's stocking evoked a tug on my heartstrings. At the Crane Road house decades later, our stockings always held tangerines and mixed nuts in their shells. A tradition in keeping with the story of St. Nicholas and his sacks of gold. During the Great Depression when money was tight, locally available fruit and nuts replaced gifts when families lacked the means. The same held true for the recession of the 1970s when inexpensive filler of fruit and nuts paired well with a few "gold coins" of chocolate. And I do recall some lumps of charcoal briquettes. Yes I do, they didn't cost much either.

What a blessing for my mother. Back then, in 1939, in the absence of family, her Christmas stocking was still stuffed.

December 26 - *"Went to Phi Delta dance with Bob Barton – first to Chatterbox, then to dance. Joe Ravel's orchestra. Had a lot of fun. Danced with Forrest Buster Bedford (Columbia), Bill Ray (Cornell) George Slather (Temple) Al Stromberg, Chuck Simmons (ex-Annapolis) Jim Sand (Florida). Had tennis date with Bill Harvard – Beach party at Eustis's. Met Ed Douglas and Chuck Simmons. Ping-Pong, breakfast, etc."*

So, it was *here* on December 26, 1939, at the Phi Delta Theta fraternity dance that Forrest Buster Bedford lurked among a well-heeled bunch of other eligible young men. My mom and my dad connected toe-to-toe and cheek-to-cheek, dancing to a big band chart topper. The sound of Glenn Miller is a safe bet. This is where their story slowly begins. Two days later, aboard the *Silver Meteor*, Florida's first streamliner train, my mom made her way back to a New England winter, set to ring in a new, and not to be forgotten, decade.

Of Skiing, Romance and Social Malice

Chapter Seventeen

I've come to understand that if my mom's passion for skiing did not exist, and if she failed to enchant Buster with the sport, the trajectory of my life would have been way off course. I might still be living in New Jersey, or somewhere in the northeast, where the highest snow skiing elevation tops out at 6,288 feet on Mount Washington, New Hampshire.

It's possible my mom learned to snowplow as a young child in Chile. Likely at Farellones, on a hill located in a village nestled within the skinny mountain chain of the Andes, about twenty-five miles from Santiago. At 7,800 feet above sea level, stellar snow crystals made for champagne powder that she'd be too short to appreciate. The same altitudes and dry air hold true for the Rocky Mountains of North America. Choke-able powder is sometimes so fine and deep a person could drown.

Alpine skiing boomed in a worldwide way in the 1930s. This is a bit counter-intuitive for the U.S., at the height of the Great Depression. No matter for my mom, Buster or the constellation of sporty folks living in cold climates with a few greenbacks to spare. Skiing offered an alternative to ice skating, sledding and tobogganing with greater opportunity to show off in the company of friends. Rope tows proliferated as a rather easy installation. People bought in to the glamour of the sport depicted in magazines and film. Think dimpled face blonde, Sonja Henie, cute and bubbly, whose Olympic champion ice skating talent transferred to skis in the movies *Thin Ice* and *Sun Valley Serenade*.

To discuss the sport, and more importantly to see and be seen *doing* the sport, defined a person as rather upscale and outdoorsy, then and still today.

Anyone who has taught their own children how to ski knows it takes effort *and patience*. As I worked with my own kids (skiing between my legs from the time they could walk) I had to hand it to my folks who saw to it that my siblings and I took up the sport. Parents put up with cold hands helping kids get geared up. Chiseling snow off the bottom of the boot, at first with the tip of their ski pole. Often resorting to scraping with mitted fingers. Cursing when conditions, cold and slushy, demand fingernails as the primitive tool required for the job. The mission is simple enough; get the binding to click. Before the first run, the little dears whine about cold hands and feet. That's why parents invest in ski school.

As a kid, I had wooden skis with cable bindings and leather boots that laced. And in keeping with the Princeton theme that permeated our house, my wooden skis were painted black, with orange pin stripes. Once "quick release" bindings came along, lack of safety straps (unmandated at the time) gave runaway skis the chance to do just that, at high speed, downhill. Other panicked skiers screamed "ski" at the top of their lungs, people riding the lift would chime in, too. No one wanted to witness an impalement. Those below stood like statues looking uphill, like a game of freeze tag, until the ski went by or sailed off into the woods. Eventually the safety strap requirement took hold. Mine was a short piece of black leather, attached to my binding, with a metal snap hook clipped to my boot strings. My dad used what he called a "long thong." It was attached to the ski and wrapped round and round his ski boot. Good enough to satisfy those patrolling the lift line.

Returning to the end of Robin's Christmas vacation in 1939, a new decade began on the ski slopes. New Year's Day of 1940 she skied at Haystack, *"chasing up and down the hill after a beer."* And the day after, *"feeling pretty tired."* Not tired enough to keep her from attending *"Hamlet"* that night, starring Maurice Evans, his name lit by the naked bulbs on the marquee at the 44th Street Theatre in New York.

Maurice Evans rates as one of the best-known Shakespearean actors of my mom's time. Maybe she was a greeting card nut, because it was through the *Hallmark Hall of Fame* that Evans brought the likes of *Hamlet* and *Macbeth* to the American television viewing audience. I personally counted on him to invite trouble as "George the Warlock," father of Samantha Stephens, whenever he appeared in the TV sitcom *Bewitched*. And his distinctive voice stands out in his role as Dr. Zaius in *Planet of the Apes*. My mom taught me to recognize and appreciate Maurice Evans, as one among so many other talented celebrities of her day, imprinted on hearts like feet on the Hollywood Walk of Fame. It explains why the MeTV Network was the channel of choice at Franciscan Oaks.

Coursework resumed that January of 1940, in bacteriology, chemistry, zoology, and sociology. Mom wrote an observation paper on "social malice" anonymously researching and recording human behavior. Obviously with malice in the title it was not good behavior. Conceivably the launch of her love for people watching? The paper was finished at 5 a.m. one morning, a happy truth for me. I never, *ever* suspected she was the all-nighter type. It was more than a handful of times I sat up all night cursing our ugly black Royal typewriter, a standard *manual*. IBM had introduced the original "Selectric" in the early '60s, and I relished their snappy keystrokes in Mrs. Wilcox's typing class at Mountain Lakes High. But into the wee hours, with appropriately dark subject matter, I manually pecked out an analysis of *Cancer Ward*, a 1970 Nobel Prize Winner for Literature: Alexander Solzhenitsyn's multi-leveled ugly representation of social malice and the Soviet Union. I love this quote from the book that characterizes my mom's dating behavior and Buster's courtship: *"Like a bicycle, like a wheel that, once rolling, is stable only so long as it keeps moving but falls when its momentum stops, so the game between a man and a woman, once begun, can exist only so long as it progresses. If the forward movement today is no more than it was yesterday, the game is over."*

So it was on February 7, 1940, that my mom finally noted a date with Buster in her diary. He wasn't bold enough to ask for her "contact information" at that fateful dance six weeks before in Florida. He was bolder.

Like a lover's chase scene in a romantic comedy, he bought a ticket to ride north on the *Silver Meteor*, the train he knew she'd board. Why? To bird-dog "Skip," the "eligible" she'd met December 23, just three days before she went cheek to cheek with Buster. It was Skip that took Robin for a drive, told her about the Florida land boom, introduced his mother and his boat. He had a head start and, quite possibly, the advantage. Not one Buster could afford to ignore. Recall, Robin wrote this about Skip: *"Could go for him in a big way"* and *"Smoothest boy I ever saw."* He was *"planning on riding from Washington to N.Y.C. with me."* Where my dad would, strategically, already be aboard getting to know all about her.

Buster sprang for a steak dinner at the Tavern. They spent the rest of the evening at Rahar's Inn. A week later, on Valentine's Day, she was taken with *"an awfully sweet card from Buster"* and salutations of the day from multiple admirers in the form of boxed chocolates and telegrams.

Their first date obviously met with success. On Sunday, February 18, Buster was up well before the birds and met Robin at 7:30 a.m. Feeling thoroughly modern, they *"whipped on out to Brattleboro"* and skied all day from ten to three, until *"he strained his leg pretty badly."* The "ski area" on the Charles Clark Farm opened to the public in January of 1938, just two years before. Lift tickets were thirty-five cents. It's hard to understand how anyone could ski for five hours at an area that had one rope tow, except that my dad was a beginner. Their leather gloves, put to the test toiling on the tow rope, were left wet and distressed. Sadly, my mom's diary left no hint of a romantic movie-like scene, fireside in a rustic lodge, like I'd hoped for.

The day after their big ski adventure my mom wrote to Buster. She confessed to being very stiff from the rope tow, but it didn't keep her from heading off to Black Panther Ski Hill the next day. Heck, her leather boots and gloves had dried by then. She reported the snow conditions... *"Over two feet of snow – all unbroken – not too great skiing."* Proving my point that New England does not generally boast about its fluffy snow. A Utah translation would sound like this: *"Over two feet of bottomless powder – untracked – best day of the year."* Bragging rights of "face shots" reverberate around those kinds of conditions.

The history surrounding all the little ski areas of New England that "once were" is sentimental territory. NELSAP (New England Lost Ski Area Project) is a treasure trove of the sport.

Of the ski areas in New Jersey where I learned to pick a line and hold an edge, chattering over icy boiler plate, there are a few on the "lost ski area" list. Great Gorge, located in McAfee, New Jersey, harbors my Mountain Lakes High Ski Club memories. As teens we schussed under the lights, showing off our very lame tricks (by today's standards) on Kamikazee, a black diamond run. Flasks harbored in an inside pocket were filled with fiery warmth swiped from unsuspecting parents' well stocked liquor cabinets. Some tried to do homework on the bus. Sweethearts "going steady" found it dark enough to "make out" in the back. The teacher chaperones were too wiped out to care.

On weekends as a teenager, I stood shoulder to shoulder with cigar smoking New Yorkers in forty-minute lift lines waiting for the "Summit Chair." Hugh Hefner's development of the Great Gorge Playboy Club in 1972 switched up the ski clientele in a big way. Swizzle sticks with bunny heads were new to me. In retrospect, I imagine that Mafioso types dealing drugs and laundering money stood in the same line.

The reward for that miserable lift line wait was about ten minutes of skiing top to bottom on cherry red Fischer Quick skis. They constituted my first big equipment upgrade from the wooden pin stripes. The look was complete with "step in" Marker Bindings made famous by ski idol and Olympian Franz Klammar. I wore Henke Plastic *buckle* ski boots in a fashionable '70s mustard color, planting each turn down the mountain with my Scott USA poles.

Snow Bowl was a step down from "The Gorge" in glamour, lift service and crowds, with two double chairlifts and a couple of T-bars that sufficiently serviced the 400 vertical feet. It found its way onto the "lost" ski area list.

The smallest "resort," a great family place with the most mischievous memories for me was Craigmeur, lift-served with a rope tow and T-bar. It was among those that opened in the late 1930s. Unusual by design, the lodge at Craigmeur was located at the top of the hill. At one point in its history, a ski jump stood in the center of the hill. Mountain lore was that the jump had burned, but the truth, as I understand it, is the timbers rotted over time. It was removed for safety reasons, leaving a few lumber stumps standing like dinosaur bones at the top and "the pit" in its wake.

When the end of school day bell jangled at Briarcliff Junior High, my mom happily drove my near-Irish twin, and me to ski. We'd meet up with the Peacock girls, a kindred sister set, from Mountain Lakes. Well-matched for mischief in age and skiing ability level, the "pit" worked for us like a half pipe, nearly twenty years before half pipes were invented. Feeling cocky with confidence we'd hang our tips over the edge of what felt like a suicide chute, drop in, shoot across on the diagonal and pop out the other side. The objective was to catch max air off the lip. In truth, other than the "airs" we put on showing off, our flight distance wasn't much more than that of a penguin. All momentum was lost on the uphill side. Waves of laughter ensued as we stuck our landings in follow-the-leader style. These were spectacular high-five moments. Except the high-five hand gesture wasn't a thing yet. Ski poles hung limp, dangling from wrist straps, for the 1960s equivalent; a low five glove slap.

The T-bar invited its own circus tricks. Designed to load two for the smooth ascent to the top, we'd ride single, maverick style. By restraining the bar when loading, a playful "liftie" could "jet-launch" the otherwise slow ride to the top. Like trapeze artists, we looped ourselves round and round, often skiing well outside the parallel tracks thinking we might trick some novice into wandering off course. Our fearsome adolescent foursome owned the mountain. The snack shack hot chocolate was watery by today's gourmet standards, lacking dollops of whipped cream, but it warmed icy fingers. The cost of a lift ticket in the late 1960s: $3 for the afternoon; a day pass for an adult on weekends: $5.50.

But enough of that. Let's get back to the end of February 1940. My mom had made her way off the dreaded Registrar's List! And a hopeful indicator of my dad's continued interest appeared. *Telegram from Buster for Jr. Prom this weekend. Damn! I'd love to go."*

Damn, she had plans for a different dance. An opportunity missed to further forge the relationship.

A week later, my mom ran out of Chem lab at 4:30 on Friday afternoon and caught the 5:20 train to New York. Buster met her at Grand Central. In keeping with conventional standards of propriety, she registered at the adjacent Biltmore, the same luxury hotel she'd comfortably overnighted in on her way to Florida at Christmas. It was a fine place that historically appealed to lovers. The solid bronze clock in the lobby proved a strategic rendezvous point for young couples. I imagine Buster took a seat on one of the leather couches near the clock. When a youthfully radiant Robin appeared, off they went to the Lion's Den for the evening. Chinese food had made its mark in New York, the result of waves of Chinese immigrants holding visas that came with restaurant work. And not unlike many hard-working immigrants of today, they were in this country to save, get ahead and send money back home.

After dinner and beer drinking, my mom and dad went walking *"over Riverside Drive to watch traffic."* Why on heaven's earth were they watching traffic on Riverside Drive? Clearly it was a distinctly different experience back then. The meandering headlights along serpentine curves held some attraction, as a relief from the street grid of Manhattan. Boats along the broad Hudson River waterway, a view westward of the Palisades rolling into New Jersey hills, the moon shining on water, and stars in the sky, went hand in hand with the ardent experience. Better than watching *just* traffic, at least from the perspective of a romantic.

My mom accompanied Buster to classes on a Saturday and found them to be *"strange."*

Strange? Possibly a lecture on corporations, learning that a corporation is a "person," maybe? It might have led to an exchange between professor and students on the topic of corporate fiction, assuming facts to be true for the sake of convenience to achieve justice. Yes, this *would* be strange from the perspective of a student of chemistry, biology, and zoology. Hopefully her study of social malice resonated at some level.

My mom met Bob Driver, a Columbia Law classmate, whom she deemed, *"a very nice boy."* The few women in the classroom, who were studious, determined and slightly older than the socialites at Smith might have struck any outsider as "strange." Picture a Bella Abzug type. Bella enrolled at Columbia in 1942, then took a break to work in a shipyard during the war. She graduated from the law school in 1947, the same year as my dad. She and her hat stick with me in my mind's eye, a compassionate fighter for equal human rights of all types; women's, civil, gay. Bella grabbed the attention and devotion of so many girls during the tumultuous 1970s, winning admiration with her political flair and cutting wit: *"I began wearing hats as a young lawyer because it helped me to establish my professional identity. Before that, whenever I was at a meeting, someone would ask me to get coffee."* It was Bella that represented the West Side of Manhattan for three congressional terms, 1971 – 1977. My dad called her out as a belligerent agitator from his place at the head of the Crane Road dinner table. My near-Irish twin and I were old enough to think for ourselves by then. It's no surprise my mom was on board with us.

That evening of March 9, 1940, my mom met Buster's family (my future grandparents). Witness the pen of her diary entry: *"Went to dinner at some Swedish place – good food – lots of laughs. Went to art exhibit – lots of beautiful paintings – Botticelli, Verrocchio, Titian, and Picasso. Went home to dress for Rainbow Room."*

She didn't exactly sing like a canary, but here's my best Agatha Christie deduction as to how this first meeting unfolded. The "Swedish place" turned out to be the Castleholm Restaurant, New York's most popular Swedish smorgasbord at the time. Just a few years old, the warm yellow walls of the "Viking Room" artfully depicted a mural of activity in the great outdoors: skiers, dancers, Norse seafarers, Scandinavian flags and crests. Blue chairs surrounded red tables. They were greeted like family in the basement of the Parc Vendome Apartments on 57th Street.

Seems to me that some of the best eateries I know are tucked away in basements. I don't mean eating strawberry shortcake at a place like Macy's Cellar Bar and Grille. I'm talking about hidden gems dripping with ambience and rustic decor: dim lighting, brick and plaster walls, shelves with trinkets, where superbly authentic freshly cooked international cuisine is paired with fine wine. And young men propose on bended knee when the music is cued up just right.

The Castleholm, as far as I can tell, offered warm hospitality and excellent service. I imagine the evening began with cordial how-do-you do introductions, followed by the ordering of Aquavit to warm the insides. Mouths watered over appetizers straight from the smorgasbord buffet; pickled herring, smoked salmon and a selection of cheeses. Small talk spawned naturally as their eyes wandered over whimsical Scandinavian subjects on the wall; a different view from each seat had their heads turning. The universal language of laughter eased the evening. I wonder if my grandfather pulled out his funny face repertoire while regaling my mom with stories of Buster's youth, insisting the young couple join them for home movies soon.

The mention of Picasso among the artists my mom namedropped in her diary led me like Sherlock straight to the Museum of Modern Art. Its proximity to the Castleholm, half a mile east on 57th Street, sealed that tidy detail. MoMA displayed a remarkable Pablo Picasso retrospective at this point in art history, an exhibit that gained the museum international recognition. Presumably why the gift shop today stocks Picasso to go which includes souvenirs that range the gamut from dining plate sets to wall calendars.

"Botticelli, Verrocchio, (and) Titian" comprised the "Italian Masters" exhibit on display at the MoMA from January to April 1940. I wonder if these works remained stateside for a time, safeguarded from the handiwork of Hitler's thugs in the rape of Europe. It's a reasonable assumption that an industry trade secret like *that* might have found its way to a chief curator. How films like George Clooney's *The Monuments Men* picked up and portrayed, in an entertaining way, the history to remind us of the nasty business of what it took to avert cultural catastrophe.

My dad's folks, then in their mid-fifties and married for nearly thirty-three years, graciously said good night at the end of dinner and retired to their apartment in midtown Manhattan. The "kids" were left to light up the night on their own.

With the next turn of events, my mom returned to the Biltmore. There she upgraded her attire for an evening at the legendary Rainbow Room, sixty-five floors above Rockefeller Center; "30 Rock" atop the RCA building (now Comcast). Then and now a person's ears are sure to pop in the elevator to the top.

"Buster sent two lovely pink camellias." I assume she put them in her hair as a rather dramatic display, and then met him by the clock in the lobby.

The Rainbow Room opened in October 1934, less than a year after the Twenty-First Amendment passed, repealing prohibition. This star-studded venue is famous for its revolving parquet dance floor, hardwood now notably pocked with stiletto heel marks of the rich and famous. The name derived from the bending of light through a combination of glass blocks, dripping crystal chandeliers and prismed "drapes." Rainbows bounced about and into infinity like one heck of a rave party. The biggest of big band names in entertainment played here; Tommy Dorsey, Glenn Miller, Benny Goodman, Guy Lombardo, and Lawrence Welk. Imagine a crowd dressed to the nines romanticizing over thirty-mile panoramic views of Manhattan's cityscape, just below today's "Top of the Rock" observation deck. Clearly my dad was set with intention to impress.

"Arrived at Rainbow Room 8:30 – lovely place – thrilled. Entertainment good – fun waltzing with Buster."

Her description of the entertainment as "good" left me with a sense of disappointment, but more disappointing still was, at the end of the evening, they drove to Hoboken. Yes, Hoboken. Which I innately remember as the butt of New Jersey jokes from my childhood in the Garden State. The best thing that ever happened in Hoboken was the birth of Frank Sinatra and the launch of his singing career in several local haunts, including his dad's bar. He split at the age of nineteen and never looked back.

Kids from New Jersey do that sometimes.

Why they visited Hoboken after an evening at the Rainbow Room is beyond me, but they did. Possibly Buster wanted to show off the New York skyline from a view further west than what Riverside Drive allowed. They returned by ferry ride across the Hudson. Maybe they each chucked a wilted Camellia into the water and made a wish. Or played some form of Poohsticks, picking a point downstream as the finish line. Whatever they did, I'll take that side-trip as a romantic return to Manhattan and the campus of Columbia University, where they talked.

"Up early to pack" on Sunday, March 10, she joined Buster for a service at Riverside Church, less than half a mile from Columbia. *"Reverend Wicks from Princeton spoke - pretty good."* Riverside Church, a Rockefeller funded awe-inspiring Gothic landmark and still the tallest church in the U.S., was only ten years old at this time, but appeared quite medieval by design. It towers above the Hudson along Riverside Drive with its pointed arches, flying buttresses, spires, and gargoyles. For lunch Buster and Robin dined on *"wonderful steak"* atop the Baker apartments on the *"roof garden,"* as reported in her diary. It must have been an unseasonably warm afternoon. New York weather can be dodgy in March and surely the garden had little color to behold. But knowing my dad, his intention was to view the Manhattan skyline from another vantage point, across the East River, on the Long Island side. It was a short trip over the Queensboro Bridge, a structure that later became the subject of Simon and Garfunkel's pop folk duet, *The 59th Street Bridge Song (Feelin' Groovy)*. Following lunch, they returned to the apartment of the senior Bedfords, just over a mile away. There my mom *"saw a lot of Buster's movies of Princeton and summers in St. Pete."*

Sure enough, I knew home movies would turn up in her script. It struck me that watching the replay of Buster's blessed childhood might have evoked a bit of sadness and even self-pity in my mom. But she was stronger than that or looking hopefully toward what the future might hold. *"Home on the 5:10. Happy, happy weekend."*

Plymouth, New Hampshire, was Robin's two-week spring break snow train destination. She pushed off campus with hat, goggles, gloves, skis, boots and poles to the White Mountains. A *"dreadful snowstorm"* kept her in

Plymouth on Friday, March 22. Intent on not wasting a day, she chased up and down Huckins Hill, the closest of three ski areas just east of Plymouth. Frontenac and Wendy's Hill, just south of Plymouth, were too far in the wintery weather. All are legends in the New England Lost Ski Area Project.

Late that afternoon, inspired by young love, Buster blazed north in a clacking rush along the rail. He arrived as the storm subsided. *"Played Fox and Hounds by moonlight. Tag, and Hide and Seek."* My mom didn't say with whom they played, if anyone. Maybe it was just the two of them amusing themselves with childhood games, in a flirty sort of way.

On Saturday they landed at Cannon Mountain. In the 1939-1940 winter season the nation's first aerial tramway, then in its second year of operation, notched its place in ski history. The "best set" loaded into the boxy red, white and black cars like cattle. Swept two miles to the top of the mountain on a cloudless winter day, they stepped out nearly on the roof of New England. I imagine Buster filled his lungs in a cleansing breath, then took his ski pole in hand like a professor's pointer. He would have impressed my mom with a geography lesson, circling northeast to the west with the tip of his pole: Maine, Vermont and New York. Canada, too. *"Came down Ravine Trail twice – lots of fun."* The Ravine Trail, now considered a legacy of the Civilian Conservation Corps, opened in 1939. I picture my mom streamlining down the hill in her well-fitted gabardine ski pants flaunting her stuff. Buster gave quad-burning chase. The stem of his pipe clenched in his teeth.

"Sat by fire tonight and talked to Buster. He loves me."

Forelsket! Eleven weeks into this blossoming relationship, did she intuitively "know" he loved her? Or, did he stare longingly into her alluring blue eyes, lean in, and whisper the words? As I imagine them fireside, the scene is punctuated with his soft southern lips locking on hers. Cheeks flushed, ignited hearts pounded. Do you understand *Forelsket*? If you've ever been in love, you do. It's a Norwegian word for which there is no English translation, but it boils down to the euphoria young lovers experience when they fall head over heels, all things amorous.

It's enough to give a young woman hives. I know from personal experience.

The weekend time-warped, as it does when young and in love. Buster left for the Columbia campus on Sunday's noon train. My mom *"felt very lonesome."* Fortuitous since it was a feeling she'd have to get used to over the next several months... and years. With a plan to visit Buster before the end of spring break, she left Plymouth the morning of Wednesday, April 3. *"Goodbye for a café while – to Fred and Charlie"* – a couple of ski buddies. *"Arrived in Boston at 2:00 – Rode to N.Y. reading book – 60 pages in five hours!"* Five minutes a page? A Forelsket distraction! *"Buster and family met me at station. Had steak dinner – off to trial. He made a nifty plea and got score of 84 – whee! Very high. Had long talk over beer in Lion's Den and en route uptown. Guess he loves me more than I believed."*

Buster's picture arrived in the mail that very week.

Returning her attention to coursework at the end of junior year, *"Went over to Dippy this A.M. for diagnostic clinic of 78-year-old doctor – senile psychosis. Cut up heart in zoology. Went back to Dippy in afternoon for clinic. Saw many types of mental diseases."*

Dippy? Really? I solved the mystery of Robin's reference to "Dippy" when I learned of a 1906 silent film, *Dr. Dippy's Sanitarium*. Mom taught compassion for those with *physical* disabilities during my youth. My sisters and I were often reminded, *"do not stare!"* But mental illness is often invisible or ignored. That's where my family ran into trouble with situations and conditions not to be talked about.

As May flowers bloomed in 1940, my mother's diary came alive, brightly dotted with notes of time spent in Buster's company. In New York and Princeton, she wrote of an inexhaustible smorgasbord of social life: cocktails, formal dinners, dances, sitting on the porch, leisurely reading *The New York Times*. A movie-like scene of a walk home after losing keys. Picnics, a baseball game, crew races, and a drive to Lawrenceville, where Buster had attended prep school. Drinking on the terrace at Princeton's Nassau Inn all morning. And afternoon. In Northampton, a garden party and dancing, cocktails followed by dinner at Toto's, and more dancing.

"Read paper after breakfast – for houses, etc. Sat in sun all afternoon – played first set of tennis. Beat me 6-2. Whale Inn for Dinner. Left after giving me his football. Will call me on Wed. and Sunday nights."

For me the question of marriage, yet unwritten in her diary, hovered like a butterfly waiting to light. What is the common denominator of "best set" and "yuppie?" Drink coffee. Read the morning paper. Be happy. Look for houses? Yes.

No doubt Robin snuck a peek at the engagement and wedding announcements, too.

At ages twenty and twenty-one, in a very grown up way, they perused the classifieds in search of a home. The going rate at the time: south of $4,000. It was Bruce on the man score that talked eastern picket fences. What a pain in the ass they are to maintain. Small matters like home maintenance fall far from the fairytale of young lovers, as do property taxes, I suppose. Their quest: to live an upwardly mobile perfect suburban life with the "best set."

The thought of homeownership was understandably heady brew for a young woman like my mom. I doubt she had ever felt "at home," anytime or anywhere in her twenty years. This was more than a hunt for a Tudor-style charmer or brick bungalow with pillared porch. She held out hope their search would turn up the one place she'd hold everything and everyone she loved.

Unlike Ossie on the man score, Buster didn't have a fraternity pin to proffer as a placeholder for an engagement ring. Greek letter organizations were not part of the social fabric of Princeton. His football, however, sealed the deal for the next several months. And in fact, like a lucky charm, the very same football had a presence in the Crane Road house for the forty-six years my parents lived there.

Who would guess, in any form of romantic symbolism, the color of love could be pigskin?

Equanimity

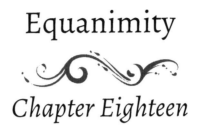

Chapter Eighteen

May 21, 1940, marked Buster's twenty-second birthday. His first year of law school at Columbia was buttoned up. In quiet contemplation he strategically weighed the pros and cons of his enlistment in the U.S. Army, the spillover effect of deeply ingrained social responsibility. His gift of equanimity, presence of mind, reflected cultural markers of his southern upbringing. Germany was advancing in France. His faith was strong as he calmly assessed world affairs and uncertainties he believed America would soon face in the stark reality of war.

Like propositional logic, his perfect pass at my mom earlier in the month filled his soul with hope, and his body with the physical perkiness of Forelsket. Nothing was set in stone with respect to marriage, but to Robin he stacked up like Romeo.

My mother, never one to miss a party, was forced to skip Buster's twenty-second birthday celebration. It fell on a Tuesday, and though he was born a Tuesday's child "full of grace" in 1918, this night of the week lacks as a standout for reveling by anyone's standards. Odds are he dined out with his folks and called it good. Meanwhile, my mom's day looked like this: *"Went to dinner with Edna Mann after working in Chem lab all day."*

Two days later, an unexpected telephone call rang through to Haven House. At 7:30 Thursday morning, a robe wrapped Robin stood flatly in slippers. Right handed, she squeezed the receiver. Her left hand shot instinctively atop her head and grabbed a hank of hair. Universal body language gave away heartbreak, as her cousin Roy delivered the news. His dad, my mom's Uncle Frank, and fatherly surrogate, *"had gone."* With a one-day reprieve from school work, she traveled 300 miles round-trip on Friday. *"Lovely flowers and service."* Words of hopefulness were offered up... *"[He] played on the square, played the game, finished the race and now receives his reward."*

On Saturday, with term-end pressures looming, Robin finished up chemistry experiments in the morning. That afternoon, she shed her lab coat and dressed to attend a "linen shower" for her bosom buddy Ruth Smith.

Hello, bosom buddy? I hated it when my mom used that turn of phrase in the presence of my friends. It was just a bad visual image hanging, like an old worn out DDD bra. BFF, "best friends forever" is much better. Excellent work, millennials, honoring the bedrock of female friendships that grow ever more important as we age.

Can you hear the *oooh's* and *ahhhh's* spilling out over monogramed napkins, tea towels, and tablecloths at the shower? I possess boxes of linens passed down from every direction over generations. They've occupied space in drawers and closets patiently waiting a call to action for a special occasion. I've actually started to use them. Everything vintage is trendy and trading on Etsy and eBay. Personally, I slack on the ironing. They function without starch. But let me give you this tip. A friend, who was caught up in the wave of Irish emigration to England as a girl, likes to iron! Her explanation? It instills a sense of calm.

Equanimity. It can be found in simple rituals if we permit it.

Infused with the enviable energy of youth, my mom embraced that evening's activities after an already full day. A horseshow, dinner at Beckman's, and on to Toto's. Then off to "Float Night," a Smith tradition that offered up more than root beer. After sunset, blended voices of the glee-club drifted across the still waters of Paradise Pond, centerpiece of equanimity on the Smith College campus. After dark, bedecked canoes in themed pageantry slipped along the water's surface to be categorically judged for beauty and originality. The spillway gurgled peacefully with calming effect.

I trust the floats were on notice to mind the edge.

The previous year, in 1939, Bruce was my mom's Float Night escort. At that time, he was in contention with Ossie for the number one spot on the man score. She decreed: *"Tom Sawyer and Little Boy Blue* [are] *best floats."*

On this night in May 1940, Bud was her chaperone. I imagined it was my uncle-to-be, Bud McLeod, strategically winning over the familial allegiance of my Aunt Dorothy's big sis. Poised along the grassy banks sloping to the pond, they might have reminisced the best of times in unadorned watercraft at Seeley Lake.

Wrong! I am way off course. It was a completely *different* Bud of the last name Narroway. I am tricked by a young man whom my mom has dated, but never ranked on her man score!

On this Float Night, my mom wrote: *"Got beautiful flowers from Buster."* A romantic gesture affirming his love from a distance. Or was it an expression of sympathy over her loss of Uncle Frank? Either is a suitable explanation. Presumably the freshest of May blooms derailed any plan for amorous advance on the part of Bud Narroway. Her favorite pageant raft: *"Erik the Red."* A reference to the famous ancient explorer nicknamed for his red hair, as if he popped off the wall at the Castleholm Restaurant and appeared now, large as life, horned helmet and all. In a diversionary tactic, she may have described the scene when she first met Buster's parents at the Castleholm. And the evening that followed at the Rainbow Room? Feeling as though she needed to fill a void of silence, she might have gone so far as to speak of that less than impressive side trip to Hoboken.

My mom celebrated her twenty-first birthday in the company of Buster. *"Brought me a lovely rose"* in hand at 3:00. Long stemmed and yellow? When I was a kid that was her favorite. Sunny, cheerful, warm and happy. Likely he didn't know her that well. No, it had to be red and romantic, symbolizing his love like Scottish poet Robert Burns in his words, *"My love is like a red, red rose."* My dad's gift was *"a beautiful leather jewel box."* And if my memory serves me correctly, I do believe it was red leather, with a gold leaf border of *fleur de lis*. The lock and latch were similar, but just a bit mechanically different from the one on my mom's five-year diary. She kept that jewel box for a lifetime. By her own account, that evening at Toto's was dizzyingly perfect. *"Had dinner and danced all by ourselves."* Then they drove out in the country to experience equanimity under the moon and stars.

Meanwhile, under the moon, stars and Luftwaffe, the English Channel lit up. A daring rescue mission known as "Operation Dynamo" was underway. British Expeditionary Forces, French armies and some fragments of Belgian troops (following Belgium's surrender to Germany three days earlier) were in full retreat, then surrounded on the northern coast of France. Where?

Dunkirk!

Military history at its best has been captured repeatedly in book and film for generations to remember. Or, more importantly, *never forget*.

Reflecting on calmer waters, my mom's May memoranda rolled out like this: *Buster rates #1.* In a matter of nine magical months, the man score reduced from six to a single. Soon to be forced apart, each with their personal obligations, the summer of 1940 might have put either, or both, to a head-turning test. But not so much where they were headed.

I hark back to 1972, when rock music was my teenage lifeline. My mom, white knuckling the wheel of our metallic teal Pontiac station wagon in chaotic Jersey traffic, was not fond of the Top 40 on the AM radio. She regarded most songs pushed out by DJ Dan Ingram from the studio at WABC New York as "noisy racket." Yet, she'd never snap off Bobby Vinton's hit *Sealed with a Kiss*. In fact, she'd be inclined to sing along. And I now know why.

> *Though we gotta say goodbye for the summer*
> *Baby, I promise you this*
> *I'll send you all my love*
> *Every day in a letter*
> *Sealed with a kiss*

Valderi – Valdera

Chapter Nineteen

Long before "networking" became a job hunt strategy, my mom tapped Miss Elizabeth B. Moriarty, the assistant director at Camp Accomac, for a counselor position in Hillside, Maine.

Why would she do that? To appease my grandmother. Accomac offered that port-in-the-storm sanctuary for the summer of 1940. A place near Bridgeton, Maine where Robin could hang her hat rent free, earn her own spending money, and wait out the start of senior year at Smith.

No matter how out-of-character it might seem for my mother, Lelia would deem it character building. My dad would have agreed.

In the two-week interlude that preceded her cloistering in camp, Robin played Buster's exuberant wing-woman. Over a three-day Princeton Reunion weekend, she was indoctrinated into "Tiger" culture. Caught up in song, she belted *Going Back to Nassau Hall* with enthusiasm to mask Buster's godawful off-notes. (As the family sat together in the pew at the Community Church of Mountain Lakes, he'd remind me that God didn't care if he sang off-pitch. It was God, after all, that created him that way.) Picnics, big-band parties and *the* "P-rade" celebrated everything orange and black. Embraced by Buster's Tiger tribe, my mom filled her heart, in a compensatory way, with a sense of belonging.

A five-day trip to spend time with friends in Plymouth followed. *"Everybody glad to see us."* Horseback riding was delayed due to a downpour, but one of the gang took up as entertainer. He picked his guitar with song selections that resonated with Robin: *Tumbling Tumbleweeds* and *If I Had my Way*. Though Buster couldn't sing like Bing, if he had his way, he'd make my mom's "golden dreams come true" as the lyrics promised. The morning of Thursday, June 27, they rode horses, then... *"Packed and left Plymouth for Northampton..."*

Buster imparted a pep-talk before his return to Manhattan Friday morning. He left Robin "chin up." (An expression he used often with me as a kid.) She rendezvoused with other "Smithies" headed for Camp Accomac, where they would work under the wing of Miss Moriarty. The evening of her arrival, she wrote this first impression in her diary: *"A fine place – beautiful waterfront."*

It was Miss "Mori's" twenty-sixth summer at the camp. It happened that her winter employment was at Smith College, teaching physical education, which is obviously how my mother met her. The college campus and girls' camp offered Miss Mori a single woman's haven for a lifetime where she exerted epic influence on many, many young ladies. I perceive her as a tower of strength, her appearance something like the character Miss Clavel, in the children's book series *Madeline*. Do you remember the little girls in two straight lines? My mom was something like Madeline herself, not afraid of mice (she permitted several as pets in my youth), loving winter, snow and ice.

Miss Mori assigned my mom and her Smith classmate, Alameda Howard, to "Camp Craft." But that direct assignment was just the beginning. As a practical measure, on the job cross-training was a strategic investment in skill-building for all Accomac counselors. It was not unlike how the military would soon turn out well-rounded soldiers.

The first few days of that cross-training included a canoe test, followed by a canoe trip to practice paddling technique. The trial run might have started with basics; how to get into a canoe, a lesson in physics for a biology major. Crouch low, grab the far gunwale, and step into the center, one foot followed by the other. Balance is key. Paddle strokes? Forward, reverse, sweep, J-stroke and how to rudder from the stern. Maybe canoe over canoe rescue? Other strokes to push and pull out of situations and conditions.

As I digested my mother's tutorial on canoeing, I recalled the lessons that preceded my own summer camp canoe trip, through rapids on the Delaware River. I imagine my mom's lessons, like mine, contained the essentials of how to read moving water: follow the tongue, land in the chute and generally navigate holes and boulder gardens without spinning around, or swamping. Watercraft at the mercy of Mother Nature is a metaphor for life in general. I know this to be true. How? My husband proposed to me in a cyclone on a forty-two-foot sailboat in the heart of the South Pacific. Our boat went aground in the "friendly islands" of the Kingdom of Tonga, thus I have experienced those situations and conditions. At least my mom knew how to balance from within and forward paddle. There were no upsets recorded on Seeley Lake with Bill, Bud, and Dottie the summer before.

"Scrubbed grease off pots and pans. Raked campsite. Picked daisies."

Nothing beats the durability of cast iron pots and pans, especially in the days before WWII and stick-free Teflon™. In 1940, the nation's supply of quality metal was understandably redirected to the war effort. But in the "cook's tour" of Camp Accomac, Miss Mori had my mom muscle kitchenware out of winter storage and into the kitchen sink. Let's talk the characteristics of "seasoned" cookware. If you live in the south and inherited your granny's skillet, or you own Dutch ovens, you already understand this ritual. Smothered with bacon fat or lard, fired up, wiped out, those vessels were prepped for hibernation at the end of summer '39. It follows, ten months later, my mom resuscitated them for use in the canteen. She cut through the rancid odor of stale grease with an already overused sponge saved for that task. The seasoning, accumulated over many, many summers like layers of seasoned stories, remained intact.

I was surprised that in Montana, of all places, there was not one cursory diary note of poking at smoky embers or the taste of campfire cuisine. Dutch ovens are typically at the center of any real cowboy's cookery. Summer 1939 had been all about splendid and carefree summer picnics prepared by others. Compared to that, summer 1940 shaped up to be down and dirty camp work.

The cast iron pots and pans stacked in the back of the cabinet at the Crane Road house would be functional heirlooms today. I don't recall my mom ever using them. If a person could muster the strength to swing a pan of that weight, it would serve well as a first line of defense against an intruder, as in Moe taking a pan to Curly, *Three Stooges* slapstick style. The technology of DuPont's (toxic) Teflon™ cookware ruled the '60s. It made my dish detail comparably effortless swiping the surface with a pastel nylon sponge engineered for the "do *not* scratch the Teflon™" task.

The Session One Accomac campers arrived on July 1, 1940. *"Bunk 11 seems very nice. Janet slow and sloppy. Tess very good, neat, polished, cute. Ellen – fast worker – tends to business and gets it done."* My mom often reminded me, "You never get a second chance to make a good first impression." For Boomers who lacked parental advice like that, *Head and Shoulders* shampoo delivered it with a wallop of social anxiety. The shedding of little white flakes? A dating deal-breaker as lethal as tooth film.

The Camp Craft lessons were many and varied. *"Good fun, but hard work."* Tools for the job included knives and hatchets for whittling, woodcarving, wood-cutting, wood-chopping. *"One accident. More 'wind' about knives."* Camp safety taught by necessity. *"Cooking with fire. Marshmallows. Cinnamon Toast. Coffee. Reflector ovens fashioned out of tin."* The girls turned out sweet confections not unlike the ones I produced, with parental guidance, using the heat of a lightbulb in my Kenner Easy-Bake Oven. Bunk-roll. Bed-roll. Camp craft contests, not to mention breakfast cooked up by one group, and supper by another: *"beautiful brownies were made as well as a steak."*

When the bunks settled, the counselors often played Bridge. There was no escaping war news on the radio after hours. July 10, 1940, is a notable date that marked the historic beginning of the "Battle of Britain." On the same day the Vichy regime, led by Marshal Philippe Pétain, succeeded the

Third French Republic. A simple note in her diary: *"End of French Republic."* Pétain had collaborated with the Germans.

The evening of Friday, July 26, my mom stepped away from Accomac with two other counselors for a night off at the movies. Storm clouds roiled on the big screen at the beginning of *The Mortal Storm*, a film that premiered six weeks earlier. The narrator asked a Chapel-talk kind of question: *"How soon will man find wisdom in his heart and build lasting shelter against his ignorant fears?"* In their starring roles, Margaret Sullavan, Jimmy Stewart, and Robert Young delivered a relevant lesson, depicting the brutality of Hitler's regime as it ripped a family apart. The praiseworthy website IMDb tells us that Hitler banned this MGM film from release in Germany. He did not appreciate its anti-Nazi sentiment. In fact, for good measure, all MGM films were banned by the Third Reich.

Thought provoking films like that make a person appreciate the blessings of their own life. Unbegrudgingly, Robin picked up on *"other duties, as assigned"* at camp, as she prepared the staple order. "Staple" meaning a basic food item like flour, sugar, and rice for the mess-hall menus. Not to be confused with a bent piece of metal or the office supply store, where if you've ever looked for them, finding a box of staples *in a Staples* plays out like a game of hidden pictures. She also took on new identities with a "commercialized" camp face. She hit the stage as a winged Angel for one show and as a *"Frow-Frow"* girl, frilled in a white ruffled red dress, for another. Having never studied German, it was "Frau-Frau" (not *"Frow"*) she intended. *Three Pills in a Bottle*, a one-act fantasy tale for children (circa 1917) came to life. As did the one-act play, *Queen Puff-Puff* (circa 1937). Good grief, can you imagine how the combination might be re-scripted as a single title today, with the setting in a rehab center? Queen Puff-Puff with three pills in a bottle?

All this may be why, in the Crane Road house, my mom supported dramatic endeavors for me and the neighborhood girls. I was a painfully shy child, but don't recall feeling bashful when dressed to the nines performing in the variety shows we kids produced in the 1960s. Chairs set in our broad, flat driveway equaled ticket numbers sold door-to-door around the neighborhood (plus a few extra chairs, in hopes that word of our performance traveled further down the street). Our stage, backdropped by the garage, supported small-scale live theatre, which included song acts, scripted skits and science magic (before Bill Nye made it cool). Our pixie haircuts did not allow for updos, but the makeup was brilliant. As a sometime Avon rep, my mom had plenty of bright samples to spare.

Reflecting on letters sealed with a kiss, anyone who's ever been there knows when a young couple is in love, nine weeks of separation over the course of a summer feels like an eternity. Sadly, the handwritten words of mutual adoration between my yet-to-be parents escaped the box in the back the closet, though I know for a fact letters traveled back and forth. She wrote in her diary about receiving mail from, and writing to, Buster. She reported on camp craft, canoe trips, and care packages, the contents of which were sometimes shared as "bunk presents."

More important in the evolution of their relationship was this: My mom wrote twice in her diary about Buster coming to visit at Camp Accomac. It is no short trip from Manhattan to Maine, but the travel distance did not deter my dad's mission.

On Thursday, July 18, eight days after the German *Luftwaffe* launched their first bombing raid against a British shipping convoy (first strike in the Battle of Britain) the young lovers *"stayed out 12 hours after getting late permission."* (Unlike the Smith campus, there were no curfew violators at Accomac.) Their conversation hung on tumultuous times in Europe. I believe Buster held her close, conveyed his sense of duty, social responsibility, and patriotism. Then stated his motives. Both spoke from the heart and together weighed decisions to be made.

The second time Buster petitioned my mom for a break from Accomac it was for two days: July 31 and August 1. This visit delivered like nothing less than a drum roll. The day before, on Tuesday, July 30, 1940 he'd enlisted in the National Guard of the State of New York.

Stationed in the Squadron "A" Armory, at Madison Avenue and 94th Street, Buster was assigned to the Cavalry Division of the 21st Reconnaissance

Squadron. He'd committed to serve three years. Driven by his ability to see the wider canvas, he anticipated further unraveling of world events and the inevitability of U.S. involvement. Presumably this tactic was discussed with Robin at the time of his July 18 visit. He'd formalized his deal with Uncle Sam, then hastened to my mom to seek reassurance that she would stand by him. His life's path was altered and, by association, so was hers.

Then one small clue, a single letter addressed to my grandparents shortly thereafter, revealed Buster's approximate location in Canton, New York. Why Canton?

He'd packed up and moved fast, to find himself in the company of over 100,000 men from twelve states and the District of Columbia. They were called up from the Regular Army, National Guard, and organized reserves for a rendezvous beginning Saturday, August 3. Some arrived by plane and truck. Most, like Buster, arrived by train.

The genesis of the 1940 maneuvers grew out of FDR's realization that existing U.S. troops were poorly trained, with little modern weaponry. Why? Because WWI was supposed to be "the war to end all wars." Casualties were such that no one wanted to relive another bloody event like *that*. Foreign policy leaders in the 1930s championed isolationism. Aviator Charles Lindbergh played a central role as a non-interventionist and critic of FDR. Lindbergh was convinced a Nazi victory was certain, and the U.S. should not enter a war unless it had a reasonable chance of winning.

It's the truth. In 1940 our country was militarily "mightless" whereas Hitler's forces embodied strength. The foot soldiers of the German infantry were well supported in the scaffolding of a modern and well-equipped military. They had it all: motorized, panzer, mountain, cavalry and airborne divisions trained with combat experience, prepped to take on the world.

Enter General George C. Marshall, Roosevelt's Army Chief of Staff. Marshall was the man to advise FDR, and win congressional approval, with a plan to re-arm America in a crash effort to develop effective combat strength. Training and experience was gained through "sham wars," transforming men and machines into a force to be reckoned with.

Pvt. Bedford, 21 Reconnaissance, A.P.O. 401, Canton, N.Y.
(postcard) – August 9, 1940

Dear Folks,

Received your Monday's letter yesterday (Wednesday). Mail seems to travel pretty slowly through the Army.

Things are moving along more smoothly now, as we are better settled and better organized. I can't think of anything that I need right now, but if I do I will write and ask for it. Wouldn't bring my good field glasses up here.

Your loving son, Buster

If mail traveled slowly through the Army at this 1940 moment, there were life lessons to be learned in the not too distant future. Lieutenant General Hugh A. Drum was the officer supervising this whole shebang from a field headquarters in Canton, N.Y., seat of St. Lawrence County; twenty miles from the Canadian border.

Pvt. Bedford, 21 Reconnaissance, A.P.O. 401, Canton, N.Y. – August 12, 1940

Dear Folks,

We arrived here (God and the Major only know where it is) after driving all Sunday and Monday. Somewhere in the Adirondack foothills near Canton, this is about the most God-forsaken town I have ever seen. Our tents, nice big ones, were all pitched when we arrived, but they had not been ditched and we didn't have time to do it before taps last night. About 4:00 this morning a terrific rainstorm struck and we were nearly drowned out. Our tent held up pretty well compared to the others, so only a few things on the floor got wet.

There is a river only a few hundred yards down the hill from camp, so some of us managed to get in a bath before dinner last night. It felt mighty good after our hot, dirty trip up. Thank goodness we will be able to keep fairly clean, anyway.

Don't worry about me, for I am really quite comfortable. I will try to write as often as possible, but they keep us awfully busy. Will try to at least send a post card every other day.

Your loving son, Buster

The troops lived in a "tent city." And though the nights in Canton were cold, pity the recruits of the massive military maneuvers held three months earlier. Those poor boys soldiered up in Louisiana sweltering on the battle-field proving grounds. A smiling variety of stinging insects, biting chiggers, ticks and snakes snuck into their stuff.

Pvt. Bedford, 21 Reconnaissance, A.P.O. 401, Canton, N.Y. – August 18, 1940

Dear Folks,

Just received your Friday's letter a few minutes ago. That makes four that I have had from you now. I enjoy them very much. Keep it up.

I was particularly glad to hear in your yesterday's letter that Robin's family meets with your approval. She is much too wonderful a girl to have anything but a nice family anyway. I hope that you are satisfied now.

Heck, I was happy to hear it, too!

Except for this. "*I hope that you are satisfied now*" smacks of, I told you so. It also implied my Bedford grandparents were not convinced my mom was good enough for their well-bred, pampered son. Possibly they called her nomadic upbringing into question? Was her lineage up to snuff?

My dad went on to describe camp life, "*fairly comfortable in a crude sort of way...weather is quite cold at night.*" So cold he slept in his Princeton sweater and wool socks with two army blankets. By mid-afternoon it was nearly one-hundred degrees. *"However, being on a hilltop, there is almost always a breeze, and we have been able to go swimming almost every day before supper."*

The men were not allowed to keep food in their tents. (Savvy campers follow that rule still today, minding critters great and small.) *"But if you want to send some nuts I think that it would be all right."*

Rulebreaker!

"I have four tent-mates who would be glad to help me handle them."

Presumably several cans all sporting the image of an iconic Mr. Peanut arrived posthaste. Planter's mixed nuts and almonds? A morale boost for discriminating palates of Busters tentmates, all college graduates: Harvard, Williams and Rutgers. Buster didn't remember where the fourth received his degree, but the chap liked nuts nonetheless.

The scout cars are running fine now and the machine guns are all mounted and cleared for action. We have been firing blanks in them, of course. I still have not been assigned to any particular car, but I hope to be before the mimic war starts. Meanwhile, one advantage of being changed around is that I have more chance to meet all the fellows.

I must write Robin a letter now.

Your loving son, Buster

Lighting his pipe in contemplation, Buster mentally assembled chivalrous words in a letter to Robin, rather like Mozart composing music in his head. The scent of aromatic tobacco filled the room. (A visibly blue cloud that gave me a headache as a kid.) He filled the opening sentence of this letter with news of his parents' "approval."

You must understand this was still a period in history when parents carried a large measure of influence in nuptial decision-making. Buster and Robin's plans fell short of an "arranged marriage," as defined by other cultures, but it met the definition of an "approved union" in no uncertain terms; principles of behavior consistent with the times.

Who, exactly, did my dad's folks meet for this calculated approval? Or did they? I know for a fact, they were not acquainted with my mom's parents in Chile. Not even by letter.

Based on geographical proximity, I might tell you they met my mom's recently widowed Auntie Rhea and her son, Roy. The trajectory between Amsterdam and New York, New York, (though lacking interstates and toll roads at the time) was well within reach.

But I'd be lying.

Using deductive logic and reasoning, here's what I believe. Like a film noir hero, my grandfather Bedford possessed resources and connections as part of his "businessman" skill set. If he couldn't do it on his own, he'd put someone up to unearthing the Skinner lineage. I don't know that he would go so far as to hire the Pinkerton Detective Agency, but I wouldn't put it past him. Evidence there would be no risk-taking with the Bedford "name-capital."

I'll hazard a guess the character reference came via a thread running between the McLatchey and McLeod clans. Recall Mr. and Mrs. McLeod orchestrated Montana magic for Robin, Billy Hoblitt, my Aunt Dottie and Bud. It happens that Mr. McLeod, father of "Buddo," was a model citizen. A prominent businessman in one of the largest business concerns of the Pacific Northwest, he also served on several boards, including the Ninth District Federal Reserve Bank of Minnesota and the Northern Pacific Railway Co., among others. It was a smooth discovery for my grandfather who sought out the Who's Who of Montana. Both men knew people in important circles. It was not hard to find common ground discussing financial strategies to make America great.

It's unfortunate the good ol' boy network left my Grammy Bedford out of the conversation.

The McLeods were longtime friends of Auntie Alta (McLatchey) and Uncle Dix; each family held the other in high esteem. Add to that Bud's interest in my aunt Dottie.

Take a hypothetical. Would Walter McLeod have objected to plans of his first born and only son, Bud, to wed my aunt Dottie?

Based on impressions of summer, 1939, Mr. McLeod would reflect on how he'd personally bonded with my mom over picnics and pitching horse-shoes. How would he describe her attributes? Decent, kind, virtuous, capable, knowledgeable, and rather athletic. Her biggest fault: bad teeth. Not that they were misaligned. She had a pretty smile, but she'd spent days in the dentist chair after all. I believe Mr. McLeod vouched for my mom: yes, indeed, *born of a respectable family!*

Pvt. Bedford, 21 Reconnaissance, A.P.O. 401, Canton, N.Y. – August 20, 1940

Dear Folks,

I have been trying for three days now to get off a letter to you, but things have been going so hot and heavy since Saturday that I have been unable to find time. Right now I am sitting in the middle of a battlefield with airplanes flying all around and the enemy attacking with tanks and artillery just a couple of miles down the road.

The nuts and almonds arrived safely Saturday and have been invaluable during the last couple of days while we have been fighting and scouting (time out to fight off a couple of dive bombers) and have been eating and sleeping irregularly.

Am very happy to know I passed Torts O.K. Must have really done well to get a C in spite of leaving out a question.

Don't worry about me, for even though I am a bit dirty and grimy I feel quite chipper this morning and am tough as nails.

Will probably be home sometime Saturday afternoon as this war is over Thursday and I believe we start home Friday.

Haven't time to write more now as I must look to my guns and ammunition. Will mail this as soon as we stop in a town.

Your loving son, Buster

The war games were a test to see if troops could mobilize and travel long distances while attacking, defending and counterattacking. The Blue Army began in Gouverneur, twenty-four miles south of Canton on U.S. Route 11. The Black Army began in Winthrop, twenty-four miles north of Canton. This two-sided exercise commenced August 19, and it was "hot and heavy" until August 22. The Blue Army was declared victorious. I will never know my dad's color on this count, but if assigned to the Black Army, he would most certainly have sported a flash of Princeton orange for effect.

Back at Accomac, my mom's diary revealed *"lots of songs and wonderful food"* as the summer consummated with the thirtieth birthday celebration of the camp. Her Smith College superiors, Miss Mori and Mrs. Wolfe, thought it strange Robin hadn't joined the Smith "Outing Club." Were Mori and Wolfe faculty advisors sweet talking new club recruits? For the "best set" in 1940, I am certain my mom believed the cool factor of the Cosmopolitan Club far outweighed membership in the Outing Club.

As the clock sped toward the end of summer 1940, the inventory on pots and pans began. Naturally, greasing them for winter storage was a chore with my mom's name on it. She *"wrote personality cards frantically."* As a counselor, it was her job to report on the unique combination of traits of each girl in Bunk 11. Parents then and now are interested in hearing others' perspectives on their prodigy. Provided it's good. Or at least constructive.

Both Miss Mori and Mrs. Wolfe hoped my mom would return in the summer of 1941. Both told her so. It's nice to know they appreciated her amiable demeanor and newly acquired skill set in Camp Craft and canoe tricks. And surely they recognized the value of veteran staff who, willingly or not, returned to clean the grease off pots and pans.

I don't know when the train left Maine, but I do know my mom arrived in New York City on Friday, August 30 where, before breakfast, she *"got parents and children connected."* It seems impossible to me a camp counselor chaperone from Maine to NYC would pass muster today, but my near-Irish twin tells me it still happens in the Adirondacks. Seemingly safe and logistically simple.

Once relieved of her counselor duties that morning, Robin reconnected with Buster like a magnet. Following breakfast *"at home,"* in the apartment of my Bedford grandparents on 54th Street, she *"got settled in the Sutton Hotel on 56th Street."*

The next several days Robin and Buster were enveloped in the company of the senior Bedfords.

"Went shopping and spent $50.00. Bing!"

Factored in today's dollars, that would make a fine one-day "cha-ching" spree in the neighborhood of $850. (Though it would not, by today's standards, stretch very far at, say, the New York institution of Bergdorf Goodman.)

I suspect the elder chaperones paved (and paid) the way for their future daughter-in-law. They bypassed the window shopping and attended straight to business; promenading with purpose right past the door attendant at Saks Fifth Avenue or B. Altman & Co. A favorite sales clerk would see dollar signs, give her hands an instinctive little rub, and enthusiastically step up to greet them just beyond the perfume and cosmetics counter.

As a kid, I found Saks and Altman garment labels galore in my mom's closet. Not that I paid much attention to them while foraging though her pockets pilfering loose change and chewing gum. (It wasn't until I had my own kids that I understood why nearly every pocket held Kleenex in some state of linty decomposition.)

In 1939, when the Skinner family toured across the nation, there was comparatively less emphasis on shopping. The girls were dressed in practical terms. Purchases amounted to functional, timeless classics with a fashion accent or two. My mom's back-to-school wardrobe à la 1939 amounted to the reliable skirt/sweater combo, simple and conservative. Shoes were practical Oxfords in brown or black with a low stacked heel. Loafers hadn't stepped onto campus yet. Pajamas, hosiery, hats, leather gloves and a purse? A coat with a simple cut.

I'd like to believe my mom's 1940 brown paper packages tied up with strings contained garments suitable for her senior year at Smith. But don't be fooled. Over the next two weeks dress code etiquette on the tennis court and golf course took priority. Hour glass outfits, destined for dinners, dancing and theatre, hung on wooden hangers awaiting their turn to twirl in sartorial splendor on my mom's petite frame. Fresh tubes of redder than red lipsticks branded by rival cosmetic queens, Elizabeth Arden and Helena Rubenstein, kept company on the bathroom vanity, and in her coat pocket, too. Were I the author of a New York society column, I'd pen an entry contrasting the families like this:

The Skinners win culture points.

The Bedfords win fashion style points.

The Skinners and Bedfords were equally matched seeking out (thriving actually) on both live theatre and film... high scores for entertainment in general.

Like millions of Americans, they sought distraction from tough decisions facing the Roosevelt administration. By necessity the predominantly isolationist attitude of our nation gave way to strengthening U.S. troops at home.

Buster's patriotism dropped him smack dab in the middle of that undertaking.

Game On

Chapter Twenty

Despite the fact that Buster would soon report to the Columbia campus for his second year of law school, and my mom needed to buckle down for senior year at Smith, the house hunt resumed in September. They picked up right where they'd left off in May, scouring the newspaper classifieds. Their outlook was metaphorically more than a glass half-full. To me, this escapade set up like a fractured fairytale about to unfold.

In the company of the senior Bedfords, Buster and Robin piled in the back seat of Grampy's art deco inspired coupe. Its chrome grille sparkled like the well-brushed teeth of a Cheshire cat, the eyes of his snapping turtle face lit up behind the wheel. Wide whitewalls whisked the family along, bound for the north shore of Long Island, Promised Land of the suburbs. Destination: the hamlet of *"Manhasset,"* my mom specified, *"for a house tour."*

Realtors in 1940 had already discovered the use of open houses to get acquainted with potential homebuyers. I was surprised to learn the Multiple Listing Service had been around since the later part of the 19th-century. A house tour was fair game where a residential agent could size up new prospects and profitably assist with alternative listings held in their back pocket. Smart marketing. I have no evidence Grandfather Bedford employed that tactic in the Florida land boom. His niche revolved around the sale of vacant lots.

Presumably the Bedfords toured Plandome Heights or Munsey Park, which was upper crust then and quite blue-chip today. Custom homes (many built in the early '30s) were a hallmark of the area, character-defining architectural design and sturdy construction tapped the artistry of the best craftsmen using the finest materials. By today's standards they contained a lot of quirky features. (Not a right angle in the house.) I honor the champions of historic preservation, lest homes like these be sent right to teardown in unprotected areas primed for redevelopment.

Was the seed to own property on a waterfront, like that of the Crane Road house, planted on this very tour? The name Manhasset derives from a Native American term meaning "the island neighborhood." Another weighty consideration? Commute time to mid-town Manhattan. The "L I Double R" (Long Island Rail Road) delivered city workers from Manhasset to Penn Station in well under an hour.

Buster's dream home would offer a place to swim, sail and fish fifty feet out the back door, with a commuter train station close at hand.

My mom's diary notes of September 1 divulged this: *"Found a little white house that we liked."*

Then it dawned on me, the "we" my mom wrote about equated to a collective use of the term. This house hunt endeavor was intended to find a residence to serve my grandparents. Robin and Buster were just along for the ride, not at all playing pretend, but rather smartly, getting their feet wet in this business of home buying. Remember that Buster, an economics major, dabbled in investments and reported to my grandfather on their mutual earnings. A home in the right neighborhood, where home values were ready to skyrocket, was more than a stable holding in the family portfolio, if the timing was right.

Revealed by the postcards Buster addressed, the senior Bedfords resided at 405 East 54th Street, apartment #6-0; smack dab in midtown Manhattan. The street bustled (by their standards, not yours, nor mine) six floors below. Brassy six-volt car horns of the day communicated a message without sounding off like an urban monster. Give me this word association test: "New York City." Instinctively the word "horns" drives from my mouth, "sirens" a close second. When *Tonight Show* host Johnny Carson defined "A new york minute" as *the interval between a Manhattan traffic light turning green and the guy behind you honking his horn,"* it wasn't a joke to me.

The Bedford's apartment was charming (still true today in the afflu-ent enclave of "Sutton Place"). The building façade of "clinker brick" was a decidedly sturdy material, dense and heavy. Like a brood of ugly ducklings, their darker patina and knobbly finish derived from close proximity to the heat source when fired. Imperfect according to masonry standards, their unlikely choice in construction resulted in fifteen stories of distinctively artsy detail. A doorman welcomed them home by name, into a lobby with stunning stone floors, wooden beamed archways, decorative metalwork and non-pastoral, random pattern architectural stained glass in happy pastels. Whatever their reason for wanting to leave this residence, home equity investment, or peaceful surroundings, I look upon their strategy as pre-war trendsetting.

On September 2, the Labor Day holiday found the family on Montauk Point, the eastern tip of the south shore of Long Island. There they dined at the ocean front resort of Gurney's Inn, a 20-room summer retreat for New Yorkers, built during Prohibition in 1926. *"Beautiful Idyllic"* wrote my mom.

Yes, it is an idyllic spot, though it's been "Hamptonized" since.

Located on what is an especially pristine stretch of beach, they were pleased to order a cocktail or two and breathe the salt air. They enjoyed the soothing effect of the water's aquatic hue, a view of infinity in the distance; the hypnotic sound of rolling waves and gently rocking bell buoys.

I wonder how many women like me packed a soundtrack like that in their Lamaze bag.

Then, ruining the sea breeze I conjured, my mom confessed: *"Smoked my first cigarette in front of Mrs. B."* Did my dad suavely pull a silver Ronson from his inside pocket and offer a light? I have reason to believe her smoke was a *Parliament*, one among many branded cancer sticks in the Philip Morris portfolio. I wonder if she inhaled. Buster would have appreciated the "recessed filter." Innovative at the time, it might have a cooling effect on the smoke, rather like the stem of his pipe when he took a relaxed draw.

The blue and white *Parliament* packaging was common to the Crane Road house, and consequently, my first "sneak." I soon learned to prefer the natural menthol blend the likes of R.J. Reynolds' *Salem*, but never considered it an addictive practice. I'll label it situational use that ended when I moved West.

Thankfully her habit was not life-long. As I recall, she quit for good less than ten years after the U.S. Surgeon General issued his first warning in 1964: smoking causes cancer.

By now, the Presidential election of 1940 was just weeks away, a watershed moment in American history. Very briefly, let's talk politics. It was at Gurney's Inn where the Women's Republican Club of East Hampton sponsored a bridge-party tea.

The guest speaker Mrs. Robert Low Bacon, wife of the influential GOP congressman from New York, appeared before a group of moneyed movers and shakers. At this politically propitious moment, the ladies of the Republican Club sipped tea with gloves off, pinkies out. Mrs. Bacon was there to champion Wendell Willkie, the candidate who carried the Republican nomination that year. Willkie had neither a political nor military service record. He'd never even held a top government post. However, he was a successful businessman, distanced from the so-called political establishment, with a willingness to serve.

Also significant, the Democratic Party broke with "two-term tradition" and nominated FDR for a third consecutive term. In the end, Roosevelt won 54.7 percent of the popular vote. The electoral vote was a landslide, 449 for Roosevelt compared to Willkie's paltry 82. The simple explanation for Roosevelt's victory: a disinclination to change leadership in the face of world crisis.

Enough politics, let's talk parties!

It had been two years since Johnny Early, my dad's Princeton skeet teammate, set up a blind date on the eve of the Tiger's skeet match against the New Jersey Game Wardens. Now college graduates, both young men have found steady girls. Robin and Johnny's sweetheart, Scottie, squared up a foursome for fun this September.

A dinner party at my grandparents' apartment on Wednesday, September 4, was followed by an evening at the Imperial Theatre, on W. 45th Street, just across town. There the two-act comedy, *Louisiana Purchase*, with genius music and lyrics by Irving Berlin, portrayed sex and corrupt politics in the South. The song, *It's a Lovely Day Tomorrow*, one of many musical numbers, stuck and became an anthem of hope to buoy British spirits.

Through the lens of history, we know the proverbial "tomorrow" was years away. Hitler dripped with hate. The Royal Air Force was yet to be destroyed according to his plan. Nearly two months into the Battle of Britain, the RAF courageously continued to beat back the *Luftwaffe*. Churchill, less than four months into his first year as Prime Minister, stood strong.

In the *Playbill* for *Louisiana Purchase*, the bright and shiny face of Philip Morris' iconic cigarette boy smiled innocently at every theatre-goer. The previously published price of fifteen cents a pack was missing. Go figure. Soon to be *free* to soldiers, cigarettes would find efficient distribution through C-Rations, and the Red Cross, too!

Following curtain call, my future parents dashed out of the Imperial in the company of Johnny and Scottie. The Princeton Club was favorably located a short walk from the theatre. There they sipped Manhattans and Martinis.

That evening my dad stayed with the Early family, who had put him up after the Tigers went down in defeat to the Game Wardens. My mom overnighted at Scottie's.

Johnny and Scottie conveniently hailed from the same hometown, Summit, New Jersey. The commute to Manhattan was short. The town's history, on the other hand, is long. Landmarks dating back to the Revolutionary War are common.

A few of my favorite observations are not revolutionary, but worth a mention: First, the town had *two* movie theatres in 1940. The Strand and

The Lyric are no longer around, yet for those who "got lost" there during the Great Depression, nostalgia lingers like the smell of popcorn with *real* butter. (It's a fact, Proctor and Gamble didn't patent buttery-flavor until 1980.)

Second, being a Jersey girl myself, I assure you a local diner serving classic American comfort food was mandatory, ingrained in the culture of the Garden State. The Summit Diner is the oldest in Jersey with bona fide railcar character, red leather booths and retro counter seating. A place to pocket a Taylor Ham, egg and cheese on a roll, before the dynamic dash for a Manhattan bound train.

Like icing on the cake, I'll bet dollars-to-dumplings Johnny, Scottie, Robin and Buster stopped at the diner for a little something. Perhaps a small confection, one of an assortment made from scratch daily on the premises. They used real butter, too.

As a kid growing up (and especially as a teen), Paul's Diner on U.S. Route 46 was the eatery where "Lakers" were schooled in the Jersey diner culture. Just three minutes from the Crane Road house, Paul's continues to carve its own rich niche in history: art deco chrome façade on the exterior, retro red leather booths; counter seating. Serving a larger market, their dining area seats larger foodie groups and multi-generational families (ours among them) bonding over eggs, any style, and home fries. For me, this place was parent-approved for post-prom early morning breakfasts. On those occasions E.T.A. (estimated time of arrival), a military acronym Buster often used, went out the window. I imagine most every student in the Mountain Lakes High School yearbook dating back to 1947 (when this establishment opened) has a story (or confession) staged here. Speaking from experience, the boxed-in booths worked best for teens behaving awkwardly, a safe harbor to straighten up before going home. At a different time of day, young parents effectively barricade squirming toddlers, where the odor of Crayola out-competes sizzling bacon. It wasn't until a visit years later that I realized it's easy to hang an ear over the back of a booth and surreptitiously eavesdrop on the table behind. The truth is, it's safest to keep your ears to yourself in a Jersey diner.

Enough of my personal retro digression, let's get back to 1940.

Filled with energetic zest for privileged lives they didn't fully appreciate, my mom and Scottie arose the next morning to suit up in pleated skirts, Wimbledon white compliant. When Buster and Johnny presented themselves preppy-dressed in "whites," off they went to re-kindle their appetite frolicking on clay courts. Wooden rackets sported the Wilson typeface. Kids in Keds on the run-around in mixed doubles formation, they chased fuzzy white balls popped fresh from a pressurized metal tube. Fact check! Wilson introduced their three-ball sleeve in the late 1920s.

Weirdly, as a kid, I loved the scent of air escaping pressure-packed tennis balls. Now I'm left to imagine if the odor in 1940 was any different. This I do know: optic yellow balls were a 1970s invention, designed to be visible to a growing television viewing audience.

Following an invigorating morning of lobs and drop shots, where a light touch trumped manly might, my mom wrote: *"Had lunch at Club and dinner party at Scottie's. Played games afterwards."*

I wager it was a board game, followed by parlor games? *Anagrams* was popular at the time. I see it like this: Ivy Leaguers out-wordsmithing one another in multisyllabic splendor using building blocks of letters on wood tiles. Long Island-based Selchow and Righter published their version of Anagrams in 1934. The subtitle *"or Words Alive"* used imagery of Egyptian cobras on the box top. Effective branding.

The very next day, Friday, September 6, 1940, my mom wrote: *"Went down to beach for day – played in sand and rode waves. Went to Princeton Inn for supper – out on lake afterwards..."*

How did this eventful day unfold?

Long Branch was my best guess as to where Buster, Robin, Johnny and Scottie were whisked by railroad that morning. Known historically as America's oldest seaside resort, Long Branch once held the reputation as a summer colony for the wealthy and, in 1940, was still considered upscale.

The ensemble of four marked their spot with beach umbrellas planted firmly in the sand along a stretch of Jersey shore nearly five miles long. My mom, her appearance rather like a shapely pin-up? She, in her swimsuit fully formed with bra cups, tummy control panels, and a flirty skirt, didn't just bob about. She *'rode waves.'* "Lastex," introduced in 1930s (think women's girdles) was the new miracle fiber applied to swimsuits.

Pity my grandmothers in their youth. A woman would have to be wildly spirited and full of personality to overcome the dreary and shapeless attire of their day; dark, saggy puff-sleeve woolen dresses. They moved like manatees through the water.

As for Buster, he sported swim "briefs." Changing the privacy settings for a moment, I believe they were cut rather like the white Jockey undies he flashed dashing across the hall, bathroom to bedroom in the Crane Road house.

After their day in the waves, the foursome likely napped on the rail back to Princeton then dressed for dinner. Whatever the fashion, it permitted a venture out onto Lake Carnegie that evening.

Just as canoes were popular watercraft on Paradise Pond at Smith, Princeton had a Canoe Club at this time. According to my near-Irish twin, a boathouse provided storage for privately-owned craft along the banks of Lake Carnegie. With or without permission, my dad must have borrowed one. He put his accomplices, Johnny and Scottie, up to the task of silently placing it at the water's edge. A Feather Brand wooden paddle in hand, he mastered the moment.

Did my mom suspect the astronomical event that was about to unfold beneath a waxing crescent moon? Her canoe training at Accomac paid off big time here.

I'll set the scene, using my own after-dark experience floating in a boat out the back door of the Crane Road house. Stars reflected brightly on the water; songs of crickets, frogs and katydids filled the night. A shrouded owl hooted. Bats dove, feeding on mosquitos and moths.

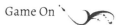

There was no engagement ring, unless my dad took a cue from the book *The Count of Monte Cristo* and used a string. Did he get down on bended knee and, using situational humor, ask "Are you ready to take the plunge?"

She finished the description like this in her diary that night: *"...out on lake afterwards Buster proposed – John and Scottie very excited about the whole thing."*

In the spring of 1974, my graduation from Mountain Lakes High loomed. I don't recall what prompted it, but my mom advised me on a matrimonial point that stuck in my teenage brain. As I set the table for dinner in the Crane Road dining room, she looked directly at me from the kitchen over the pony wall where knick-knacks collected dust. With gravity she said, "When a man proposes marriage, tell him you'll think about it."

I get the impression that's not exactly how she answered Buster that night.

Her advice blew through my brain during the cyclone in Tonga when my boyfriend (now husband) proposed to me. And I admit, when the shoe was on my foot, it wasn't an immediate "yes." But not for reasons you'd think. The wind and rain buffeted so loud that words were lost over the water. I asked my boyfriend, "What?" Then, "Are you serious?" Did my beau think we might die? Weighing the peril of our situation, I felt flat out of time to "think about it." As we prepared to cash in our chips together, I said, "yes." By the grace of King Neptune's trident, we lived to see our wedding day.

Obviously, so did Robin and Buster.

Mustering Resources

Chapter Twenty-One

The day after Buster's proposal was a dark one. Not for my folks by any stretch. I have proof of that: *"Played a little golf in P.M. Had formal dinner at Johnny's – and a toast to us. Went to dance at Short Hills Country Club."*

Like a split screen display, with northeast trajectory 3,500 miles across the North Atlantic Ocean, Saturday, September 7, 1940, marked the day German bombers appeared in mass numbers over London. Sirens wailed. Bombs fell and flashed. Fighter planes attacked with ferocity. Docks were blown to smithereens. Debris flew. Fires burned. Buildings? Annihilated. "Black Saturday" was day number one of the London Blitz; the relentless bombing that would last until May 1941.

While the people of London wore gas masks and sought shelter, life in my parents' world was *tickety-boo* and right as rain.

On September 8, Grampy turned fifty-five years old. Somewhere on the north shore of Long Island they celebrated his double-nickel birthday. My mom's words revealed the worst news of their week: *"Went out to find little white house sold."*

It seemed to me the senior Bedfords never tired of dining out. Robin and Buster often joined them in unique settings offering fresh menu selections. Less shopping, cooking and kitchen cleanup for the women. Good for them. I knew this pattern would break eventually. It happened, apron clad, when my mom stepped up to demonstrate she'd make a fine wife and considerate daughter-in-law. The proof was in the pudding when she wrote: *"Dinner with Bedford's where I broiled a 2" steak – whee! – 'twas very good, too. Sent Mrs. B. a dozen American Beauties' – ouch!"*

The events that followed displayed omens of future happiness, as my mom recorded September days with Buster: *"Went to dinner at Rainbow Grill, even in dance contest. Drove up to Columbia for a long talk 'til 5:00 A.M."*

Making wedding plans, I suppose.

"Went to Zoo with Buster for afternoon." Presumably she meant the Central Park Zoo, a respite from the hardscape of the city and yet another WPA endeavor under FDR's New Deal. Did they have a zoo strategy like searching out baby animals? The darling of any cathouse for my dad was the Bengal, which is the majestic Tiger of Princeton mascot fame.

By the time I was a kid in the '60s, visitors called into question the antiquated animal quarters at the Central Park Zoo. Wet, cold concrete sticks in my mind's eye for good reason. "Habitat" exhibits were atypical at that time. In the early 1970s hoofing it to and from outdoor rock concerts in Central Park's Sheep Meadow, beleaguered animals behind bars presented like a side show; monkeys, mongoose, llamas and the like. The zoo was re-built and re-opened in 1988.

Notably, the original sheep of Sheep Meadow were shipped out during the Great Depression for good reason: Hungry citizens in desperate times targeted them as an attainable food source. Today there are sheep in the petting zoo.

"Out to dinner with Mr. and Mrs. B. and Mr. Scherback, a Czech. Planned a career – airline stewardess, receptionist secretary to diplomat, journalist."

That's a colorful palate of womanly vocational options that could work with, or without, a Smith diploma. No mention of medical school? I don't know where her biology major was taking her, but her Mrs. degree was a bird in the hand. The question yet to be answered?

When?

The young betrotheds escaped for an evening to themselves on Saturday, September 14. Rodgers and Hart's musical comedy *Boys from Syracuse*, the film adaptation of *A Comedy of Errors*, was the first Shakespearean play ever to be adapted into a Broadway musical. Did Buster, schooled in the works of Shakespeare, give away the plot points? Slapstick and zesty music were a fresh twist. Neither had seen the live Broadway show two years before. Too bad. There were seventeen catchy tunes in the stage production. Only four of them were used in the 1940 film version. Hollywood actor, Allan Jones, sang this: *Falling in Love with Love*. The lyrical cynicism was a little awkward for a couple newly engaged, but his romantic tenor was smooth. Over the years, versions by Frank Sinatra, Andy Williams, Sammy Davis, Jr. and Diana Ross and the Supremes played differently. Bernadette Peters, step-mother in Disney's 1997 film release of *Cinderella*, spun it with this revelatory opening line: *"This isn't about Love! It's about Marriage! Have I taught you girls nothing?!"*

On Grammy Bedford's fifty-fourth birthday, September 15, the family hopped in the polished coupe, Connecticut bound for more house hunting. *"Had dinner at Silvermine Inn - lovely place"* wrote my mom. They were drawn to yet another waterfront setting along the banks of the Silvermine River, in Norwalk. *"Home early,"* she wrote.

Yes, home early. An inevitable pattern that flows naturally one generation to the next. Call me a party pooper, but the late-night scene has lost me. For years, *The Tonight Show* paired with a nightcap was my dad's thing. This apple can barely keep her peepers open past the opening monologue. Was it my grandparents' desire to get home and tune in the nightly radio serial of *Amos 'n' Andy* whilst Gramp sipped sherry? (Grammy, a temperance woman, likely abstained.) Their appreciation for spiced black dialect was genuine. More germane? Personally patchworked backstories. The comedic theme of everyday problems facing ordinary people tickled Grammy's funny bone. While she tittered, I conjure Grampy with flared nostrils hooting with laughter.

My folks gallivanted through the first two weeks of September, living life like a happy song playlist. Meanwhile, Congress was at work. Since June elected officials had deliberated language of the Burke-Wadsworth Bill. Grenville Clark, a Wall Street attorney and author of the legislation, spearheaded the National Emergency Committee. Their agenda, as if working toward a Boy Scout merit badge, was emergency preparedness. They lobbied for the first peacetime draft in U.S. history. I believe Buster had his ear to the ground on that point, hence his pivotal decision to join the Guard six weeks earlier.

On September 16, FDR signed Proclamation 2425, the Selective Training and Service Act. For the first time in history, American males between the age of twenty-one and thirty-five were required to register for the draft. Roosevelt spoke the dramatic words kids today get quizzed on in American History II.

"America stands at the crossroads of its destiny. Time and distance have been shortened. A few weeks have seen great nations fall. We cannot remain indifferent to the philosophy of force now rampant in the world. The terrible fate of nations whose weakness invited attack is too well known to us all."

Jump back to Reverend Niebuhr's Chapel talk, on the October day in 1939 when my mom completely missed Orson Welles' *War of the Worlds*. The reverend preached prophetically from Psalm 73: *"their evil imaginations have no limits."* Take pity on the students under his tutelage at the Union Theological Seminary in New York. If any demographic fit the profile of religious conscientious objector, they did. Proclamation 2425 provided for a person, "who, by reason of religious training and belief, is conscientiously opposed to war in any form." They had to qualify in the eyes of their local draft board. A satisfactory record of church attendance was relevant and necessary.

The Act broadened provisions for folks like Niebuhr's students: an option to *"be assigned to noncombatant service as defined by the President"* [or] *"assigned to work of national importance under civilian direction."* In the "Civilian Public Service," these men were based in camps doing the work of the Forest Service, Soil Conservation Service, National Park Service, and on farms and in state mental institutions. Some chose firefighting in the west, as smoke-jumpers. The fact that these duties, as assigned, were without compensation did not go over well, but based on principle these "gentle-men" were compelled to make the sacrifice.

Fast forward to the Vietnam War, when the draft picked on Baby Boomers. Conscientious objectors who participated in non-violent civil disobedience were joined by the ranks of those that burned draft cards or fled to Canada. Protest music dominated the radio. I taught myself the guitar chords of Staff Sergeant Barry Sadler's *The Ballad of the Green Beret*. (It isn't hard. Just three chords: C, G7 and F.) My throat constricted as I sang the lyrics alone in my bedroom. The music added chutzpah to the neon anti-war handiwork on my walls. That ballad was the #1 Billboard hit in 1966. Then along came Woodstock, August 1969. Too young to attend, I wore out the three-LP set released in 1970. *The Fish Cheer*, among my favorites. You know it. Country Joe and the Fish; *"Gimme an F."*

Unsettling as world news in the fall of 1940 continued to be, life carried on with normalcy for Robin and Buster. The betrotheds marched back to school. Mom returned to Smith where I imagine Haven House looked the same, but she saw it differently. Would it be the last place she'd reside as a single woman? Moral standards being what they were at the time, "shacking up" was out of the question. Until their wedding date was set, the time to set up housekeeping as man and wife would remain open.

In New York, Buster began his second year at Columbia. I daresay coursework in civil liberties and human rights complemented his experience as a National Guardsman. The summer maneuvers heightened his perspective on national defense. He applied the rule of law, or lack thereof, to actions of other world leaders. His studies were filtered through a personal arsenal of democratic principles.

On October 2, my mom wrote: *"Had first Chem quiz and got 23! A beautiful example of non-comprehension!"* Indubitably, like weak tooth enamel, I inherited her gene for that subject. In fact, it's the only class I ever flunked.

Then the smitten twenty-one-year-old added: *"Wrote Buster a letter on why I love him, which he appreciated."*

Her concentration was askew. In dreamy distraction, she was often lost in ardent thought. It led to a befuddled moment on October 3 that had consequences. She wrote: *"Had one of the worst days of accidents in bacteriology lab ever. Everything spilled everywhere."*

Oh, that's not good. In 1940 every vessel was made of glass. Even worse, diagnostic functions were closely aligned with clinical work in infectious disease. Broken beakers of urine? Shattered agar plates; petri dishes with throat, nose and who knows what cultures? Colonies of bacteria crept through the lab. My mom consistently overreacted when, as a kid, I spilled milk at the dinner table. After recoiling in horror, I suppose she owned the task to clean it up. (And, for the record, I learned at an early age to mop up mine.)

On a wing and a prayer, the rest of the afternoon looked like this: *"Went to Red Cross."* I trust she took this work seriously, possibly rolled bandages. Given the time and circumstance, she might have been lucky enough to be on the front line of the "Blood for Britain project." The technology of how to "bank" blood for transfusions was new. One responsibility of the Red Cross was to collect blood and ship plasma to England to aid those injured in the Blitz. Hands down, more meaningful work than packing off a supply of cigarettes.

Pause here for a moment to appreciate how necessity was the mother of invention in the timely birth of America's nationwide blood banking program, which we too often take for granted. Let me introduce Dr. Charles R. Drew, a brilliant individual who completed pioneering research and a doctoral dissertation on "Banked Blood." He received his medical degree from Columbia in June 1940. Not long after, this young doctor was appointed to head the "Blood for Britain" program. He rolled out a game-changing plan in a matter of *weeks*. The first trial shipment was sent to England at the *beginning* of August and by *mid*-August 1940 the program was officially underway. This was the guy who wrote the standards for collecting, processing and storing blood.

Based on this short narrative about the good doctor, allow me to share these insane facts about blood segregation. Dr. Drew was a D.C. born African American. Do you agree it's a slap in the face "Blood for Britain" from America was segregated based on race? Heck, the Brit's in the Blitz didn't give a hoot about skin color. Across the pond, blood supply for transfusions was the difference between life and death. As the Red Cross Blood Donor program evolved here in the U.S., Dr. Drew stood by the argument there was no scientific evidence, based on race, to support the need for blood segregation. The Red Cross Blood Donor program adopted a discriminatory policy anyway.

What a waste of resources. Neil deGrasse Tyson should have been alive at the time to make this point: "We have competent people thinking about this stuff. We're not just making shit up."

Yet, the segregation policy of donated blood lasted for years. It owned its very own civil rights struggle.

And I am not through with this bloody conversation.

On Friday October 4, Robin wrote this: *"Got thru workin' in lab on rabbit and caught 5:40 train."* This entry, to me, was clear as Mars on a summer night in Montana.

In my mom's elder years, one battery of blood tests followed another. Phlebotomists at work did their best to bulls-eye a vanishing vein and be done. If they didn't get it right, she schooled them with this: "Go back to the lab and practice on a rabbit's ear." Curious expression? Working in a lab in 1940 she had learned how to draw blood from a rabbit's tiny ear veins. I believe she was a likely Red Cross candidate to assist in the Blood for Britain Project. She learned, hands on, all about the good work of Dr. Drew.

On the *"5:40 train"* Robin was New York bound for an all-around town weekend, the kind she'd become accustomed to. It began with dinner for two at the Lion's Den. On Saturday, in the stands of Palmer Stadium they cheered "sis-boom-ah," Princeton's distinctive "locomotive" cheer, adopted fifty years earlier. Like a train leaving the station, it started slowly then picked up speed. (By way of Tigertown transparency, *"ah"* is an expression of awe, as in awesome, never to be confused with *"bah,"* a declaration of disgust). They celebrated the Princeton Tigers' wafer-thin pigskin win over the Vanderbilt "Commodores," from Nashville, Tennessee. I know this because my mom wrote: *"7-6, Whee!"* The "Vandy" mascot, "Mr. C" (for Commodore) led a futile "Go Dores" cheer against the sharp "game-over" whistle of the referee.

Lest our modern minds forget, scoreboard countdown clocks were yet to be invented.

Monday evening, October 7, the busy day distilled to this diary note: *"Was lonely today for Buster – couldn't get down to work. Went to all classes and spent almost 4 hours in Chem lab. Letter from Buster tonight. Went to Red Cross."*

Since Buster had cast his lot with the National Guard, my mom was unaffected when, on Wednesday, the sixteenth day of October 1940, in keeping with "Proclamation 2425," over sixteen million Americans registered for the Selective Service.

There is also no diary mention of FDR's October 29 radio address to the nation. I envision many American families, ears glued to the radio and wringing hands that Tuesday night. The selection process was explained, and in the luck of the draw, chance decided fate. The first lottery number was broadcast. Some young men were called up, others were left hanging in suspense.

Settling out year 1940, here is what I know about my Bedford and Skinner grandparents.

The Bedfords' house hunt was over. They left Manhattan following their purchase of a 2,500-square-foot home built in 1937. In the village of Pelham Manor, Westchester County, the four-bedroom, three-bath residence sat on a nicely manicured quarter acre. It was a rather large home for near empty-nesters. But it was the one I remember, as a child. Dark hardwood floors rested beneath my tapping black patent leather shoes. Oriental rugs. A fireplace in the sitting area. An elaborate tea set of Georgian silver atop a stunning mahogany sideboard. Of course, they employed help to polish pretty much everything, the likes of a small-scale PBS *Masterpiece Theatre* stage set.

1283 MANOR CIRCLE   -   PELHAM MANOR   -   NEW YORK

Extrapolating the occupancy of this new abode was assurance my mom had a place to comfortably light for the holidays. What a relief to Lelia's *"any port in the storm"* worries.

In fact, Lelia didn't need to find refuge for my Aunt Dottie or Skeeter this Christmas.

Why? After sixteen years stateside, the two teens beat it back to Campamento Americano. They were sheltered in place with their folks.

Factor this news, too: Skeeter, a son born to two U.S. citizens in South America, was ineligible for the U.S. Draft. The *Chilean rules* would apply.

Where In the World

Chapter Twenty-Two

L.M. Skinner, Rancagua – Sewell, Chile – December 29, 1940 (airmail)

Dearest Roberta,

A Happy New Year!

I hope this will catch you at Pelham Manor since I missed the last airplane [for airmail] to get one there for Xmas day. I had one started but we had to take it to the P.O. before 1:00 <u>A.M.</u> and I didn't want to keep Daddy up as we were leaving Santiago the next morning for a health resort where the Doctors sent Daddy for several days for his bronchitis. The nose and throat specialist thinks it is more of an asthmatic condition and wanted him away from the coast or any body of water.

I don't buy it. Breathing problems and a persistent cough were, and still are, symptoms of occupational lung disease in the mining industry. We know it as silicosis. Lucky, as an engineer, he spent more time topside with hands-off the aptly nicknamed "widowmaker" drill. Though once a man set foot in the tunnels, silica dust particles did not discriminate.

We stayed several days and are now in Santiago on our way back home. I expect you received the check of $150.00 I sent the last days you were at Smith and I'm sending you $50 in this - $35 is your 20-Dec. – 20-Jan. allowance and the other $15 *is extra. You should keep us better posted as to your money needs. We can't estimate just when you need it and how much you need...*

Hope you had a nice Xmas yesterday. I certainly did think of you and wondered if you were at Pelham Manor. It was very nice of them to invite you. We had Xmas lunch at the resort and at 6 P.M. took the train back for Santiago, and at 10 P.M. went to the late show, "The Boys from Syracuse." I wish you would write a letter of inquiry to Mayo Clinic – Rochester, Minn. and see if you could get a laboratory job there in June. We inquired when we were there what you would have to do or rather just how to go about getting a 6 mo. job, and they said send in an application before you graduated. There are hundreds of laboratory girls there, it seems like.

Do work the hardest you ever have on your semester exams, after you get back to Smith, won't you? Don't let Forrest turn your head, as Jack did Dottie's, and not make your exams, will you, dear? Daddy is just all broken up over her, and I think it would about crush him if you were to disappoint us by failing your senior year. Give Daddy a little consideration – He hasn't been at all well the past 6 mos. and I don't want him to have any extra worries heaped on his shoulders. Write me a letter right back – airmail – if you receive this check – because it won't be back in my cancelled checks for 2 mos.

All good wishes for the New Year. Make a lot of good resolutions and use a lot of common sense in the next 6 mos. won't you, Darling?

Hugs and love from all of us, Mother

Grandma's bunched up year-end letter sounded as if she was on helpless watch, praying the Jenga blocks didn't topple. Sparky, yet fretful, she advised on health, money, and love, like a toast to the New Year minus the cheer.

I deconstructed the time and place like this: The "family tree" points to the fact that my grandfather, then age fifty-three, lived to be eighty-four. The health issues she disclosed did not dramatically alter his lifespan. Though I believe her time spent proactively minding his physical well-being did, in a good way.

I wager he was stubborn about doctor visits, like many men are today. (Do *you* know one?) She was too well-educated to put up with that behavior. In 1940, physical signs were palpable. Turn your head and cough. Lab work was on the uptick. (There was no colonoscopy avoidance, because that procedure didn't come into play until 1969.)

Did it ever occur to her that medical research was undeniably male-focused? Women would wait. Again.

As I weigh the odds of what constituted genuine peril for T. Wayne, it boiled down to the act of tons of ore flying out of El Teniente. One-off accidents (poor Mr. Spectzen) and calamitous disasters turned a life-story arch in a snap. Ore mine mystique gained traction with mythical creatures called Tommy Knockers, wee beings harboring the souls of departed miners. They tapped on tunnel walls before disaster struck, so I'm told.

Grandma was granted her wish to spend the holidays with (two of her three) children at home, but a clipped one-sentence summary of Christmas Day conveyed little, if any, joy in her voice. Was she dismayed they were grown? Santa lacked believers and the summer weather melted white Christmas traditions. Cola de Mono, a Chilean milk punch concoction, replaced traditional eggnog begging raised glasses to prosperity and good health. No mention of merriment here: *"We had Xmas lunch at the resort and at 6 P.M. took the train back for Santiago, and at 10 P.M. went to the late show, "The Boys from Syracuse."* Roger that. Not one snip of comedic film commentary. *Falling in Love with Love* fell flat. Christmas spent with two out of three children lacked the magic. Family traditions decomposed, poof, in a seven-year calendar shift.

And the newsiest news leak? My Aunt Dottie would not graduate from Smith in the class of Cute '42s. Presumably Skeeter finished high school at George Junior Republic and lacked a next step. While my mom was occupied at Accomac, my non-Spanish speaking aunt and her *hermano pequeño* steamed from New York to Valparaiso. They returned home to Campamento Americano in August. A lesson for all mothers: Be careful what you wish for.

On the heels of Lelia's letter, Aunt Dottie volleyed her own volume of even juicer news to my mom. Top of mind for me? Where *was* my uncle-to-be, Bud, in all this drama? Sister to sister, Dottie laid it out in this tell-all.

D. Skinner, c/o Braden Copper Co., Rancagua (Sewell)
Chile – January 6, 1941

Hiyah Keed –

I suppose you're still there and haven't eloped yet. One would never know by the profuse amount of letters we receive from you – again!!! I suppose it's quite in order for me to wish you a happy new year and all that sort of thing while I'm about it – and tell you the only reason you're getting this slight note from me is my kindly first of the year cheer.

It's not a "slight note." She wrote to ask favors.

So, you'd better write and tell me all about you 'n Buster - vacation, etc. Mother and Dad as you can well imagine – are having cat fits because you haven't written – and at least once a week comment that you ought to be left without money for a month (and then they guess you'd write). I kinda dampened their hope tho' by telling them that Smith is a great place for borrowing – and if out of 2,000 strong you can't get enough from friends to live on a month – something is radically wrong.

One month's borrowing power was validated between sisters. News that left their mother sighing in disgust.

I don't know whether you've seen Leavell or not but in my last letter I told her the status of my love-triangle – and I think you'd better know too – so as to prevent a possible serious faux paw [sic]. Bud once more reigns supreme! Oh yes – ain't love grand! His feathers are all smoothed down – and we're very happily writing per usual once a week. He sure was mad at me for a while – but all is as it should be finally... I know we'll be married now as soon as we can.

I expect to receive his fraternity pin – the White Cross any day now – the one I returned to him in May when we had our little huff – He said he had the rest of my silver set waiting for me when I return" ... and "something else too." What I can't dare imagine.

The white cross is emblematic of a Sigma Chi affiliation. In New York, Bud's personalized stationery revealed his affiliation with the group nicknamed "FIJI," Phi Gamma Delta. The FIJI pin is black diamond shaped, with a white star. I dug deeper and learned more. Before moving to New York, Bud affiliated (in his father's footsteps) with the Sigma Chi's at the University of Montana. He's right there on the Sigma Chi page in the 1940 University of Montana *Sentinel* Yearbook.

... Sweet old faithful – how I love him – and by the by – he was very disappointed that you didn't answer his letter – He wants very much to see you and the Smith campus... Be a pal to your future brother-in-law please (you bum)... just remember how nice he was to you out in Montana "all one summer."

The summer of 1939 would not ever be forgotten. Proof laid in my mom's underwear drawer.

And oh yes – the other corner of the triangle – Well, letters from Jackie-boy started getting scarcer and scarcer – like chicken's teeth – and I knew something was up...

He fell quite in love with a *"beautiful blue-eyed blond."* (And, for the record, chicken don't have teeth at all.)

Seems she is quite well-to-do – lives with mother in a large beautiful home – with cook, colored chauffeur, houseboy, etc., etc. – is tops socially – was a Powers model – went to finishing school in NYC after going to prep school in Washington and practically was engaged to someone when Jack blew into town.

Enough said, he's marrying money.

... although says he still loves me more than anyone else in the world – which is rather hard for me to believe – knowing that fickle streak of his... guess the worms turning now. He's sending me "Life" for an Xmas present by the way – and while very nice could have been more original – as that was what I gave him last year – but I should talk because I didn't give him anything.

That pillar of the world, *Life Magazine* was ten-cents an issue at the time, $4.50 for a yearly subscription. Standing fourteen inches tall by ten-and-a-half inches wide, the red and white *Life* masthead branded the upper left corner. Cover subjects, in sepia tones, were varied. Some smiled, some didn't: celebrities, soldiers, athletes, diplomats, fashion, film, fun. Faces of Churchill, Roosevelt and the Statue of Liberty piqued interest, possibly boosted sales at the newsstand. Photojournalists delivered "do or die" action from around the world to the coffee table for consumption.

He says he wishes we had gotten married before I left – and then the problem would never have arisen... he doesn't know what we would live on now – but wants to know if there isn't some way I can hurry back – so we can be married. He has Nancy's happiness to think of too... doesn't want to ruin her life by going around with her until I get back and then suddenly strand her – and up and marry me.

... So-o-o Being plenty fed up – I wrote back a letter and said I was returning his pin as soon as I could find someone going north – and would he please send my Emma Willard ring back to you. Hope he hasn't lost it – cause I want to give it back to Bud... I told Jack it would be better for him to get himself married to Nancy – he at least won't have to worry any more about money – told him to forget me as I had other plans..."

What was the backstory on Jack? He was a "best set" New Canaan, Connecticut, kid on his way to a Dartmouth diploma. Like Louie, he was a serious player on *my mom's* dance card when Dottie lit on the Smith campus in 1938. Robin was the sparking conduit between Jack and Dottie. Then, when Jack bumped off the man score in August 1939, the timing to win Dottie was impossible. Her heart was full of one love: Bud. Robin and Jack mixed it up until Buster danced into the picture in 1940. *Then* Jack won Dottie over. The huff with Jack (when he found out about Buddo) laid the foundation for Dottie's messy love triangle. It's convenient for Dottie that she chose to date her sister's ex-beau, for no other reason than to retrieve her Emma Willard ring.

Bud sent me a sweet New Year's cable – and made me so lonesome to see him again – he is the most thoughtful boy. Hope you take him around and introduce him to Leavell – I know she'd love to meet him... Tact old girl is all you need to make us a happy family – so see what you can do for a pal.

This afternoon mother, Russell and I have been planning a birthday dinner for 10 people including Russell and me. We're planning to have it on the 10th – and it's going to be a lot of fun.

January 10 fell smack between Russell and Dottie's birthdays. He turned eighteen on January 9; she turned twenty on January 11. Upside down for a person in North America to think of them as summer birthdays.

Wish you could be down here with us enjoying all this wonderful summer weather – instead of being in mid-winter facing exams – Ha Ha – By the way, I told Bud I wasn't planning to return to Smith and Mother told me I wasn't going to any expensive Katie Gibbs – Guess she's trying to get me married off to Buddo – and the sooner the better to my mind...

Katharine Gibbs School of Secretarial and Executive Training for Women was known for its standards of excellence at the time. Of course, so were the Women Ivies. I should think training at Katie Gibbs might be practical. And economical, compared to the tuition expense for a liberal arts education at Smith.

Spent a very quiet Xmas and New Year's compared to last year. But nice just the same – even though the family keeps us well under thumb – if you know what I mean – and I think you do... Been going riding almost every morning at 8:00 for quite a while – and along with golf twice a week – plus hikes – and swimming I'm getting good and tanned up - 'Bout as brown as you me thinks – Mother has a fit because I haven't a hat to shade my face – and even if I had one I wouldn't wear one – or the visor she tries to make me wear – It's really a healthy life – and I love it...

I understand why my grandmother nagged her to wear a hat in the high-altitude, mid-summer sun. It was less about ruination of her beauty, premature wrinkles and age spots. It was more about health. The correlation of UV radiation and skin cancer was understood early in the 19th-century. Sunblock had been invented in the 1930s and was commercially available. But what young woman wanted something of *that* consistency to clog her pores. What surprised me? Creamy white skin was fashionable during the fair skinned '40s, offering a canvas for the reddest of lipsticks emphasizing a kissable cupid's bow. The rebel in my aunt ignored fair skin as a symbol of wealth and refinement. She preferred a "healthy tan" as a by-product of her outdoorsy activities. Pep, ginger and playfulness defined her.

Hope I can get up to the States for summer. Wouldn't you like to have me for your graduation chum? I'm aching to buy millions of clothes in U.S. stores – I sure do miss good stores here.

She went on to report a new section of the mine would soon open. Five-hundred Chilean laborers were to be added to the work force. More men meant faster production for the war effort.

Damn war anyhow – makes the mine work Sunday – so with the three different shifts going night and day – none of the mine boys can get down to Coya to play golf – ride or swim with us... Oh never fear – Bud's my man from now on – I wouldn't get married and stay down here for any amount of money or love in the world...

Remember me to all the cronies – and loads of love. Dottie

Hope you can read this mess! I can't. Did you see picture of N. Houston in "Life" Dec. 16 p. 107?

I didn't locate the picture of N. Houston on page 107, but the *Life Magazine* cover on December 16 shows a Greek soldier blowing an allegorical trumpet backdropped by Parthenon ruins. Through the pages of a *Life* cover story, another set of European front lines had crept into American living rooms. Greece was defending itself against Mussolini's military in the Greco-Italian War, the beginning of what history dubbed the Balkans Campaign of WWII. Overall, the magazine content remained broadly palatable and informative, pleasing to an American audience still at peace. Conscripted soldiers classified as 1-A, "available for military service," were training, but not yet in harm's way.

So were men like Buster.

**Note – Family sends love. Write Soon. Me. A boy down here received an <u>air</u> letter from the US, which had been opened and passed through a US censor inspection. He received it a day or two ago – and it had been held up on the way down – took

exactly three weeks – just as long as boat mail. We don't know what the score is –
Hope none of your letters get held up when you want something in a hurry.

Insofar as Dottie and Skeeter switched up their lives in the southern hemisphere, Buster, too, faced a transition in residence. He forewent second semester, as a second-year student, on the Columbia campus and moved north. Fort Devens, Ayer, Massachusetts was his new home. His "REPORT OF PHYSICAL EXAMINATION OF ENLISTED MAN ON INDUCTION," prepared in quadruplicate, was dated January 30, 1941.

Joyously, for Buster and Robin, the travel time between Ayer and Northampton was about ninety minutes, via U.S. 202 and Massachusetts Route 2. Even with newfound geographic proximity, they penned ten letters during the short month of February, with evidence of their first tiff! Her letters were addressed to:

PVT N.F. Bedford
Headquarters. 2nd Squadron
101st Calvary
Fort Devens
Ayer, Mass.

Shangri-La

Chapter Twenty-Three

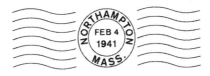

Roberta Skinner, Haven House, Northampton, Mass. – Tuesday night, February 4, 1941

My darling –

The ole professors are back at it again. They had us lack our midyears and then proceed to give us enough work to keep us busy 'til June – and say, "get it done by Easter" – so the slave yoke is back on.

...Our measles casualty list doubled itself over the weekend – nine cases – now we should have a rest 'til the next round starts in.

Fact check measles! The childhood vaccine against this dreadful disease, released in 1963, rolled out too late even for me. My mom, a worldly traveler in her youth, was well beyond worry. For Buster, on the other hand, there was cause for concern. Deafness was a not uncommon result, even death.

Went to the movies last night and saw "Santa Fe Trail" – Lots of blood and thunder all over everywhere. Raymond Massey does a superb job as John Brown, tho'. It's worth seeing just for him.

Warner Brothers went wild with both the script and cast in this 1940 year-end release. For me, it's a star-studded roster of Hollywood icons: Raymond Massey, Errol Flynn, Olivia de Havilland, Ronald Reagan and Alan Hale. Take it a step further, who would have gone out on a limb to predict a U.S. President in the making? One who loved jelly beans, no less.

No more news, dearest – 'cept that Mrs. Roosevelt is coming Thursday night to address Smith – (and that's no great news.) I shall write you about it later on.

Take care of yourself and remember I love you.

Your own, Robin. Xx

Eleanor Roosevelt lumped in as an afterthought? The prime news source on campus was the *Springfield Republican*. That conservative New England newspaper came across, editorially, as an oppressive doubter of the First Lady. As inspirational and influential as Eleanor was in the flesh, the poor woman's face was an object of caricatured proportion.

Roberta Skinner, Haven House, Northampton, Mass. – Friday morning, February 7, 1941

My darling –

Your letter arrived this morning amidst all this rain and "slosh." It must be awfully messy in camp with such weather. It's the first rain we've had for months – and here I was planning to get out on the old boards this morning for a couple of hours.

I am praying you can get over here tomorrow. Joyce and another boy (not Cousin George) have asked us to play with them Sat. night and Sunday. Please come dearest – not only to see me but to meet part of your future family. I guess they are still planning to come this weekend, either Saturday or Sunday.

Take a moment to meet more of the social circle. Joyce Thompson, a Haven House-mate was another bosom buddy. Her sidekick "Cousin George," may actually have been Joyce's cousin for all I know (but *not* the George on my mom's 1939 man score). They're part of the "gang." As were Braxton, Dizzy (Virginia "Gina" Solly's fun-loving beau) and a few others guilty of infringing on my mom's GPA.

I didn't flunk my chemistry exam (praise Allah).

An apolitical expression in 1940, genuinely thanking God for the gift she did not receive, namely a "flunk notice."

I went to hear Mrs. Roosevelt last night and she was very nice. Newspaper reports are very deceiving I guess. She talked in a very general way of "the responsibility of youth to the future."

What kind of understated eyewitness account of a living legend is *that*? Politics aside, Eleanor's words were practical, non-partisan and universal. I hope they honored the First Lady with a closing hymn. Eleanor's favorite? *Brighten the Corner Where You Are*. Activism and social reform cloaked in song to send the girls singing the message all the way home.

Before her lecture, I had dinner with all the counselors in "Hamp" who'd been to Camp Accomac. Three out of four have gotten engaged since last summer – some record!

Robin's Accomac counselor contemporaries waved engagement announcements like patriotic flags. Giddy in their good fortune, those women influenced my mom to set her sights on summer fun.

If I start working in a hospital in the fall, I think I'd rather have the summer to play in, even if I don't go to Chile.

She was not going to boomerang back to Accomac. Enough was enough when it came to scrubbing grease off pots and pans.

Roberta Skinner, Haven House, Northampton, Mass. – Monday, February 10, 1941

My dearest:

I had such a wonderful time playing with you this weekend. After you left I had that old feelin' again – that I wanted to get married to you right away. (You have the unanimous approval of my aunt and uncle – and they're twice as bad as Mother and Dad would ever be.) Doesn't that make you happy? They liked your family so much, too. They said when we come out to Sun Valley we have to stop and stay with them. They're only about 100 miles away.

Glory be, those *"how-do-you-dos"* spun faster than Disneyland teacups. Buster and the senior Bedfords mixed it up over a barrel of laughs when Auntie Alta and Uncle Dix passed through. No doubt the McLeods of Montana came up in conversation. Did they speak of Buddo and Dottie's long-distance romance? Not in a million years would Grampy reveal Walter McLeod as the character witness for my mom and her "respectable family." He played that hand close to the vest. It was men's business.

With the awkward meeting of family members behind them, the circle of love closed like a slipknot. For the first time in years, my mom lacked fancy chocolates, telegrams and flowers from multiple suitors on Valentine's Day.

Busy in love, she was taken with this simple card from her Buster.

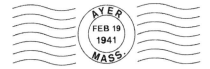

This is a very special day
To tell you that I love you —
That you are always in my heart
And I am thinking of you
This is a special time to send
My wishes fond and true
And a Valentine to let you know
My heart belongs to you

AYER
FEB 19
1941
MASS.

PVT N.F. Bedford, Fort Devens, Ayer, Mass. – Wednesday, February 19, 1941

My darling,

Just time for a note today as I went to the movies to see "Turnabout" last night when I usually write you. The movie was very good light comedy, I thought, and it cheered me up considerably.

I may be able to get off this weekend, and if I do I will fly home Friday night to see if I can finish this cold. Can you come down Saturday on the 11:53? If so, I'll meet you at Pelham at 4:08 and we can go back together Sunday. I'll telephone you tomorrow (Thursday) night at about 7:15.

All my love, Your own Buster.

Turnabout, a 1940 comedy classic may be silly but is stereotypically sexist in a husband/wife trading places theme. Glad it cheered my dad. It would be appalling in the #TimesUp era.

As for Buster's reference to "fly home Friday night?" At first I believed this to be strictly metaphorical. But the truth is, air travel between Massachusetts and New York was a suitably practical option in 1941, if a person could afford it.

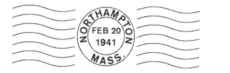

Roberta Skinner, Haven House, Northampton, Mass. – Thursday noon, February 20, 1941

My dearest -:

Measles, measles running all over – Even Scottie came down with 'em yesterday... But the saddest blow of all arrived when the Doctor's office decided that Haven House couldn't have Spring Dance 'cause that would be right in the middle of the 4th round – So we'll have a private dance in the spring – with picnics and baseball games later.

I had a letter from Mother yesterday and she is happy that we decided not to get married in June. I hope you don't regret it, honey. She hadn't received my letter asking her about December yet...

Unraveling the next one-sided, lightning round of letters, here's the set up. Buster opted out of flying home Friday night, and instead the senior Bedfords drove to Groton, Massachusetts, located less than five miles due north of Fort Devens. They checked into the Groton Inn, a Colonial-era mainstay of the town at the time. The oldest wing dated to 1678. It featured charming white clapboard siding, muntin windows, shutters, multiple chimneys, and pillared wraparound porches with broad, shaded decks. A lovely place to sit and sip lemonade in the summer.

Saturday, February 22 was considered the Washington's Birthday holiday, but my mom was obligated to attend chapel that morning. She'd written to explain it. *"No excuses accepted. Required chapel is an age-long tradition on that day."*

Lest we forget, this was not the long weekend Americans have become accustomed to. It wasn't until 1971 that the Uniform Monday Holiday Act permanently fixed a three-day President's Day weekend on the February calendar, honoring more than just our first POTUS.

It had been nearly a year since the evening of laughs at the Castleholm, when Robin was introduced to the senior Bedfords. Then on this Sunday evening of the holiday weekend, seated in the fine dining room of the Groton Inn, Buster's equanimity wore thin. Pray it was not a tantrum sufficient to draw a hush in the room.

Let's let the principals speak for themselves, but first meet Mary Liz, another Haven House-mate and a swell sport. She played emissary for damage control.

Sunday night, February 23, 1941

Dear Buster,

Please don't let this surprise you too much, but after all your secret admirer must write you sometime, and this seems quite appropriate. Robin is very, very unhappy that she was so "grubby" a short while ago. She wants to apologize, and will write you tomorrow after she has punished herself enough!

So please, please forgive her, and disregard the whole matter.

Our love – Mary Liz

P.S. We just love your candy!! Very good.

Buster appeared to enact the "silent treatment" in written form. Robin's letters flew in one direction.

Roberta Skinner, Haven House, Northampton, Mass. – Monday night, February 24, 1941

My dearest:

Just a little note to tell you I'm well, and happy, and most important that I love you very much.

It seems like I've done a million and one things today like going to chapel, and hearing a Vocational lecture on Bacteriology, and defaulting an opposing ping pong team...

I had a lot of fun in lab, today, watching three photographers for Year Book take pictures of two <u>very</u> <u>beautiful</u> photogenic models equipped in earrings, brilliant make-up and long sleeved silk blouses – in front of a lot of apparatus I had set up. (That's exactly the type of girl these laboring chemists are – and their latest working clothes! <u>Huh!</u>)

Must jump into bed to prevent one of your little viruses from catching up to me. He's already on the march, including all his war paint – but I'm hoping to fool him. Get rid of your little tribe, too, real quick.

All my love to you, Your Robin.

Even with my mom playing up details of beautifully appointed lady chemists and their photogenic features, Buster didn't bite. She followed up the next day with an apology and solicitous explanation.

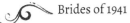

Roberta Skinner, Haven House, Northampton, Mass. – Tuesday night, February 25, 1941

My dearest:

Where are you? How are you? Your Daddy just called me and wondered if I'd heard anything from you, and he said you were in the dumps Sunday night when he left. You shouldn't have been unhappy, honey - 'cause I was unhappy enough for two of us!

I'm sorry if I made you unhappy by scolding you, dearest – But it's really 'cause I love you so much. If I didn't it would go by – and I'd never speak about it – and just remember it as an act I dislike intensely.

As for any children of ours I shall never allow any of them to speak so rudely to you, or to me, or to any other older person.

I can attest she stayed true to *those* words.

Goodnight, baby – a great big kiss and a little one from Tigger.

Demonstrating respectable maturity with that explanation, she softened the message in closing with a kiss from "Tigger," a stand-in security object when her Princeton tiger was away. One of many anthropomorphic characters of A.A. Milne's 1920s invention with timeless, universal appeal.

Roberta Skinner, Haven House, Northampton, Mass. – Friday, February 28, 1941

Hello, sweetheart –

Today, it's awfully cold around Hamp and it must be terrible around Ayer. Hope you're not out on one of your 10 mile strolls. How's your cold, honey?

Safe conversation opener talking of the weather, with concern for his health.

I wrote your mother a "thank you letter" the other day – after receiving yours. Honey, she didn't talk to me about the party on the way home from Ayer. She said just a little about it in Groton, while you were out on your self-imposed walk on Sunday and nothing that you hadn't said before mostly, that it was not any kind of an announcement party – rather one for your friends – a tea on Sunday afternoon. That's all. – Oh, also that she would have to know in plenty of time – so's to make out invitations, etc. As you had told me all this before, I didn't think about mentioning it to you. Understand?

Now we know there were *words* about "the party." Witness a communication situation between mother, son and sweetheart; quintessential grounds for wrangling. A "self-imposed walk" seemed like an excellent idea, my dad puffing on his pipe.

Yesterday, Mrs. Priest [Haven Housemother] *gave an awfully nice tea for the engaged Seniors – (She likes you so much.) She sent us all corsages.*

It begs the question, exactly how many seniors in Haven House were engaged? Here come the brides of 1941.

Wednesday, we gave Dottie Davies a party at the Tavern for her birthday – 'mid champagne and birthday cakes and candles. I guess she's nineteen now. She had a wonderful time with Joyce and Gina, a couple of other girls and yours truly. After that we rushed off to see "This Thing Called Love" which is nifty – with Rosalind Russell and Melvyn Douglas – lots of fast dialogue, and a laugh a minute. You <u>must</u> see it.

It's a movie about newlyweds where the wife insists on celibacy for three months after the wedding. Would Buster find *that* funny?

Honey, what are we going to do for the party? If it's a party for your friends, I should think that you would make out the list of people? How many invitations is your mother going to send?

The content for an invitation to a tea in 1941 was not that different than any social occasion today: who, what, when, where; but "why" is still a bit of a mystery. Proper etiquette dictated that the invitation be as formal as the occasion; sent two weeks in advance.

I'd like to send your mother a corsage for the party – Do you think that's alright? Write soon honey, I'll be waiting for a letter...

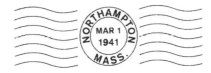

Roberta Skinner, Haven House, Northampton, Mass. – Saturday night, March 1, 1941

My dearest -:

I went to see "Lost Horizon" tonight and loved it. It was so beautiful, and so ideal that I could go back and see it all over again.

A film that offered complete escape from world news headlines. It happened that German troops swarmed into Bulgaria, within striking distance of Greece and Turkey that very day.

I know I'm a dreadful idealist, honey... I thank God for letting me know you, and for letting me make you happy. I shall try to do that 'till my last breath, my dearest... in peace and happiness, free from conflicts, and petty jealousies and selfishness.

Step back a little further in time for a minute and consider this. The origins of a mythical mountain paradise called Shangri-La was fabricated by British author James Hilton in his 1933 novel *Lost Horizon*.

The legendary brilliance of Frank Capra delivered Hilton's Shangri-La larger than life on the big screen. The historically significant 1937 Columbia Pictures film, *Lost Horizon*, conjures a movie-induced daydream. Robin probably fancied herself playing the part of a horseback-riding Jane Wyatt. Her co-star love interest Ronald Coleman, a dashing substitute for Buster,

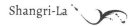

had slicked-back dark hair (though parted on opposite sides), ears of comparable size and shape, and kissable lips.

The appeal of this utopia went well beyond enthralling my mom. Even FDR named his presidential retreat Shangri-La; what we now know as a rustic and woodsy Camp David in the Catoctin Mountains of Maryland.

What matters most is this: Robin's tactful use of storyline content softened the party-planning squabble.

Quarantines and Camellias

Chapter Twenty-Four

Roberta Skinner, Haven House, Northampton, Mass. – Saturday A.M., March 8, 1941

My dearest one -:

How are you today? I hope you're better. You know, you'd look awfully funny all polka-dotted with scarlet fever. You'd better not catch it. – Now you'll have to be a fugitive from a scarlet fever – 'stead of a measle. Furthermore the legal quarantine for that is pretty long and you might not be able to come to your own party – if you caught it.

...Yesterday I saw something in the N.Y. Times which made me very unhappy: That the National Guard's training had been extended to at least six months additional training and probably a year's – That's an awfully long time away, isn't it honey. That means a postponement – doesn't it, of our getting married. Gee, it seems a shame we can't get married real soon and be together while we're still young and happy.

Witness the skew of youth's perspective. Silly girl, she spoke as if they would be old and unhappy in no time. It is now fourteen months since their introduction over Christmas break in Florida. Six months since the proposal on Lake Carnegie, when my mom said "yes," without "thinking about it."

I had a letter from Mother this week – and she commented on the picture I sent her to put in the paper with the announcement – but said nothing definite about it.

Like when she would place it? Or where it would be placed?

She also said that Dad wrote you one letter quite a while ago, but she would have him write you another.

Presumably Buster wrote my grandfather Skinner, formally asking for my mom's hand in marriage. Upholding tradition, he covered the points: how much his daughter meant to him; why she was the only one for him; promising to take care of her for the rest of her life. Anxiously my dad awaited T. Wayne's fatherly reply. It must have been awkward for both, having never met.

While letters crisscrossed continents, the "why" to be printed on the invitation my grandmother Bedford prepared for "the party" became clear. Did she try and fail to plan an engagement soiree under false pretense, playing trickster in cahoots with my grandfather?

Or did she plot against the whole notion of the engagement?

Darn the sticky wicket of mid-twentieth century etiquette. It haunted the nuptial process and often spoiled the fun.

In many cases, it still does today.

Roberta Skinner, Haven House, Northampton, Mass. – Sunday, March 9, 1941

My dearest -:

Your mother said you looked so healthy when she saw you – healthier than you'd looked since you entered law school. Gee, I wish I could see you...

Joycie and I were talking about men in general last night – and what we like about certain individual ones – the things about you we like are your sweet nature, your clean mind and high ideals, honey – your gentleness and fine moral values. I want you to always keep those qualities, sweetheart 'cause with them you'll make the perfect husband (for little me), and the kind of a man that will stand out so sharply against a group of others, with their "smooth" and worldly ways.

Every time I think about how wonderful you are, and what a lucky girl I am, I make a silent little promise that no matter how long that (G.D.) Army keeps you or what may happen in the next two years I'll still be waiting for you, - waiting 'till the day when we can be together forever and ever, and I can live with my perfect – or should I say – "my wonderful" husband.

Oh, my! Mom paid attention in that 1939 Chapel-talk marriage forum. There is no such thing as a "perfect" partner.

Now Buster wrote, clearly on edge about parental blessings from Campamento Americano.

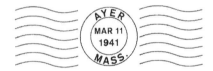

PVT N.F. Bedford, Fort Devens, Ayer, Mass. – Tuesday, March 11, 1941

My darling,

Tried to phone you yesterday to find out what you had heard from your mother, if anything. Time is getting short before spring vacation and I am a little worried. I certainly will be glad when we have finished with this stage of the getting married process.

A thought common to prospective grooms?

My chances of getting off this weekend look brighter now and there is rumor that the quarantine will be lifted on Thursday. If so, I will call you Thursday night at 7:15 to let you know. You can take the 11:05 out of Hamp Saturday morning, Mom and Dad will meet you at Pelham station at 3:08, and you can all drive out to the airport to meet me at 4:27. Maybe if we can all get together this weekend we can get everything cleared up and the stage all set for the party on the thirtieth.

A man with a plan to finish "this stage of the getting-married process."

You have been very good about writing, darling, and I do appreciate it. If you are always as thoughtful about everything else you are going to make the most wonderful wife in the whole world...

Meanwhile, on this March 11, 1941, faced with increasing international unrest, President Roosevelt cracked a tough nut. Countering bold opposition from isolationists, FDR signed the Lend-Lease Act: the means to provide material support in the form of U.S. military resources, answering Britain's need for assistance in their defense against Nazi Germany.

Playing off Buster's hopeful words to Robin, let's apply them (hypothetically) to the tip of Churchill's fountain pen. A letter he might dash off to Roosevelt: *"If you are always as thoughtful about everything else you are going to make the most wonderful [ally] in the whole world..."*

Roberta Skinner, Haven House, Northampton, Mass. – Sunday, March 16, 1941

My dearest:

It was so wonderful seeing you yesterday – Now maybe I'll survive somehow till the 28ᵗʰ – 11 days is still a long time tho', isn't it?

All the invitations arrived this afternoon – and thank heavens I was in Chem lab. Even then, there was much talk about it at dinner. Gee, but the party's so wonderful. I get so excited about it I can hardly study! I got a letter of introduction today to a doctor down in P. & S. [Columbia University College of Physicians and Surgeons] *who wants somebody who's had zoology and chemistry but to start work in June. I'll see him sometime during vacation – maybe he's got a friend who'll give me a job in September.*

We are leaving here on Wed. and arriving at Plymouth about midnight – Joyce says that on our way back down – (she's driving us from Boston to N.Y.C. after skiing) we will probably stop off and see you – i.e. if the Army doesn't frown on four little girls whipping thru the Fort. Does it?

Love you very dearly, Your Robin

Easter vacation began mid-week on Wednesday, March 19. A "Pituitary paper" due after the break remained unfinished. Bothersome, like a paper cut, but not to worry. She was proud of important accomplishments of late. Invitations to the engagement soiree were hand-addressed, stamped, postmarked and on their way to those on the guest list. Presumably, my mom enlisted the help of friends with practiced penmanship.

Unlike today, almost everyone's penmanship was practiced in the 1940s.

Robin and Buster rendezvoused at the Groton Inn for a far more pleasant and palatable dinner than the petulant event three weeks before. As he returned to business at Fort Devens, my mom and Haven-mate, Joyce, launched the spring break odyssey north on the evening rail, bound for Plymouth, New Hampshire. Destination: Huckin's Hill. In the railcar, they bumped into that good sport from Haven House, Mary Liz. Animated girly adventure chatter filled the train compartment.

The first RSVP to the engagement affair was a personal note to Buster. It revealed common themes running through the lives of young men at the time.

Princeton football teammate, "Sawbones" Sawyer had this to say:

March 20th, 1941

Mr. Nathaniel Forrest Bedford '39

1283 Manor Circle

Pelham Manor, N.Y.

PLEASE FORWARD IF NECESSARY.

Dear Buster –

Thanks very much for your invitation. So our quadruple threat man is finally taking the leap! Seems these announcements come along in the mail about every three days telling of one classmate after another and here I am still on the single list. Congratulations, Buster, and the very best luck to you and the bride-to-be. She must be a fine girl.

Your announcement reached me here at home just as I arrived from the Canal Zone. I've been there for the last eight months, following a six month trip bumming through Mexico and Central America...

...I won't be able to attend [your engagement party], *although I'd certainly like to. The U.S. Army is rather uncooperative at times...*

I'd like to hear from you and find out what you've been doing, so if you can spare a minute from preparations and such drop me a line. Address is Flying Cadet J.E. Sawyer Jr. Darr Aero Tech, Albany Georgia.

Yours, Sawbones

Meanwhile, my mom beat herself up on the ski slopes over the next four days. She wrote these diary samplers: *"Skied and spilled hard on trail on Huckin's. Muscle bruise."* Then: *"Skied part way down trail on Huckin's and hurt my knee. Damn!"*

Damn! Meaning something along the lines of confound it. She didn't use the Lord's name, as in God Damn It (or abbreviate it, "G.D.") but her knee hurt enough to garner more than a darn or dang it.

Lord knows I've used worse in similar circumstances.

In keeping with the spring break itinerary (at least in part) my mom and Joyce boarded the train out of Plymouth on Monday morning March 24. But rather than motor with Joyce from Boston to New York (with the proposed four-girl, head-turning stop at Fort Devens) my mom stayed aboard, day-dreaming over scenery out the window for hours. The train pulled into Grand Central at 10 p.m. Joyce's parents embraced their house-guest with gracious hospitality. Mom tucked in for the night.

The next few days of indulgence rolled out with sheer delight. It started with my mom's arrival at the Pelham Manor house on Tuesday. Witness (no surprise) a spending spree financed by her future in-laws. Finishing touches on party planning followed:

March 26, 1941 – *"Shopped and bought blue dress for Sunday – also girdle. Buster arrived by plane 11:40 P.M."*

March 27, 1941 – *"Shopped some more – for gloves, shoes and Mrs. B dress. Lunch at Seymour with Doug Johnson."*

Doug Johnson was a clean-shaven friend of Buster, and a rising pianist. His long slender fingers spanned an impressive Steinway keyboard reach. Pomade slicked hair, parted on the side, stayed put through head bobbing crescendos. He'd recently returned from gigs in Havana and Miami where he'd spiced up his live performance repertoire.

Doug resided in an apartment at Hotel Seymour, 44 West 45th Street, mid-town Manhattan. Buster met Doug while living "off-campus" at the Seymour, as a first-year law student at Columbia. This twelve-story "Beaux Arts" brick and limestone architectural statement was perfectly situated for a musician, in the heart of the theatre district. The positively exclusive "Apartment Hotel" catered to prominent citizens, successful entertainers and (apparently) Columbia Law students who could afford it. The dining room at the Seymour was a convenient place to pencil out the set list of music for the engagement party.

Amused chuckles spilled out at the suggestion of Gilbert and Sullivan's *When I Was a Lad.* A happy song from the comic opera *H.M.S. Pinafore* about a young man who served a term as an office boy to an attorney's firm; a kindly poke at Buster. *Rosenthal's Fantasy on Themes from Johann Strauss* promised sparkly virtuosity at Doug's fingertips. You know the tune: *The Blue Danube Waltz.* Music of Vienna that universally draws forth a sense of peace. A musical masterpiece that a kid like me first experienced watching *Looney Toons.* Later it raised iconic imagery; floating in outer space. Recall Stanley Kubrick's 1968 epic sci-fi mind-bending release: *2001- A Space Odyssey.*

On Friday, March 28, 1941, my mom wrote: *"Day of Day's – Engagement was finally announced. Whee. As Cousin George says – 'I've got the chain on – all I need is the ball.' Had dresses fitted for Sat. and Sunday."*

Personally, I wouldn't tag this day as the *"day of day's"* since it preceded the engagement party. But for my mom, I believe she excitedly waved the news clipping under people's noses like an exclusive scoop. A diamond soon to follow? I'd guess the senior Bedfords purchased two dozen or more copies of the newspaper that day.

Let's pause for a moment to keep the historical record straight.

A little poking around tells me Saturday's event had nothing to do with the wedding. Spring Formal for Columbia law students, better known as the Barristers' Ball, was held in the Jade Room on the third floor of the Waldorf. Tickets: $3. Music by Art Kahn and his Orchestra; one of the hottest jazz dance bands in the 1920s. In 1941, they still had the Fox Trot touch. She wrote about the day like this: *"Had lunch at Princeton Club with Buz. Had hair set at Saks – Mr. Wighton very English... a nifty time at Barristers' Ball in evening – then to the Monkey Bar (of all places!)"*

It's safe to say a trip to the Monkey Bar (located in, and inextricably linked with, the Hotel Elysée on 54th Street) was a spur-of-the-moment après party choice; a hot spot to roast and toast the young couple. No doubt Buster's Columbia law buddies trumped that up. It's a short walk, just five blocks, from the Waldorf. Did they play monkey-see-monkey-do in the mirrored panels of this dimly lit piano bar? It invited that kind of foolish mimicry. Doubtless, the Florida boy in my dad had a heyday. Not every-one is genetically predisposed, in a dominant way, to wiggle ears, roll their tongue and flare nostrils. (Are you trying it now?) At least Robin did not ruin her hair trying to keep up in that contest. All that styling by Mr. "very English" Wighton needed to hold tight.

Pelham Manor waited for the young couple to return from their night out with porch lights lit. In the wee morning hours of March 30 (the longed-for party day), Robin and Buster slipped into the house. There they presumably slept until noon; then rallied for the afternoon tea in their honor. That night, my mom wrote this:

"Had a most wonderful party today at Waldorf-Astoria. Everybody happy – Doug Johnson played piano – lots of pictures for album. Bed early. Wore a red camellia in my hair – Blue dress – Oh! So beautiful!

For Buster, it was a fleet-footed long weekend. His round-trip itinerary, arriving near midnight on Wednesday, commanded him to report back at Fort Devens Monday morning. Whatever uniformed duties were on his to-do list that day, he surely uplifted all within earshot regaling tales of the Monkey Bar. I suspect the bugling of *Taps* at dusk was a relief; full license to hit the sack as the twenty-four languid notes of the tune invited sleep.

Meanwhile, my mom was off for yet another night on the town.

Remington Ready

Chapter Twenty-Five

Bud McLeod stepped in as Robin's escort for dinner at the storied Plaza Hotel, and a three-act comedy, *Charley's Aunt*, at the Cort Theatre, on Broadway. Her diary revealed they capped the evening with a *"drink on [the] house"* at the new and swanky Copacabana night club. A Latin themed legend now, its doors had opened just months before.

I can't smile without reflecting on pop-musician Barry Manilow here. While he had little to do with this *"hottest spot north of Havana,"* his 1978 hit *Copacabana* is a veritable disco earworm right up there with Alicia Bridges' *I Love the Nightlife (Disco Round)*. I'm no "Fanilow" (the well-known moniker of his fan-base) but, to his credit, he crossed generations and genres over a lengthy career.

To my surprise, this momentous spring break of senior year also found Robin responsibly chasing a job prospect. Recall she wrote, in her March 16 letter to Buster, about one *"who wants somebody who's had zoology and chemistry but to start work in June...I'll see him sometime during vacation."*

It was appropriately April Fool's Day when she acted on her intent and met with Dr. Werner of the Columbia College of Physicians and Surgeons. With respect to that meeting, she wrote in her diary: *"Saw Dr. Werner of P. & S. – no luck."*

Roberta Skinner, Haven House, Northampton, Mass. – Wednesday, April 2, 1941

My darling -:

I meant to write you Monday night to cheer you up a little bit at camp – but fell asleep on Joyce's bed and didn't wake up 'til Bud was 'sposed to be there.

That night we went to the Plaza for dinner, and then to "Charley's Aunt" as we could get better seats there (8ᵗʰ row). I don't think I ever laughed so hard in a play.

(Anyway, now we can see "My Sister Eileen" if you want to. Happy?)

Seemed unlikely that they went to Broadway on a Monday night. Why? Nowadays, Monday's are mostly dark. Buddo happened to get tickets before history played out. Let me explain. A colonial blue law dating to 1695 prohibited fun, including anything theatrical, "on the Lord's day." It held for nearly 250 years. In November 1940, Sunday shows were first authorized by the council of the Actors' Equity Association. The transition took years, but it's how the new norm (Tuesday through Sunday afternoon) evolved on Broadway.

And why was my dad uninterested in *Charley's Aunt?* Perhaps he'd already seen it. The original Broadway production reached back to 1893. It's not inconceivable to think Buster had either viewed it more than once or even played a role. Why? Revivals of this Victorian farce dot history right down to high school drama class.

Mom went on... *Tuesday I had an appointment with some awful doctor at P. & S. I came back on the train last night with a girl who had seen him Monday – and she also didn't care if she ever saw him again. As a matter of fact he had kept her waiting for two hours in his office before he interviewed her, despite her appointment – and then wound up by telling us both, he had a lot of other people to see – so we wouldn't hear anything 'till April 10ᵗʰ. However the salary was $1,400 which is good for us unexperienced graduates.*

No more news, dearest – but I have to tell you again how happy I am – and that I want to get married in Dec. definitely. I don't see how I can wait any longer than that. Do you think we can? At times I wish the war would be declared so I'd have an excuse to marry you even sooner.

The picture she painted for Buster about Dr. Dick Werner at P. & S. exposed the real dirt on how *"no luck"* played out in detail. (Truthfully, I have no evidence that the doctor's name was Dick, but any modern woman would agree he is one.) If all the young women interviewees dittoed the narrative of these two train companions, maybe the doc was looking for a man to fill the position. Sixty-seven cents per hour: was there equal pay for inexperience?

The due date for her unfinished written report on "Pituitary" was now imminent. Her entry on Thursday, April 3, read like this: *"Tried to finish paper. Wrote Buster. Buster called. Out with Louie. He announced his engagement March 30."*

Go figure the coincidence. On the very same day, former beaus Louie and Robin proclaimed their respective plans to wed...other people. With evidence at my fingertips, they had not seen or heard a peep from one another since June 1, 1940. (Recall it's the same day Jack found out about "Buddo" and was plenty mad; when Buster was #1.) Evidently, Louie was thrust into a new phase of life at that time and moved on. It's satisfying to know my mom had a bestie-like male friend in her old beau, like a pair of worn jeans; familiar, comfortable, and not likely to let you down. The kind a girl remembers fondly looking back over the years.

PVT N.F. Bedford, Fort Devens, Ayer, Mass. – Sunday night, April 6, 1941

My beloved,

Many thanks for your considerate little note of Thursday night. Your thoughtfulness in letting me know that you were going to be in New York instead of Northampton saved me my Friday night telephone call and considerable worrying. The result was that I spent a very happy weekend instead of one of those awful fretful, stewing ones of which I have endured so many in the past. You are either learning to be more considerate, dear, or else you love me more than you used to even as late as last Fall, but whatever it is I appreciate it and love you for it. I hope that you had a very enjoyable time in New York and learned a great deal. Please write me a nice letter and tell me about some of the more interesting details.

Most of this weekend Ben Wood and I spent gardening, since we were unable to leave camp. We transplanted two six-foot pine trees to adorn our front door, carried several gunny sacks of humus from the woods to furnish top-soil for a lawn, sowed the lawn with oats from the stables and planted sweet-peas along the edge of the building. In a couple of weeks 2nd Sq. Hq. is going to be the garden spot of Camp Devens.

Your own loving Buster Xx

Did my dad rib Ben Wood about being a crimson man? Of course, but not because Ben had contracted German measles or overexerted himself hauling gunny sacks of humus. "Chalmers Benedict Wood," was a class of 1940 Harvard "Crimson." The two young soldiers were ideal compatriots. As much as Ben appeared to enjoy gardening, he knew football, too. "Captain Wood" proved to be a fine leader for the St. Marks High School team in Southborough, Massachusetts, about thirty miles south of Fort Devens. He played positions of defensive tackle and offensive running guard. Strategic skills he would soon use in the U.S. Army Air Force (the predecessor of the United States Air Force).

Not only that, as practically a "local," Ben had wheels at his disposal!

On her return to Northampton Saturday night, Robin took a room at the Brass Knocker. Presumably Haven House was still "on break." She wrote Buster the next day.

Roberta Skinner, Haven House, Northampton, Mass. – Sunday, April 6, 1941

My dearest -:

Another beautiful day, sweetheart – I wish you could be here to enjoy it with me. I guess I'm getting a little curl in my tail about you now! I'd much rather take care of you than let the Army have you – but I guess they know a good man when they see him, too.

Let's unwind the *"curl in my tail"* Robin spoke of. Did she make that suggestive expression up? Had she revealed to Buster the "anatomically social" behavior of a pig's tail, as described by her Montana cowboy? Buster would perk up at the insinuation of her excitement.

I got home safe and sound last night after reading just pages and pages of "Mortal Storm."

Juxtaposed with her fantasy of domestic bliss, worry festered over "what if" events that might alter her promised life with Buster. Phyllis Bottome's novel, *The Mortal Storm*, churned introspection. Snug on the train with this first edition (1938) mass market Penguin paperback, she thought back to that night off from Camp Accomac when she saw the film. As she read *"pages and pages"* of the frighteningly authentic narrative, film icons Jimmy Stewart, Margaret "Freya" Sullavan and Robert Young loomed. Mom put a face to Freya Roth, an eligible, college aged female. Her fictional "non-Aryan" father Viktor Roth (played by Frank Morgan: The Wizard in *The Wizard of Oz*) taught there is no scientific difference in the blood of an Aryan and that of other races. (Raise a glass to Dr. Charles Drew.) For this, Viktor was arrested and sent to a concentration camp where he died. Mysteriously.

As to the family post-mortem on the engagement party, recall Robin's ruddy-faced cousin Leroy, the Union College grad who returned home in 1933 to live with his parents in Amsterdam. Following the death of his father nearly a year ago, Roy followed an employment opportunity in D.C. and relocated south to Alexandria, Virginia. At age thirty, he was gainfully employed as a statistical analyst for the U.S. Department of Agriculture.

As the only blood relative my mom could muster, Roy attended Robin and Buster's engagement party. Because T. Wayne and Lelia (obviously) couldn't be there, he made a promise to Robin. He would write an objective third-party report c/o Campamento Americano. In his own voice, he captured details like the Philomathean Society champ he'd become whilst attending Union College.

Roy Huntington, 212 E. Howell Ave, Alexandria Va. – April 7, 1941

Mr. and Mrs. T.W. Skinner
c/o Braden Copper Co.
Rancagua (Sewell)
Chile
South America

..... Having rambled about on our own affairs to this point, I'll now try to turn to the basic purpose behind the writing of this missive: to keep the promise to write you my impression of Roberta's party last Sunday, which I agreed to do at her request... on condition she didn't consider my report as excusing her from the necessity of writing you.

After having received the very formal invitation, I was very pleasantly surprised to find the party quite informal and most congenial and enjoyable instead of being stiff, cold as Antarctica, and boring like all previous similar affairs which I have experienced. In fact I continued to go sightseeing around New York for two of the three hours the party was scheduled instead of going to it when it began, because of my certainty that it would be a boring and unenjoyable affair.

He's an introvert.

On arriving there and discovering the enjoyable congeniality of the hostess, host, and guests, I regretted having adopted such a course of action. Most of the guests were young people who are friends of Roberta and Forrest from Princeton, Columbia Law, the Army, and Smith. The suite of the Waldorf-Astoria in which the party was held was very nice and most appropriate for such an affair. I would estimate about fifty were present at one time or another during the period I was present. While there I had very enjoyable conversations with Mrs. Bedford, Mr. Bedford, Roberta – or "Robin" as the Bedfords all called her in common with many of the guests, Forrest – or "Buster" as he was called by many, "Bud" McLeod and several other guests.

Assuming you would be interested in my impressions of the Bedfords and of "Bud" McLeod, all first time ones and hence all subject to the deficiencies and errors of appraisals based on first meetings offering about 10 minutes conversation with each, plus observations made during my hour stay at the party; I'll attempt to describe my impressions of these persons, taking them individually: -

Mrs. Bedford: Appearance: - Neat and orderly, features good for a woman in middle age. In build she is rather short – say 5'2" or 5'5" tall and just fleshy enough to give her a well-proportioned figure.

Personality: - Pleasant and such that she was a fine hostess. She is rather quiet and retiring, however the speaking she does is in such a manner as to leave one with the feeling that gives thought to and is earnest and sincere in her statements.

Mr. Bedford: Appearance: - Well-ordered and neat without being "Showy". That with his smooth, well-formed features would make him one of the better look-ing men in any group. He is about my height – say 5'7" or 5'8" and medium build. His dress, features, build and carriage render him a very good looking man although not one I would term either commanding or handsome in appearance.

What about the sparkle in his mischievous eyes?

Personality: - Very pleasant and congenial. He proved himself a wonderful host. It is his fine poise and smooth, easy manner – neither ostentatious nor commanding, yet seemingly always appropriate to the occasion – and his agreeable, friendly personality; which make him really outstanding and attract others to him even more than his fine appearance.

Roy certainly appeared attracted to Grampy!

For the sake of giving you a yardstick by which to evaluate my impressions of "Buster" I will use "Bud" McLeod, one whom you have seen and had an opportunity to judge for yourselves, for comparative purposes.

Evidence T. Wayne and Lelia met a twenty-one-year-old Bud in the summer of 1939.

My first meeting with each (Buster and Bud) was at the party and I conversed with each about the same length of time, so my appraisals of each are without prior knowledge or bias and are subject to equal likelihood of errors.

Forrest "Buster" Bedford:

Appearance: - Neat and tidy with smooth, well-formed features which make him a very good looking young man. In height he is slightly taller than I, possibly as much as an inch. His build is quite slim and youthful, although not to such an extent as to render him thin. His carriage is erect and his posture good, thereby utilizing to the utmost his features and build to produce the maximum in a fine appearance. "Buster's" features and build are such that I think he is at present better looking than "Bud" McCloud. However "Bud" has a 2" to 3" height advantage on "Buster" and has facial features so formed that with filling out and his outgrowal of young fellows' typical facial trouble from early shaving, (assuming his carriage to be equally good with "Buster's") he may develop into a man more handsome and commanding in appearance than "Buster's" features and build will ever permit him to become. The features and build of each of these fellows is such that I feel the filling out, likely to come with additional years, will improve rather than detract from the already good appearance of each.

More analytics in this business of measuring up: Buster stood five-feet-eight-inches on enlistment in July 1940; Bud was seven months older.

Personality: - "Buster" possesses a very pleasant/likeable personality and an easy, congenial manner which to me appeared smoother than "Bud's" manner. His manner, like his father's, reflects a cultured individual. He already possesses considerable poise, although he still needs additional practice to develop it to equal his father's.

From every standpoint, judging merely from the impressions I could obtain during my short time with "Buster" plus observations made during the remainder of the time I was at the party, I would term him an intelligent, sensible young fellow possessing a fine appearance and very agreeable personality who will prove a husband striving continuously with his best efforts to make Roberta proud and happy to be his wife and her life most enjoyable.

"Bud" McCloud [sic]:

Appearance: - You already know his and I have therefore used it for comparative purposed in describing "Buster's".

Personality: - He appealed to me as being another very congenial and likeable fellow. In making the statements I have that his manner and poise were not as smooth as "Buster's", I fully realize that he was under the handicap of being familiar with a much smaller number of those present than "Buster", whose party it was. This might account for the difference, and even if it doesn't, there is no apparent reason why "Bud" will not be able to acquire just as much poise and smoothness of manner as "Buster", given some time and the opportunities for such development.

To me, both "Bud" McLeod and "Buster" Bedford appeared as very fine looking and most congenial, likeable fellows such as I would enjoy meeting and associating with at all times.

That "Buster" has dark hair and the color of his eyes Roberta has undoubtedly long since informed you, I made no attempt to note them anyway.

Doubtful Robin educated anyone on Buster's brown eyes.

Roberta herself looked very nice in a pretty and becoming blue dress and a big red camellia, which "Buster" said is his favorite southern flower, in her hair. As always, I enjoyed greatly the time I had with her and from her actions and manner I feel sure she was enjoying the party tremendously – for which I am very glad.

Roy was sensitive to Robin's happy demeanor. I hope my Skinner grandparents were equally happy to hear of it.

Think I have covered the party and the principal characters about as fully as I know how, they took some pictures of the affair showing Roberta and "Buster" and the general scene so they will probably be sending some of them. Suppose the next thing now will be Roberta's graduation – when and if…

By way of Auntie Rhea, Roy was obviously privy to Robin's fight to the finish. Two months remained.

She asked if I would come up to it, to this I replied that my decision to go would not be made definitely until it was certain she would graduate, and she invited me after such certainty of graduating.

This has developed into a regular volume, I have finally become unsound, there-for to each of you,
Best wishes, Roy.

Evidence that it's sometimes worth spending the money for news to travel faster by air, my grandmother had <u>yet to receive</u> this detailed "volume" penned by Roy while other letters crisscrossed the ocean by both air and sea.

On the day before Easter, Lelia wrote about the buzz in her world like this:

L.M. Skinner, Rancagua – Sewell, Chile – April 12, 1941 (airmail)

Dearest Roberta,

We had the surprise of our lives a couple days ago. Mr. Klugescherd (Dad's assistant) came walking into the office, handing him the clipping of your engagement announcement – No picture attached – but it looks as though a photo might have been cut off – probably was sent to him air – so someone had cut off the photo on account of air weight. I noticed the editor had cut out Buster graduated (with honors) and the wording was changed a little. It was in the paper 27th of March, which gave one day more before Mrs. B's party. Some class having it in the Waldorf, no?

Grandma was understatedly wowed by this fame-attracts-fame "best set" glamour venue, the world's tallest hotel at the time. Like the solid bronze timepiece strategically placed at the Biltmore Hotel, smack in the middle of the luxurious lobby of the Waldorf stood another historically significant "meet me at the clock" rendezvous point. A two-ton, nine-foot Westminster quarter chimer topped with a decorative statue of liberty replica. A plaque at the base reveals the Goldsmith Company of London executed its production for exhibition at the Chicago World's Fair in 1893. Imagine the eyeballs to infinity that have rolled over that ornate pedestal. It depicts bronze plaques of various sports, iconic scenes and likenesses of six U.S. Presidents, Ben Franklin and Queen Victoria, too.

With so much to inspect, did anyone bother to consult the clock face for the time?

Grandma continued:

Bud wrote a hurried note and told us it was lovely. He liked the Bedfords greatly and thought Buster a fine fellow – said he would tell us more in his next letter. Hope he doesn't forget. Still haven't read any description of it from you.

Nor Roy.

Haven't rec'd Mrs. B's invitation yet either. I'm going to write her a letter just to start a friendship – when it arrives – that will give me an opportunity or an excuse to write.

I'm sending this check for your April-May allowance $35.00 + $40 extra toward Senior expenses that you will be receiving bills for. So don't spend it for weekend trips etc., and have nothing to meet the Senior incidental expenses as they are billed to you...

It looks more and more as though the States will be in the war – shortly. Do you know when Buster will be sent South or elsewhere? Any further plans about getting a job or coming to Chile – which? I read in another magazine – National Guard might be kept on indefinitely, looks rather certain don't you think?

Hugs and kisses, Mother

I get so cross at Dorothy she won't attend to writing any letters except Bud and an occasional letter to Mary Leavell.

An answer to my grandmother's line of questioning, *"plans about getting a job or coming to Chile,"* remained open. Meanwhile, the Smith Vocational Office crusaded for their seniors with leads like this:

Smith College
Northampton, Massachusetts
The Vocational Office
April 14, 1941

My dear Miss Skinner:

A letter has come from Dr. R. Teichner, Head of the Duplicator Supplies Division of Remington Rand, Inc. in Bridgeport, Connecticut, saying that he expects to have openings on his staff for women trained in chemistry and interested in industrial research. Remington Rand is at the moment doing work with pigments, dyes and oils. Dr. Teichner says that the starting salary will probably be $25 a week and that there is excellent opportunity for advancement.

I suggest that you write a letter of application directly to Dr. Teichner so that he will have it on file when the next vacancy occurs. You may refer him to this Office for your letters of recommendation.

Sincerely yours,

(Mrs.) Louise Thomas Newman
Assistant Vocational Secretary

Industrial research is a cool trajectory to think about for a woman in 1941. My mom's marginal chemistry grades would not make her the best candidate for Remington Rand, but it wasn't in the interest of the Vocational Office to rat out that fact. They measured success by student placement results.

As Assistant Vocational Secretary at Smith, it's obvious (Mrs.) Louise Thomas Newman was married, or possibly widowed. Odds are she worked out of economic necessity. Highly efficient with office correspondence, she'd expertly sandwich carbon paper the color of midnight between two pieces of white cockle finished "onionskin"; set to imprint a file duplicate for systematic record keeping. The papers were delicately fed, rolled around the platen of the typewriter, then carefully straightened. Manicured nails blazed above the keys. The carriage return batted in a swoop at each "ding." Common office din at the time. Letter upon cheery letter in modified block style delivered notice of a job prospect.

Is that special treatment from a vocational office a modern college senior's fantasy? It's vintage truth: personalized letters were the network for introductions in 1941.

Why exactly was Dr. Teichner on the hunt for girls from Smith? He knew Remington Rand's corporate contribution to the war effort extended well beyond business machines in the form of armament manufacturing. All but the men classified "4-F" (due to some physical defect) would soon abandon his Duplicator Division for a division of military persuasion. He proactively cued up female reinforcements to smooth the transition. These young women would work with the "Dexigraph," a copy machine that utilized cameras, film, developing agents and fixers on special paper.

Seems an elaborate process to make a "photocopy" compared to the effortless way we depend on ink and toner cartridges today. Pushbutton technology everyone takes for granted.

As much as Robin waffled on whether to commit to a post-graduation visit to see her parents, she'd already signaled her intentions in a letter to Buster weeks ago. "If I start working in a hospital in the fall, I thinks I'd rather have the summer to play in, even if I don't go to Chile." Mom had twenty-one years of experience trusting the winds of destiny to blow her in the right direction. Whichever summer escapade suited her would be bankrolled by one set of my grandparents or the other.

Provided a twenty-something is sufficiently funded, it seems fair enough to take a holiday after caps are tossed high and *Pomp and Circumstance* fades away. I lacked the means for a (then popular) post-grad breakaway the likes of backpacking Europe on five-dollars a day. Though at the time, my residence in Utah (land of Mormons and the Great Salt Lake) seemed altogether foreign to the good people of New Jersey.

While Robin's summer itinerary sorted out over the next eight weeks, more celebratory events lined up on the horizon. Spring Dance, cancelled for the sake of the Haven House measles quarantine in early March, lit up the next round. The promised *"private dance in the spring – with picnics and baseball games"* was about to unfold.

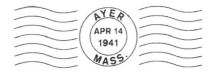

PVT N.F. Bedford, Fort Devens, Ayer, Mass. – Monday night, April 14, 1941

My beloved,

Tonight seems to be party night at 2ⁿᵈ Sq. Hq. as one of the Sergeants just contributed a pitcher of beer to the cause of good fellowship. However, seeing as how I love you more than beer or anything else in this world I am determined to write you in spite of everything.

You were very sweet to come over for Easter, dear, and share our simple church service with me. I enjoyed the week-end very much, more than any other I have ever spent around camp, and even more than a lot of others that have been more exciting but less full of real substance.

There doesn't seem to be much more for me to tell you tonight – most of the important things I told you last night, I guess – so I will have to tell you my two termite jokes.

1. As the termite said to the barkeeper; "Beat me, daddy, I ate the bar!"

A person had to be party to the times to make any sense of this corny joke. The up-tempo song *Beat me Daddy, Eight to the Bar* was a 1940s hit. Eight beats to the bar (rather than four) made for better boogie-woogie. Daddy (as in "Daddy-O") referred to the drummer who would key off the command "eight to the bar," then kick the beat up to double-time.

2. *The termite's nightmare: "I dreamed I dwelled in marble halls."*

Just noticed there was an R.S.V.P. to Mrs. Priest's invitation to your dance on Saturday, so must drop her an acceptance now. Will see you then, darling, and hope that this week passes very quickly.

All my love, Buster

Robin and Buster dressed in Easter Sunday best.

Roberta Skinner, Haven House, Northampton, Mass. – Tuesday night, April 15, 1941

My darling -:

Enclosed please find one certified statement from Mary Liz – We were both so busy yesterday – we couldn't write you.

However, we thought of the weekend that we'd just spent and felt very happy.

Very little news has developed since Sunday – Last night I went to "Le Bourgeois Gentilhomme" which the faculty of the French Dept. gave for French War Relief. I wish you could have seen it – It was very delightful.

Tomorrow, we seniors wear our caps and gowns to chapel for the first time – Wanna bet it'll rain?

Please don't forget what I told you Sunday night – coming back – I meant every word of it, dearest – from the bottom of my heart. So every time I say something silly, don't worry about it – just laugh – and remember what I said Sunday –

Yours forever and ever. Robin

My Dear Mr. Bedford,

This is to certify the fact that Miss Roberta L Skinner drank one entire glass of milk on Sunday evening at 9:30 o'clock. In fact, she manages to consume one every single evening! At any rate, I'll guarantee that none of her front teeth will be missing, unless of course she gets pugnacious again, the next time you see her.

Don't worry, Buster

Love Mary Liz

That jokester Mary Liz acted like a promotional partner of the USDA. The first federally subsidized milk program for schools was less than a year old. Qualified kids paid a penny for a half-pint served up in a short bottle. In the interest of public health (and the dairy industry), widely distributed posters took aim touting the virtues of milk for health. They pitched good teeth, vitality, endurance and strong bones, sold with big, whiter than white smiles.

Mary Liz paid attention in April 1941 when this government program migrated into the state of Massachusetts. You can be sure tall drinking glasses dotted each place setting in the Haven House dining room, just as they do in the iconic *Our Gang/The Little Rascals* comedic episode "Mush and Milk."

Recall these classic words of warning whispered between small children (Spanky among them) seated around the table in the Bleak Hill boarding school:

"Don't drink the milk."

"Why?"

"It's spoiled."

If it doesn't ring a black and white bell, I suggest you Google "Mush and Milk" right now and have a laugh. It's not my place to reveal why it's spoiled. MGM originally released this hilarious short to theatres in 1933. I, of course, watched the often-played re-run from my spot on the orange convertible sofa in the TV room of the Crane Road house.

Back at Haven House, I dare say regular milk deliveries arrived farm fresh from Northampton's local Sunnyside Dairy; possibly in ten-gallon milk cans. On the other hand, reusable glass bottles depicting a pyro-glazed Guernsey cow were another delivery option; containers sized for the milkman to off-load into a deco-inspired General Electric refrigerator.

Who could predict seventy-odd years later the USDA would be petitioned to remove dairy milk as a requirement of school lunch menus. Health benefits are called into question. Nowadays, research suggests milk consumption does not improve bone health and lactose intolerance is classified a digestive disease.

Circling back to Robin's mention of *Le Bourgeois Gentilhomme*, the French Department faculty drew on the talents of many with music and dance skills to pull off that five-act comedy by Molière. Pray the house sold out and the financial contribution to war relief, however small, was meaningful. The Geneva-based International Red Cross in Switzerland, the group tasked with daunting responsibilities to organize relief assistance for civilian populations, needed every cent.

PVT N.F. Bedford, Fort Devens, Ayer, Mass. – Wednesday night, April 16, 1941

My beloved,

I have several interesting things to tell you, but I'm afraid I haven't time tonight as I have to take my final examination in Radio Procedure tomorrow afternoon and have had to spend a good part of the evening in cleaning my pistol prior to shooting on the range tomorrow.

Many thanks for your sincere letter which arrived this morning, also for the certificate from Mary Liz. She is a good sport to join in our little jokes.

Spring dance was just three days away and Buster lacked a ride. *"Ben Wood is using his car so I can't get it."* He would resort to the train.

Robin recruited Cousin George and Joyce to pick him up at the station. At Buster's suggestion they drove *"an extra 10 miles"* (more accurately twenty-five) to meet the train at Athol at 2:03 p.m., rather than Greenfield at 2:43. Obviously he was hoping to spend an extra forty minutes with Robin in the back seat of the car, but it didn't work out that way. She needed time to primp and polish top to toe for the weekend kickoff event.

Here's what my mom had to say about the evening: *"Had a slick cocktail party at Admiral Inn. Danced in evening. Buster got sleepy after 10:30. Lots of fun."*

The Admiral Inn was yet another clapboard sided, double chimneyed white colonial classic with black shutters. The unimaginative moniker comes alive with the backstory. It was the historic homestead of Francis

Augustus Cook, a Northampton-born hero and 1863 graduate of the U.S. Naval Academy. A veteran of both the Civil and Spanish-American war, he retired in 1903 as a rear-admiral, and returned to Northampton where he died in 1916. It appeared traditions of old New England hospitality were offered up posthumously in the form of a storied (hence marketable) seafarer's inn. I imagine, in the visiting room, a prominent life-size oil on canvas portrait of a handsome man in uniform with artfully painted eyes. The kind that follow a person. They paired well with hearsay of hauntings.

Sunday morning the happy couple grabbed breakfast at *"the Foodshoppe,"* then packed off for a picnic... *"with... just everybody."* Enough folks for a baseball game.

That evening, *"drove up on Reservation – very beautiful,"* she wrote. The vast acreage of Mount Tom State Reservation is a noteworthy Massachusetts forethought; public land preserved in 1902 by their state legislature. Here, too, the CCC improved roads and trails under FDR's administration. The silent backdrop offers sweeping panoramic views of the Berkshires to the

Object lesson: How to eat a watermelon.

Playing tag on Mt. Tom.

Blissfully happy and at peace relaxing in the woods.

236

west; the Connecticut Valley to the north and south. The kind of spot young people enjoy in the moment and return to over time.

All the promises made to the girls in Haven House for, *"a private dance in the spring – with picnics and baseball games"* were kept, fulfilling the Smith tradition with far more than a dance.

Surprisingly, under the magical spell of social satisfaction there was no mention of what I know to be a "wildfire sunset." The evening views from Mount Tom must have been unmistakably pink to orange. Tequila sunrise psychedelics played along the horizon's edge. Why? Forest fires were raging in seven eastern states. They'd been burning all weekend.

Buster wrote a short, to the point pre-drill thank you note early Monday. *"Found an extra five minutes this morning to write you a little note thanking you for a very lovely weekend and telling you that I love you more than ever."*

His day was about to change fast in an unexpected way.

Godless Lot

Chapter Twenty-Six

PVT N.F. Bedford, Fort Devens, Ayer, Mass. – Monday night, April 21, 1941

My beloved,

I had better write you a nice letter tonight, for I don't know when I will be able to write again...

All day long the woods fires have been raging around the fort. Although I spent the morning on the pistol range coaching the men who have not shot yet, I was called out this afternoon to fight the fires. We were put in a pretty hot sector where the flames were whipping through the tree-tops and had almost surrounded a poor little farmhouse. When we arrived on the scene the meadow was all ablaze and we had to work like the very devil with shovels, pickaxes and wet gunny sacks to put it out. Then the fire, whipped by a brisk breeze, came tearing through the adjoining woods. It looked bad for a few minutes, but by digging up a grass-covered road, chopping down overhanging trees, and starting a backfire, we managed to clear out a fire-break that eventually stopped the progress of the wild fire and let it burn itself out.... Unless we get rain soon it looks as though this is likely to become a daily routine...

The slash left three years earlier in the wake of the Great New England Hurricane of 1938 made ideal tinder in the recent dry weather spell. Buster fought shovel in hand, like (a yet to be fabricated) Smokey Bear. Hot, dirty and choked with smoke, he wrote about his own muddy boots on the ground as if a Princeton football play by play. *The Chicago Tribune* of April 21, 1941, legitimized the broader tragedy with this two cents worth of news. (It's the truth, the paper cost two cents.) There on the front page: *"Forest Fires Rage in East; Enter Towns."* Seven states, including Massachusetts were affected:

"Fanned by 40-mile an hour winds, fires for a time endangered the barracks at Fort Devens, Mass. Several homes were destroyed and many families forced to flee. Six hundred Fort Devens soldiers joined firefighters at nearby Leominster and then were called back to battle two blazes inside fort property."

The travel distance of an ember was just as far then as it is today; a mile or more. The travel distance of a virus, immeasurably short. The red rash of rubella bloomed in the spring air and then marched indiscriminately through camp. Buster was forced into sudden isolation.

Roberta Skinner, Haven House, Northampton, Mass. – Wednesday afternoon, April 23, 1941

My dearest -:

I really had to laugh at you this morning when you were placed in quarantine for German measles! Let the voice of experience tell you that they are terribly contagious – and to watch out for and stay away from all people who complain of swellings in back of their ears, or lumps on their neck or head... remember the 2nd cases won't break out for 18 – 21 days from Sunday.

I guess you are going to get your long-awaited rain storm tonight... I wish I could have seen you Monday as a little fire-fighter...

Roberta Skinner, Haven House, Northampton, Mass. – Tuesday A.M., April 29, 1941

My dearest -:

I expected a letter from you today at the latest – but no such luck – so have decided that you must be sick – or lost the use of your writing arm. A week really is a long time not to hear from anyone, isn't it. Maybe you have the measles – Heaven forbid! – or else they must be keeping you horribly busy.

He had forewarned her that he didn't know when he'd be able to write again.

I had a very nice time in N.Y.C. this weekend on the religion field trip... We spent almost all day Saturday in Harlem going to the Abyssinian Baptist Church, the Harlem Library, the Y.M.C.A and ate dinner at St John's Baptist Church.

Presiding over the Abyssinian Baptist Church in 1941 was the Reverend Adam Clayton Powell, Jr. He'd been groomed for the position under the wing of his father, the Reverend Powell, Sr. I hold this mental image: A thirty-three-year-old Powell leaning on an Italian made marble pulpit, offering a personalized and compelling oratory before a gaggle of cardigan-ed Caucasian women. On TV in the Crane Road house, Powell performed as a 1960s congressional rabble-rouser. A charismatic character sporting dark wavy hair slicked back, a mustache and movie star smile, he championed federal social programs under President Johnson's "Great Society." Racial injustice was conventional Crane Road dinner table conversation. Egocentrically, and ignorantly, I presumed most folks shared our views.

We also visited some of the new Fed. Housing Projects in Harlem... In one day we learned a tremendous amount about the problem of racial discrimination and how senseless and stupid it is. In talking to a lawyer from the N.A.A.C.P. under Wm. Allen White, I got the full force of your ideas for the future – one of social justice, equality, and democracy for all, which I never had applied specifically before... Here is a tremendous field for work, dearest.

Nearly eighty years later, how it can be so many fellow Americans and members of the U.S. Congress *still* question the equality of basic human worth? In 1941, Robin identified as a "best set" Republican. Yet her belief system was positively progressive. Freedom, with opportunity for all, to advance the common good.

I saw Bud this weekend, and he sends his best to you. We went to St. Thomas's Church on Sunday and sat in his Uncle's Pew – way down in front.

A charitable feather in the McLeod family cap.

The boys' choir is magnificent there. I said two or three prayers for you that day 'cause I missed you so much.

Your own, forever Robin

L.M. Skinner, Rancagua – Sewell, Chile – April 30, 1941 (airmail)

Dearest Roberta,

Haven't had a letter from you since I wrote about April 15 (just before we went to Santiago) in which I sent a check for $75 which included your Apr. – May 20 allowance and $40 extra for Senior expenses.

The door to correspondence once again darkened with dollars.

We have since had a letter from Bud saying you were going to be down to New York April 25 week end. He said that might be the last time he would see you before graduation (Isn't he going up to Smith? He has expressed his desire so many, many times.) Haven't you a weekend you can give up to entertaining him up there before it gets too near examinations and commencement time?

No, she didn't. Besides, Bud was on the brink of exams, too. As if a wild mouse ran around on a wheel between his ears, Buddo wrote Robin a dubious note. There were many young men just like him filled with uncertainty that spring of 1941. *"I'm awaiting a reply to a letter inquiring the date of my call to active service. How truly wonderful it would be if the reply would state sometime in August! Then I could fly to see Dorothy! But considering past questionnaires, and present conditions, this hardly seems possible... I received such a nice letter from your mother inviting me to visit them. It is so kind of your mother and father.*

As cordial as Lelia came across with her invitation to Bud, was this a conniving plot to marry off Dottie? Then in the pages of a personal, inky rant, Grandma kept on and on like a fugue. She fished for Robin's acceptance of the plan laid out for her little brother.

...I didn't have time to explain in my last letter we were making the trip down below (to Santiago) *to take him* (Russell) *to the Cavalry School – He has to do his year of military service. We were fortunate to get him into the Cavalry – instead of the regular Army.*

Taking kindly credit for making it easier on her son? Grandma believed the South American Cavalry School was like U.S. Officers Training, where the men were better treated and well fed. Living quarters were reportedly cleaner, too, but she did not actually set eyes on the place. Methodical in making the best use of limited time, she and Dottie went to the dentist, while T. Wayne bid farewell once more to their youngest.

The school is out in the country on a "hacienda" that belonged to a millionairess originally. Daddy said the grounds were beautiful.

They'd considered "buying" Russell's way out of the service. She confessed why they didn't.

...he has come to the place where he must have strict discipline and that's the only place where he will get it.

So much for the regulatory routine at his alma mater George Junior Republic. Russell's tough teen years were delegated when his parents abandoned him at age eleven to be raised like a guinea pig among other "at risk" youth.

He wanted to stay up ¾ of every night – sleep every day until noon.

The Chilean Cavalry boys in training rose at 5:30 in the morning, with fifteen minutes to bathe, shave and dress.

Wouldn't lift his hand to do a tap of work of <u>any</u> kind whatsoever (wouldn't even sprinkle the lawn). He would yell "shut-up" to Daddy and me to the top of his voice whenever we tried to reason with him. He would run up big bills in both the Teniente (Social) Club and Golf Club – and just sat around and smoked one cigarette after another all day – day in and day out – wants to spend freely and yet won't earn a cent toward spending money – so something had to be done. A boy of 18 ½ years can't go on like that – has no interest in anything... Went to the show every night – wouldn't try to study or even learn Spanish. (He'll have to down there in the Cavalry.)

She cut to the heart of all they, as parents, slaved for; a college education for every one of their three kids. At the time they left the States, their design for Russell was hopeful, *"Yale or Harvard for higher education."* Expectations squelched.

Such a useless – idle – good for nothing existence. He won't go on to school any more – isn't interested in learning a trade of any sort. The Braden Co. offered him work – three months in each of several dept.'s chemical – mechanical, etc. He went about one wk. and refused to go any more – (shamed us to death). Just wouldn't get up in the morning to go to work. His only ambition is to go back to the U.S. and be "a tramp" – as he expresses it. You never saw such laziness in your life. Heaven only knows what he'll turn out to be.

Exasperated by circumstance, Grandma held out hope for a nice group of Chilean Cavalrymen, intrepid spirits, to light a fire under her son. Russell had little self-respect, and lacked parental deference, but by gum he would buck up under those caballeros.

The Army here makes <u>men</u> out of good for nothing Chilean boys – so let's hope it will do something for him.

She spat more insults, drawing Dottie into the fire.

Personally I don't think Russell is "all there" for a boy of his age. His mentality is about a 12 yr. old. He isn't a normal boy for 18 ½ yrs. and I don't think he ever will develop any further intellectually and he hasn't even common "horse sense" or as good judgment as a boy of 12 should have. He's terribly selfish – wouldn't put himself out to do anything he knew Dorothy wanted to do – just contrary. Wouldn't go swimming – hiking – or riding when she wanted to go. Would agree to – then when the time came, would back out.

A young woman needed male accompaniment, a trusted chaperone for such outings. Her brother was a slacker even when there was fun to be had—in a passive aggressive way.

Has no conscience about keeping an agreement or a promise – she gets furious at him for that. If the next three or four yrs. don't change him – he'll never amount to anything in life. So much for him.

If Grandma believed Russell is not "all there" for a boy of his age, so be it. Tit for tat, *she* was not "all there" for him with love, patience and parental wisdom when he most needed her. Not in a million years would he ever think, let alone speak Hallmark Card words, "You were always there for me, Mother." Grandma forgot this Bible lesson: "We reap what we sow."

Now, touching upon your needs – when do you have to pay for your Senior invitations? Do you have to have a new white dress for Ivy Day (another Smith tradition) or have you one that will do? Do you have to pay for any more senior pictures? Or have you gotten all you need to.

How many pictures does a senior need? Lelia assuaged parental guilt waving dollar bills over my mom's head.

Then, in a twist of Grandma's pen, we learn she is yet to receive Roy's letter of April 7. The meticulous engagement party narrative remained captive in a bag of boat mail.

You never wrote anything about Leroy going to the Bedford's party – Forrest mentioned it. Did Leroy appear O.K. and measure up with the rest of the crowd? He hasn't written us a word – he's such a queer guy.

Roy's complex identity was apparent in the unusual detail of his letter. But he was a devoted son to his widowed mother, Rhea. Lelia had no good reason to pick on her nephew. With what intention did she use the turn of phrase "queer?"

That must have cost the Bedfords at least $300.00 to have it in the Waldorf – or do you think more than that? Mrs. Bedford's invitation arrived while we were in Santiago and since getting back I've been so rushed with school – tests – and reports – Had to give a dinner party last Sunday night – haven't had time to write her but am going to this weekend. I'd rather be thrashed than write her – not knowing her type. They were nice engraved invitations I notice.

Not knowing my Grammy Bedford's "type" tipped Grandma Skinner's hand on her own insecurities. "Nice engraved invitations" were a sign of sufficient planning time and money, too. She fell into a personal purgatory of self-doubt. When she berated Aunt Dottie in this next round, it proved she was blind to the truth in her shortcomings as a mother.

Dorothy won't do a tap to help me – no ambition – such a lazy life also. She won't write to anybody except Bud – no interest in learning to cook or anything about a house. I asked her to vacuum the rug Sunday – while the maid and I were rushed getting ready for company and she answered, "Let the maid do that." Daddy and I are so disappointed in her. All she wants to do is sit with a fellow and be a butterfly. She has written only once to Auntie Alta in all the months she's been here. She won't even practice typewriter nor piano – if you come down Dad and I hope you'll be interested in something practical and think of life in earnest and realize that a person owes something to the world and not figure the world owes her a living. We do so want to hear your plans and know whether you're coming down.

Oceans of love, Mother

Grandma's signature, "Oceans of love," contradicted the garbage barge of negative energy that spewed from the mining camp. Lelia knew her eldest daughter did not knock herself out to graduate with special honors— no "laude" for her. The simplest form of unadorned sheepskin, with an A.B.

degree was good enough, but now Robin had better be *"practical and think of life in earnest."* Privileged with pressure, as first-borns often are.

Graduation now weeks away, she was faced with fast decisions to make. Then, in a bright moment, a means to entertain Buster presented itself. With scissors from her desk, she cut a two-part clipping from the *Smith College Alumni News*, tucked it into a personalized powder blue envelope, licked and sealed the flap. She scrawled *"For your amusement"* on the outside, then affixed a forest green three-cent commemorative stamp: "Vermont's 150th anniversary of statehood."

The article publicized results of a *"Survey on Students,"* dated Tuesday, May 6, 1941. Faculty, housemothers, housemaids, townspeople and a sampling of underclassmen at assorted eastern mens' and womens' colleges responded. The aggregated impression of Smith College students? Overall, the girls were considered *"moral, democratic and intelligent."* Grandma would like those data points. Princeton boys chimed in with a polite: *"Smith girls warm up as you get to know them better."* One frustrated soul took this shot: *"Smith girls make charming company and exhibit an exceptional ability to have a good time, in spite of the fact that they are shackled by college regulations."* Then, this radical view. *"You may go in conservative, but you come out a bunch of Communists."*

I prefer to think they were passionate about social justice, but what was the profundity that evoked mischief in my mom? As if entered in a competition to respond in five words or less, a "Heavenly Seven" Holyoke sister delivered a one liner that packed a punch to her Smith counterparts: *"They are a Godless lot."*

Hurried Lines

Chapter Twenty-Seven

L.M. Skinner, Rancagua – Sewell, Chile – May 8, 1941 (airmail)

Dearest Roberta,

I'm tearing off this letter the first 15 minutes in the morning at school so it can catch the air mail out this A.M. Your letter...written and mailed Apr. 29... said you hadn't rec'd any word from us for <u>weeks.</u> I sent on Apr. 12 a check <u>airmail</u> for $75 (your Apr.-May allowance $35 + $40 extra for senior expenses)... Didn't you receive it? Or did you forget?

Robin had not yet received it. It was sent by boat mail, despite the extra postage for airmail. Human error. Then came this finger wagging:

Your student certificate was in your last letter, but I'll have to return it in my <u>next</u> letter because if you're coming by boat you present it in N.Y. to Grace Line.

Steamship service to the Chilean Coast had been reduced. Three ships were taken off, strategically repurposed for military use. The three boats that remained offered limited service for passenger transport and mail delivery every *other* week. Passages were booked well in advance. Grandma had proof.

Dorothy and Russell had to wait over – for the next boat – couldn't get on the one they should have come on.... We don't want to pay extra room and board for you for 15 days up there waiting for a later boat...

Robin would move out of Haven House post-haste after commencement. By her parents' penny-wise standards, her date to sail proved time sensitive. Although there were errands to do, too.

We want shopping done for both Dorothy and myself and the house, which will probably take a week in New York. Shopping is slow in New York you remember – can't accomplish ½ as much in one day as in a <u>small </u>city shopping.

Robin will have to find someplace to stay convenient to the shopping district. A good bet, the Biltmore. With seventy-five dollars delayed due to the boat mail muddle, her ask for money multiplied.

Goodness – this $300 scared me! Does that include your May – June allowance or not? We're trying to get enough ahead to pay your passage down – of course we don't want you to run short, but don't be extravagant, will you?

Weighing dollars and common sense, Dottie and Russell's boat fare last August set the senior Skinners back *far* less than tuition room and board for all three children would have in the 1940-41 school year.

I expect I'll have to send quite a check for the shopping we need. Will you need an extra trunk or have you two? Our things will take one whole one – But you must buy a <u>Hartmann wardrobe </u>through the Braden N.Y. Office when you get to N.Y. to get 50% discount and that causes a couple days delay – we want wardrobe – as there is a demand for those here and we can resell it.

Hugs and kisses, Mother.

On Sunday, May 11, my mom worked on zoology slides until 2:00 p.m. It was Mother's Day, so understandably Grampy honored Grammy's wish to celebrate the occasion her way. The senior Bedfords motored to Massachusetts. Robin joined her future family for a late lunch. The Whale Inn, twelve miles east of Northampton, in Goshen, was an ivy covered New England treasure circa 1799. It derived its name from the Bible story of *Jonah,* a prophet, who was swallowed and sat in the belly of a giant fish for three days as punishment for running away from a mission God had planned for him. When God spoke to the fish, Jonah was thrown up. According to restaurant lore, he landed in Goshen. That's the premise of the Whale Inn moniker, unappetizing as it sounds.

Their own bellies full, Robin and Buster retired to the gardens after lunch. The magic of May flowers led to a whale of a moment. She revealed this in her diary that night: *"Sat on grass and talked about getting married earlier than Xmas. Maybe this summer – but it seemed impossible."*

If Robin wrote to T. Wayne and Lelia on a turn of hope that evening, the letter failed to arrive before yet another dire communiqué arrived from Campamento Americano:

L.M. Skinner, Rancagua – Sewell, Chile – May 12, 1941 (airmail)

Dearest Roberta,

A hurried line to send along this student certificate...

Grandma got down to business, reminded my mother (again) to present the certificate for the fifty-percent student reduction on steamship fare. Then like a drill sergeant, pressed Robin to fall in line.

The Santa Clara sails from N.Y. June 20th. Dad wonders if you could make that. It would save you having to pay board and room for 15 days until the next sailing of the Grace Line but more important than that the Santa Clara docks in Valparaiso during the wk. of my mid-year vacation – so it would be more convenient for us to meet you at that time... you will have to make up your mind in order to make a boat reservation long enough ahead of sailing to be sure of a room.

For the Skinner seniors, the timing of the *Santa Clara*'s arrival was convenient. Reality check for Robin: To make a boat in New York on June

20, following graduation on June 16 in Northampton. Tight. And with Grandma's shopping to do? Impossible.

A "hurried line" quickly twisted into monumental marching orders.

I don't know how much of a deposit you need to make when you reserve your passage. Write and ask them. Have you gotten your birth-certificate yet? You also should begin now to get your typhoid injections – They are not required but you must take them and don't wait until the last, so it would come while in N.Y. or about to sail. They don't tell you you <u>must</u> have a vaccination certificate before you can land in Valpo – Dorothy had hers but Russell didn't so he had to be vaccinated on board and their antisepsis on ship isn't as good as other doctors, and one young fellow who just recently arrived had an infected arm... he couldn't work for about a month. As I say the authorities don't require typhoid shots but everyone takes them on account of the lettuce – fruit and water on the trip down. If you happen to have had a vaccination (for Small Pox) within the past two yrs. and can get a Physician to give you a statement to that effect you wouldn't need to be re-vaccinated – but it must be within the <u>last two yrs.</u>

Time out to get this straight. The *required* vaccine is for Small Pox. The typhoid inoculation is optional. But typhoid fever is highly contagious and still today the vaccine is recommended for travel to South America. So are a lot of other needle sticks that weren't around at the time.

Have you applied for a passport yet? You can reserve passage before you have a passport – don't wait. Grace Line S.S. Office is 628 Fifth Ave. (Rockefeller Center) New York. As soon as we know you are coming and not going to take a job we will send you money to make a reservation. So let us know immediately. Dad was saying yesterday he isn't sure it wouldn't be the wisest thing for you to get a job – if you can.

Love, Mother.

P.S. I rec'd your Mother's day card. It was sweet of you. Dad's idea that it might be wise to get a job is, that he thinks U.S. is going to be sending troops to Dakar soon... (He's abandoned any pretense of neutrality.) ...and that possibly Forrest might have to go (to serve in Dakar?) and you would want to go on working. As I wrote before you can get a job much easier while in U.S. than from this end.

The messaging from Campamento Americano was practical but flagged with mixed signals. Did they want to see their daughter, or not? Robin was overwhelmed with test stress and to-do lists. Her ability to think, confounded. For more than two years her parents maintained this view: *"We have always felt it would be far wiser for you to wait until you've finished college and can spend six months at least and come in Chile's summer time."*

Screw that. A dejected daughter and forlorn fiancé, Robin procrastinated on schoolwork and wrote Buster Sunday evening. She reflected on their garden moments at the Whale Inn. Hit the mailbox, too.

He turned around this immediate response.

PVT N.F. Bedford, Fort Devens, Ayer, Mass. – Monday, May 12, 1941

My beloved,

Was pleasantly surprised by your sweet but plaintive little letter which arrived this afternoon. Please don't worry too much about these things just now dearest when you should be concentrating on your work so that you can make me real proud of you on your graduation day. We can talk more about our plans and hopes over next weekend when we will have a chance to be alone together.

He wrapped her, by written word, in the warmth of sunshine to temper the fiery coals of catastrophic thought. His reminder of next weekend offered happy anticipation, then turned the conversation (as he often did when I was a kid) to fun. A playful attitude toward work inspired his positive outlook.

Had a lot of fun this morning learning to ride a motorcycle and spent the afternoon in Radio School... They gave us a couple of intelligence tests... One was the Otis test for High School and College students (first generation SAT used for generalized classification of WWII inductees), *and the other was on general electrical knowledge. I'm sure that I did well on the first but was a bit rusty on my electricity. If*

I did well enough, however, I may rate a trip to Fort Monmouth, New Jersey (home of the Signal Corps School) for two or three months to learn the workings of radio. It would be a good break.

Must write a line to Mother now, so good-night, darling.

Yours alone forever, Buster

Buster understood Lelia complicated my mom's paradox; should I stay, or should I go? With just over a month left in her senior year, Mom lacked the mental capacity to make an emotionally charged decision. Mr. Equanimity was reassuring; optimistic about the future.

The next turnabout from Campamento Americano uncloaked a conundrum for my grandmother. It stemmed from garden moments at the Whale Inn and words my mom wrote home about a game-changing plan.

L.M. Skinner, Rancagua – Sewell, Chile – May 14, 1941 (airmail)

Dearest Roberta,

We received your letter telling us of your wedding plans. Of course we can't help but be a little disappointed that you are rushing things so. Because I was hoping to get up there in Dec. to see you married and take care of the arrangements – even tho' Daddy couldn't go. The two events a mother desires more than anything else in the world – is to see her daughter graduate from college and married. Especially the latter.

The timing was not in lockstep with her own schedule.

I think I would have caught a plane this wk. and been up there – (made a flying trip of about three wks.) if it hadn't been that Bud is arriving... After we had invited him I couldn't hardly bring myself to flying away and leaving him here with no special attention especially when the trip will undoubtedly cost him $1,500.00 before he is back in the States. Imagine he has to make a very rapid trip since he is flying – as he had talked about coming by boat all year.

What hung in the balance here? Bud needed special attention. Robin did not? Dorothy needed chaperoning. My mom's ship had sailed on that point long ago.

We, however, can see your reasons and will be understanding enough to over-look your haste. I hope both you and Buster will not allow yourself for one minute to believe – He's not coming back if called to active service. That's bad psychology.

What kind of matrimonial blessing and guiding advice is *that*?

Of course, there are chances that any soldier may not but don't admit it in your inner thoughts. Keep thinking, "Of course he's coming back" and go on planning accordingly – even though of course your personal arrangements have to be made and legal points taken care of – but after those are attended to – keep thinking "Of course he's coming back."

Disaster scenarios. No young couple caught up in the rush to marry in 1941 expected smooth sailing. Many young men yearned for a gal to count on "back home." One that would write letters and wait for his return. Grandma, who had lived through the Great War, braced for misfortune. Then came this etiquette-based flap over more checks to be written.

We must pay for the church – the flowers – and the reception and the wedding announcements. You can use the $300.00 I sent up (for your S.S. reservation) to begin buying your wedding outfit and Daddy is sending a Braden Copper Co. Draft this A.M. (having the N.Y. Office send it to you at Smith) of $450.00 (I think it is) to take care of expenses. We don't know whether that is enough – or is more than expenses will be. Later we want to get you your flat sterling service, for a wedding present. But I guess there is no great rush about it until you have a home of your own, is there? Nice that Mr. Bedford is giving you your car.

I'm sending you a form for a wedding announcement – they will show you forms in the shop – if you see one you like better O.K. I didn't put in the name of the church because didn't know which one. But don't think that need appear on the announce-ment. They charge so much a line for engraving. We would like three or four sent down here – will tell you names later.

Dorothy is disappointed she can't be Maid of Honor. Just rec'd your Father's day cable.

Much love, Mother

...If you hadn't asked Roy to give you away we would have paid Uncle Dix fare east to have done it. He is older and more like a father.

True. Auntie Alta Dixon's husband was distinguished. Not the *"queer guy"* Lelia believed Roy to be.

Despite Lelia's emphasis on all that was plainly off-target, the stage was set for a wedding sometime in June. Caught up in a cacophony of emotional noise, Robin's decision to marry was hasty, yet well-reasoned. My dad would deliver equanimity. Emancipate her from her parents' incessant obsessing, too.

Or so she thought.

PVT N.F. Bedford, Fort Devens, Ayer, Mass. – Wednesday night, May 14, 1941

My beloved,

Sorry I couldn't write you last night, but we left on manoeuver at 8:30 and didn't get home until 1:00 A.M. this morning. As a result I am pretty tired tonight. I tried to telephone you, but Mary Liz said you had gone over to another house for dinner. She also said that you were working too hard. Please take care of yourself, dearest. Get a good sun-bath every day, will you?

Tomorrow noon we leave on another all-night manoeuver, so I won't be able to get in touch with you until I telephone Friday night.

Exhausted as he was, Buster laid out logistics for their next rendezvous.

I am going to try to catch the 1:13 (daylight) out of Worcester Saturday. The 1:40 (daylight) from Hamp meets my train in Springfield at 2:18. I will try to save us a

seat and will look for you on the station platform when my train gets in. If anything
goes wrong I will telephone you at Haven House at 1:20 or earlier...

Must go to bed now, as I am very, very tired...

Robin's May 17 diary entry confessed this: *"Finished Chem notebook, not*
History paper." The paper could wait when moments with Buster were at
stake. Every letter he wrote delivered a sense of hope she latched on to like
an orphan. So very different from the letters from Campamento Americano
that evoked familial acrimony before she slit the envelope open.

According to plan, the lovebirds connected on the train in Springfield,
bound for New York. *My Sister Eileen* was live on stage at the Biltmore
Theatre. A comedy Buster was eager to see; more so than *Charley's Aunt*.
The storyline centered on two sisters from Columbus, Ohio. One pretty,
one plain, they took a leap from Midwest manners to a New York state of
mind, trying to make it in Manhattan. The hive of activity surrounding
their Greenwich Village apartment fueled the kind of folly Buster got a kick
out of.

Buster with a happy Robin on the bustling train platform.

After the show, the fiancées stepped out. *"Had a beer near Seymour,"* scratched my mom in her diary.

Miller High Life perhaps? That *"champagne of bottle beer"* overpopulated the downstairs fridge at the Crane Road house. A pilsner ripe for the swiping. On this night, seven weeks since planning the party music at the Hotel Seymour, the senior Bedfords were absent. Was this getaway planned with set intention to land in a single-occupancy hotel room for two where Buster would tip a familiar doorman and the desk staff, too? Yes. The evidence? Three months from now Robin will write to Buster. The letterhead she swiped will remind my dad of this night. A sensual vestige: *I'm still using up the Seymour's stationery – just one piece left, so here goes."*

On the Sunday afternoon train back to Massachusetts, my mom braced to return to the belly of the proverbial whale.

At Fort Devens Sunday night, Buster scripted larger than life words. They began like the young man in love that he was, then moved as if channeling the wit and wisdom of Alexander Hamilton. Then, as if tying his thoughts with a bow, he closed by paraphrasing our honorable sixteenth president of the United States, Abe Lincoln.

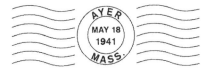

PVT N.F. Bedford, Fort Devens, Ayer, Mass. – Sunday Night, May 18, 1941

My beloved,

Here I am, not a quarter of an hour departed from you, yet missing you like the very dickens already. Gee, honey, a weekend is such a terribly short time to spend with you when I want to be with you for a whole life-time! Why, oh why do the overpowering desires of one small man or group of men have to interrupt the peaceful and useful pursuits of millions? However, I suppose that without the bitter there would be no sweet by contrast, and so without a struggle the ends we gain would not be appreciated.

My dad was so very proud of his military service, it's hard to imagine he (like every young man in the world at the time) worried in advance about what might happen to him. These words convinced me otherwise:

... Anyway, I know that in the past three months life has seemed sweeter to me than ever before, so that I have tried to live every moment of beauty as though it were my last. At least I have gained that much knowledge of the art of living, and no matter what happens I shall feel that I have lived fully. I could even be content to take whatever fate has in store for me, a useful life or a useful death, if I had someone to carry on my aims and ideals. – But that is something that involves more than just my own life.

My mom understood *she was the shining star* in his *"knowledge of the art of living,"* and exactly why he felt he'd *"lived fully."*

She was the one that opened Buster's eyes beyond *"just my own life."*

She would be the one to raise another to carry on his *"aims and ideals."*

He was counting on *her!*

Powerful words written forty-eight hours before Buster turned twenty-three. His intention to father a child before he fell into harm's way was set.

But don't let me strike on too melancholy a note. There is a story about Abraham Lincoln that is encouraging. When told by a religious adviser that God was on his side, Lincoln replied, "I am not worried about whether or not God is on our side, I am only worried as to whether we are on his side!" I think that this time we are on his side, and somehow I feel that if we have faith in Him and in each other everything will come out all right.

Good night, my darling, work hard but keep healthy and remember that you shall always have my love whether or not I am with you in person...

PVT N.F. Bedford, Fort Devens, Ayer, Mass. – Wednesday noon, May 21, 1941

My beloved,

Just time for a note now as I have to go to Radio School in 10 minutes. However, I get out of going on the three day manoeuver because of Radio School, so I will write you a long letter as soon as I can think of something worth-while saying and have heard something from you.

Good grief, Robin is doing her best to graduate, and Buster chided her for not matching his performance letter for letter. Except for this. It was my dad's birthday and the mailbox was empty.

I am afraid that I won't be able to get over for Float Night, dear, much as I would like to. I have to stay in the barracks as guard from 6:00 P.M. Saturday until 6:00 P.M. Sunday and there is going to be a dance given for the Wellesley girls in the gym that night to which everyone else is going, so I doubt if I can get anyone to take my place. However, if anything can be done I will let you know about it when I telephone you Friday night.

Guarding the barracks was a sad excuse to bail on the only Float Night my folks would ever share. Buster played "good Joe." The spoken-for soldier boy who accommodated his mates, so they could wow the Wellesley girls.

Robin explained herself in this next letter.

Roberta Skinner, Haven House, Northampton, Mass. – Thursday, May 22, 1941

My darling -:

I just got back from Hartford on a Bacteriology Field Trip to see the Connecticut State Bacteriology Lab – and have a little time to sit down and tell you what's been going on lately.

First and most important though is to tell you how much I wanted to be with you on your 23rd birthday – I thought of you so often all day – and kept telling you how much I loved you in my heart.

Just a word about the beautiful letter you wrote Sunday night, hon. It was so, so lovely– I admire and respect you so much for great ideas like those, Buster – and as Professor Harlow said – "you've got to like a person as well as love them to be happy in marriage." I do "like" you so much, dear – and you know I love you. If we were only married, my dearest – I'm sure we'd be the two happiest people alive. Thank God, for our dreams, honey!

While my mom came alive with heavenly hope, Professor Harlow was a mystery to me. Possibly one of several marriage forum speakers on campus? The message was relevant to all the up and coming brides of 1941. We've already learned men desired *"emotional stability, maturity and a good disposition"* in a wife. What did women want in a husband? Dependable character. For Robin and Buster, a "best set" education was high on the list. Mutual attraction? Yes, that too.

...Wednesday night we had Senior Supper and in the "wanted ads" was a nearer Army base for Robin.

The "wanted ad" advertised a sign of the times like a billboard. Nearer Army and Air Force bases were "wanted" for several girls who would soon graduate, and those in the class of Cute '42s, too.

The "For Sale" column included the names of all the men I've been out with for four years at one time or another. It's a nice feeling to know how I belong to you alone, my dearest.

My point about her going around good and plenty stands. Her career of cupidity came to a well-publicized end. Buster had caught the brass ring on the grand carousel of life and would do everything in his power to keep it.

I'm sorry you can't come over this weekend, dear, but I shall work very hard for my four exams next week. It hardly seems possible I'm all through in two weeks.

Am making reservations for June 20 on the S.S. Brazil, I think...

"I think?" I don't believe she thought at all. At least not beyond final exams. What about the wedding? It was now twenty-nine days until the S.S. *Santa Clara* (not the *Brazil*) was scheduled to steam out of New York Harbor.

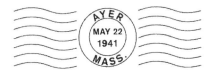

PVT N.F. Bedford, Fort Devens, Ayer, Mass. – Thursday night, May 22, 1941

My beloved,

Just for a few minutes tonight I felt happy and peaceful again, at rest with the world. It is odd – or perhaps not so odd, really, - how little it takes to make a man happy. Tonight it was two very simple things. First, a few minutes of wading around in Robins' Pond trying, unsuccessfully, to catch a fish with a completely home-made outfit consisting of a hickory branch, a piece of strong black thread, and a hook filed from a piece of steel spring wire.

Along the lines of Bear Grylls, *Man vs. Wild?* Dad pre-dated his calling as a survivor celebrity.

The fish, if there were any, didn't seem to like the frog I offered them for bait, so when the Regimental Glee Club showed up along the shore to practice singing I deserted my angling for a comfortable seat in the grass under an oak tree and an old corn-cob pipe. It was a good trade. Not for two years have I so enjoyed listening to singing. It was singing as it should be – not in a crowded, stuffy building, but under the blue sky and the green trees. Good strong male voices, glad to be alive. Wonderful. I had my choice of places in which to listen to it, too. Robin's Pond itself, now dark with the reflection of the green trees encircling it, was picturesque and restful enough. But that was not all. By merely closing my eyes I could be three hundred miles away listening to the seniors sing Aura Lee from the steps of Nassau Hall as I sat beneath the giant elms as an underclassman. Cool breezes shuffling through a still, warm summer's night. Or by closing them tighter I could travel a thousand and more miles back to my childhood, back to warm nights after a day's hunting on our farm in the Everglades on the strains of Massa's in De Cold, Cold Ground.

I know nothing of the farm in the Everglades he recollected for Robin. Whatever critters he bagged as a kid, waterfowl and wild boar were among the options. It's too late for consequences so I will digress to share this mid-1960s pets-on-planes escapade. On board a National Airlines non-stop, Jacksonville to JFK, Buster sat with a Footjoy shoebox in his lap. A captive caiman held the space where his golf cleats belonged. My near-Irish twin and I took great care in the "eco" design of an alligator's aquarium habitat, naturally warmed by the sun that beamed through the picture windows overlooking Birch Bay. What did it eat? "Ground round." A ball of raw meat served up on the eraser end of a number two pencil. Kid fingers were to avoid all contact with the bite force of those reptilian choppers. Who knew a man full of shenanigans like that could be such a romantic. He continued:

I could write on for hours, dear, if I had the time. How I would like to sit with you under the elms at Princeton, watch the sun set over the steaming Everglades, watch it rise early in the morning, red hot out of the Gulf of Mexico as it reflects on the silver back of the tarpon as they roll through the waves – how I would like to live through a thousand wonderful experiences with you, telling you that each was more wonderful because of your very presence. – But I can't tell you all now. Maybe someday, if God is good to us, if there is any beauty left in the world, if you still love me in future years as you have this past year, if the horrible months of absence pass quickly, if I am still_____.

Good night, my darling, and good luck on your exams.

All my love, forever, Buster

Songs of the Glee Club of the 101st Cavalry Regiment steeped Buster in grand nostalgia. Doing the math, it's neither more than six years, nor less than three, since *Aura Lee* wafted from the steps of Princeton's storied Nassau Hall. It was a peaceful reminiscence from where he now sat, puffing his pipe, at Devens.

But let's pick on the warm nights of his childhood. It begged a question for which I will forever lack an answer. Or, more to the point, one I would want to accept. Exactly whose voices did he hear on the strains of *Massa's in De Cold, Cold Ground?* Even in historical context, it unsettled me. My near-Irish twin informed me they were farm hands.

There is an illuminating lesson in this circa 1852 minstrel song written by Stephen Foster. (In the spirit of praising this not to be forgotten Pittsburg born and raised composer, Foster penned the likes of *Oh! Susanna, Camptown Races, Jeanie with the Light Brown Hair* and *Beautiful Dreamer.*) Long story short, and to the point for me (because I have Robin and Buster's story to finish): Foster was a childhood friend of abolitionist Charles P. Shiras. Living at a time of black-face minstrelsy, Shiras encouraged Foster to write lyrics with compassion and humanness; amplifying the cultivated refinement of the north. The takeaway lesson: Home, family, happiness are universal desires. Regardless of ethnicity, the death of family member or friend was mourned equally. The lyrics told the story of slaves who sang their sorrows over a man that had treated them well.

Snapping back to 1941, Buster (just like Bud) was a man head over heels in love. He barely got that last letter in the mail before he arrived big as life at Smith on Saturday, May 24.

Late that night, Robin revealed this juicy news in her diary: *"Buster drove over from Devens at 11:00 tonight. Wants to get married this summer – loves me very much and wants to have a child – someone who can carry out all his ideals. He means more than anything else in the world – even life itself."*

On Your Mark

Chapter Twenty-Eight

Why did Robin write *"Wants to get married this <u>summer</u>"* when a June date was already acknowledged in Lelia's airmail just ten days ago? She'd even enclosed the *"form for a wedding announcement."* Possibly Robin caved to Grandma's expressed disappointment *"that you are rushing things so"* and her parents' wish for a December wedding.

Roberta Skinner, Haven House, Northampton, Mass. – Sunday, May 25, 1941

My dearest -:

Thank you so much for coming over last night. I hope you got back safely. I had breakfast with Mr. and Mrs. Thompson, Joyce, Braxton, Gina and Dizzy this morning – and Diz said you were rather impetuous over a cup of coffee last night. I wish I could have seen you for a little longer – just so I could tell you how much I love you, about 100 more times...

Honey, I've got so much work to do before exams that I'm scared to death. Four in one week is plenty tough to take, Tues – Zoo, Wed – Bacteriology, and Gov't and Religion on Saturday. Bud wants to come up and see Smith for a little while on

Friday – but I certainly won't miss him if he doesn't come. He's leaving for the West June 1st, I guess. I hope he leaves early so I can get some Gov't done.

LMAO, there's a first time for everything. Had she *ever* ranked course-work above a social call? *"Scared to death,"* she wished away Bud's visit. It was twenty-two do or die days until graduation. And what in the world was Buddo up to? Montana bound waiting on a date certain for his call to active service? Or were all his eggs in one basket to visit Campamento Americano?

Honey, I don't know when I've enjoyed an hour with you more than last night. I just loved everything you said and did so much that I didn't want 12:00 to ever come...

Ooh la la, a sixty-minute tryst that, like a fairytale, ended at the stroke of midnight.

Sometime, you know what I wish you'd do? – Make a list of everything you want out of life, and everything you want Junior to have, or to strive for, or to be.

You've told me so many things in the last year at one time or another, but I wish you'd put them all together for me so I could have 'em all in one place.

You are so wonderful, my darling – and even if you don't come back after the war – I'll still be the luckiest girl alive to have known you, and loved you, with all my heart and soul – and perhaps to bring up your son.

Yours forever and ever, Robin

PVT N.F. Bedford, Fort Devens, Ayer, Mass. – Sunday night, May 25, 1941

My beloved,

Just a note to let you know that I got home safely and quite awake after stopping off in Amherst for coffee and hamburgers with Dizzy.

Darling, you can't imagine how happy you made me last night by telling me that you would marry me this June. I hated to ask you to make the sacrifice, for it does hold possibilities of hardship, yet I felt somehow that you would see things the same way I do – that there is something more involved than just pleasing families or trying to attain super-safe financial security.

Buster threw the covers back on Lelia's motives and possibly Grammy's, too. Boldly, he dismissed *"just pleasing families"* and convinced Robin to think likewise. As for their financial well-being? The optimism of youth, and college diplomas to lean on, would hold them up.

To my mind, after a careful weighing of all the factors involved in the international situation and in administration politics, it seemed to me to be a matter of life itself. You chose life for me, so all my life, short or long though it may be, will be devoted to your happiness.

Potent words. Despite an uncertain future, Buster was dedicated to his dreams and steadfast in his devotion to Robin. Like a statesman, he expressed the thoughts of many young American men caught up in the matrimonial storm.

With prayerful gratitude, Robin read his closing... *Good-night, my only one, and may God bless you and watch carefully over you, for you are one of his finest works of creation.*

Robin snapped out of that Shangri-La moment with the next letter-bomb from Lelia. It began with a birthday wish then scuttled into head-exploding pointers and more to-do's.

L.M. Skinner, Rancagua – Sewell, Chile – Friday, May 23, 1941

Dearest Roberta, A Happy Birthday!

Your letter written and mailed May 15th came the 21st. I think that an air letter of mine of April 12th that reached you May 5th, must have been sent on the boat. It certainly couldn't have gotten on a plane.

Redemption for Robin. Lelia had resolved the long, lost path of the floating boat letter.

Now in reply to your questions – You should write to the Grace S.S. Line in Rockefeller Ctr. sending in your student certificate and telling them when you want to sail. Tell them you are from Braden, and that even tho' the boat is crowded you hope they won't put you in an inside cabin. They apologized to Dorothy that it would be necessary to do that...

For any information you need or any help, when you are getting ready in New York, go to Miss Otterstrom. She's awfully nice. Address her 120 Broadway – Personnel Dept. - Braden Copper Co.

Miss Otterstrom was a mover and shaker. When Dottie was assigned to an inside cabin, Miss Otterstrom acted fast. She called the Grace Office and arranged for Dottie's move to an outside room with a view.

Go to her about getting the trunk and she'll take you to Mr. Early's office, next to her office, who calls up the Hartmann Agency on 5ᵗʰ Ave. and tells them to let you have export prices... The Braden Offices are high up – in the Equitable Bldg. at 120 Broadway.

My grandmother valued those connections in high places—in more ways than one. Of skyscraper caliber when completed in 1915, the forty-or-so story Equitable structure was built without setbacks. It presented at street front as a towering object of attention (and objection due to the long shadows it cast over the neighbors.) The Equitable Building's 1914 brochure flavored it this way: *"Its exterior is built of granite, brick and terra cotta in soft tones and is designed after the Italian Renaissance."* The building simulated the letter H, and for that reason offices on the inside were *"interior in name only and have nothing in common with the traditional darkness of average interiors.... It will rank as one of the really beautiful buildings on this continent."*

That's one reason it was designated a National Historic Landmark in 1978.

Lucky for my mom's legs, by intention the architect wanted the structure to have the reputation of the best-caged elevator service in the world.

Add to that 5,000 windows lighting the interior office space. A notable contribution to the magnificent Manhattan skyline after dark.

Look on the floor directory, as you enter the Bldg. Dorothy says the travel agency in Northampton can't tell you <u>anything</u>. We've looked up our schedule here and the Santa Clara leaves N.Y. June 20th, The Santa Lucia, July 4th. It doesn't look as tho' you could catch the Clara, June 20th.

The *Santa Clara* was an impossible idea to begin with.

Your baggage must go to the pier 18 hrs. ahead of sailing – and <u>you</u> need to be at the pier <u>two hrs.</u> ahead. Better pay your hotel bill the night before sailing. Dorothy said the Biltmore nearly made her miss her boat. She counted about 2 hrs. to reach the boat and go through the necessary preliminary to sailing and when she gave the Biltmore her check they weren't going to accept it. They kept her waiting while they called up banks, etc. more than an hour and she asked them what the delay was – they told her they were not accustomed to accepting checks...

Funny, for entirely different reasons, most hotels *today* are not accustomed to accepting checks.

She roostered up and told them she was leaving in an hour for South America and they would accept that check or nothing. They finally asked her if she had accounts with any New York store. She told them Lord and Taylor's and she told them she was from Smith and had been at the Biltmore several times before – finally he cashed it and they got to the pier about the very last of the passengers. She was almost frantic.

Bud wrote us this week he expects to go to Smith May 30th. Gracious if that isn't convenient for your exams, tell him so. Don't fail an exam just to entertain him. He said he wouldn't go for Float Night if you couldn't give him time over May 30th - why don't you tell him to come for commencement (providing he could go then).

He can't. Recall my mom's words in a letter to my dad a few days ago, "He's leaving for the West June 1st."

Do hope you have a happy birthday and I'm sending you a check to get something you want. I could just weep to think we can't see you graduate.

What about the wedding?

We have waited years for your graduation from college and we are proud of you. I guess you'll be our only college graduate – after all we have planned to have the three of you finish college. Doesn't look as tho' there's any chance of Russell or Dorothy ever getting a college diploma.

I can attest that family secret never leaked until now.

We rec'd your photo finally – without being broken. It's splendid we think... I'm sorry to think Leroy (cousin Roy) and Auntie Rhea can't see the jam at graduation isn't any place for Auntie Rhea. But she has done so much for you, you can't refuse to have her come, I suppose. Let's hope at the last she won't go. But she is proud of you, and I expect won't want to miss it. You'll be so busy you won't have much time to give her with the Bedfords there (with both Mrs. Bedford and Auntie Rhea being sensitive, you'll be liable to offend one or the other, when you have 1,000 things on your mind).

Can't put more in an envelope with the check for your birthday.

Hugs and Kisses – Mother and Dad.

I'll send shopping list on next plane.

Roberta Skinner Senior Portrait
Smith College 1941.

If Lelia had not put my mom over the edge with her musings, my aunt Dottie just might. She let loose like a birthday balloon in a blizzard.

D. Skinner c/o Braden Copper Co., Rancagua (Sewell) Chile – Monday, May 26, 1941

Dearest Robin,

Just a half scribbled note to wish you happy birthday which I hope gets to you in time. When are you going to answer all my letters – or do you think you're eventually going to make up your mind to come down here. Mother is preparing huge lists of things for you to bring if you do come – and I hope you will.

Mom was set up like a post-graduate pack mule. Grandma desperately counted on delivery of the goods to the South American port. *"... I'll have to send quite a check for the shopping we need."* A long list of items to be fetched in a quest through the streets of New York.

Skiing hasn't been half bad lately and it's going to be much better. It's wonderful being able to go down to our golf course as we did yesterday – and have a summer day with nice green grass and trees – and then come back to Sewell where the snow is feet deep.

My twenty-year-old butterfly of an aunt enjoyed advantages I had living in Utah at that age. With an easy altitude shift, skiing and golf were logistically simple on the same day.

I've been wondering if Bud will eventually get up to Smith – and if he does will you do me a big favor? Will you on the Q.T. find out when his birthday is? And don't you dare let him know that it is me that wants to know. It's Oct. 7, 8 or 9th but I can't for the life of me remember when. Thanks loads my pet.

What are sisters for? But then she kept on with her own pre-voyage prep-list ... *check up on the things I left... my black suitcase – and a large carton – with my treasured stamp collection – all my snapshots – and souvenirs.... I don't want to lose them.*

More sensibly speaking, at least from my perspective, she added ... *I hope you can bring a portable radio – and a dozen or so nice new records right off the Hit Parade. All we can get here are old ones – about six months old or more. They just don't get them down here any sooner than that.*

Columbia House was yet to invent its *Record Club of the Month*. In the 1970s, I wasn't alone when I got sucked into paying a penny for a too-good-to-be-true stack of vinyl. Then got stuck with a bunch of LP's (plus postage) I didn't even want. Teens like me became ensnared in that mail order marketing fly-trap.

Good luck in your exams, old thing, and I wish I could be there to see you graduate. Give my love to Leavell and all the gals... I'll write you another letter if you do decide to come down – and give you some tips that might be helpful.

Joined one of the bowling teams made up of Sewell ladies – and go busily bowling twice a week. It's really quite a sport.

Conveniently there are bowling alleys at El Teniente Club. It's the same place that good for nothing Skeeter *"sat around and smoked one cigarette after another all day."* Dottie, the social butterfly *"gave a bowling tea for 25 people one day last week"* and charged it to T. Wayne's tab.

There sure will be plenty to keep you busy if you do come down. I'll keep you baking when we haven't anything else to do. I'm getting so I can produce pretty good cakes, cookies, etc.

Happy birthday again, little one – and I'll write a decent letter soon.

Loads of Love, Dottie

Juxtapose Grandma's airmail and Dorothy's boat mail with this next piece of correspondence from Mr. Equanimity. I read it like a deep cleansing breath. Do you understand my mom's call to action? Tie the knot.

PVT N.F. Bedford, Fort Devens, Ayer, Mass. – Monday night, May 26, 1941

My beloved,

Your Sunday's letter came this afternoon. It was so sweet, dear, such a perfect little footnote to Saturday night, that I shall treasure it forever above all the other letters I have every received. You have made me so proud of you by your sincerity, your ability to face a situation realistically, your willingness to meet life as it comes and get the most out of it, and your pure and beautiful love for me, that my love for you knows no bounds. I thank God that I will be able to live my life with such a wonderful woman as you for my wife.

I am glad that Bud is going to pay you a visit on Friday, dear. It will do you good to relax a bit before your exams. But don't let him take up too much of your time. When you have two exams on one day you want to get plenty of sleep the night before, for a clear head is worth two days of study. Get home early, go through every-thing quickly <u>once</u>, and get to bed.

And put notes under her pillow?

Just to make certain you are home early I will telephone you at 8:00 P.M., so please be back at Haven by that time at the latest.

Who knows why Bud's visit to the Smith campus on May 30 became everyone else's business. Grandma, Dottie and Buster all butted in. What purpose did it serve? Then a lucky break. I have no evidence he ever set foot on campus. Mom devoted the time to exam prep, and Dottie used other resources to dope out his birth date, which happened to be October 7.

Tomorrow we are going out on a big tactical problem involving all of the New England seaboard, so I won't be back in camp until Friday. However, Friday is a holiday, so Mother and Dad are driving up to visit me.

It happened "Decoration Day" fell on Friday, May 30 in 1941. It is the historically colorful holiday we now observe as Memorial Day. In 1868, veterans of the Union Army designated May 30 as a day to "garland the passionless mounts... with the choicest flowers of spring-time." Just as Presidents Day shifted according to the Uniform Monday Holiday Act in 1971, Memorial Day moved to the last Monday in May.

My dad prepared to face a personal tactical problem he'd brought upon himself. Recall sheer jubilance in his letter of May 26: *"Darling, you can't imagine how happy you made me last night by telling me that you would marry me this June."* He looked at it as *her* sacrifice, *"for it does hold possibilities of hardship..."* His promise was pure: *"all my life, short or long though it may be, will be devoted to your happiness."*

So, what's the trouble?

He had yet to inform his parents about the change in date.

I am going to explain everything to them then. As soon as I get paid on Saturday, I will leave for Hamp and should arrive around 2:00 P.M.

Robin would be miserably distracted from studies as she awaited Buster's debrief Saturday afternoon.

Do you want to arrange for us to visit Professor Harlow sometime Saturday afternoon or Sunday? I think he might be interested in us if what you have told me is true. Maybe you would like to be married by him.

Recall Harlow's words my mom took to heart, *"you've got to like a person as well as love them to be happy in marriage."* Obviously my parents are on the hunt for a respectable officiant. Where in the world of religion does Harlow come down? Today the Universal Life Church offers instant online ordination for any interested layperson. I personally know several and like them better than the Methodist minister that married my husband and me. A telephone salesman on the side, he showed up twenty minutes late for the service. Our pump organist was pit-stained and steamed up in more ways than one, pushing pedals for nearly an hour before *Here Comes the Bride.*

I have asked Dad to get us a little second-hand convertible for this summer. I will try to have it by graduation weekend.

To fortify the sporty social façade of this young couple, a convertible would do nicely. In my practical opinion? It would stink for hauling skis.

I must write Mother now, dear, so I will say good-night.

As foolhardy as Buster was when asking his dad for a convertible, he was hypervigilant when it came to his doting mother's state of mind. Possibly he wrote her to smooth the way for the bombshell he planned to drop on Decoration Day.

Best of luck on your exams, and remember that I am rooting hard for you, so don't let me down....

Roberta Skinner, Haven House, Northampton, Mass. – Wednesday, May 28, 1941

My darling -:

Just a little note 'til the mailman comes – Two exams down and three to go – and just dead tired!

Received both of your sweet letters, honey – you really are so wonderful to write so often. It helps relieve a lot of tension to read 'em.

Tension the missives and lists posted out of Campamento Americano exacerbated.

I shall be thinking of you Friday – when you inform your Mother and Daddy.

Maybe you ought to ask your Daddy whether it's the right psychological moment to inform your mother, dear...

As well-rehearsed and logical as Buster's argument would be, the betrotheds had obviously talked about some form of emotional blowback from Grammy. To him this was *"a matter of life itself."* As the only son of an only son, the firstborn of their family would secure a lineal descendent.

Robin's diary note of May 24 made it clear. He wanted a child, *"someone who can carry out all his ideals."* Would Grammy buy it?

If there was a wedding to pull off in the next four weeks, she would have to.

Try and find out whether you could get away from camp at night this summer, dearest. It would be awfully lonely seeing you only on weekends...

On Saturday, May 31, Robin wrote about her twenty-second birthday like this: *"Two exams in A.M. – lunch with Edna - Buster and family arrived – Decided to go to N.Y. – arrived about 7:00 – Had dinner – Bed early. Rained during night and window closed. (A spiritual sign?) Buster gave me a beautiful picture of himself and a corsage of gardenia and red roses – lovely. Today we decided to get married June 22nd – Compact from Mary Liz – cigarette case from Edna - $100 from the family."*

It's surprising that my mom threw her wedding date into a list of birthday presents, like it was a gift itself. Illustrative of the early 1940s in every way: a compact for beauty, a cigarette case symbolic of sophistication, money (a gift that never goes out of style), and a date certain to wed.

Young couples across the country thought like my dad, *"...weighing of all the factors involved in the international situation..."* They made identical promises: *"all my life, short or long though it may be, will be devoted to your happiness."*

Grammy Bedford wrestled through the "psychological moment." Like any mother of a prospective groom, she allowed personal experience to guide her unarticulated thoughts.

I wager she tapped into her sixth sense and flashed on "the match" into eternity. Was Robin *the right one for her son?* Ma Grover's keen intuition represented my mom as *"determined, can be coaxed, won't be led!"* If Grammy read it the same way, would she bestow the same *"wish for happy life"*?

Then she factored matrimonial age. At twenty-one, Grammy had married my charming twenty-two-year-old Grampy in New Haven, Connecticut. Buster and Robin were older by a year. No argument.

Finally, Grammy and Gramp had been married nearly thirty-five years. Historically, in their blessed "Progressive Era," a world war was unheard of. But WWII loomed for Buster. He was not only enlisted, he was *committed* to the nation's service.

With that in mind, my dad made a most convincing plea with this: *Robin* would be the one to birth a son to carry on his *"aims and ideals."* Enough to give Grammy pause for prayerful delight.

For my mom, save for one final exam, the rush to move into the next chapter of life began.

Tassel Turn

Chapter Twenty-Nine

At a very young and impressionable age, my mom taught me the "rabbit rabbit" ritual; a superstitious act I still practice. If you are lacking in the habits of good fortune, these gentle words uttered upon waking on the first day of the month make good luck stick for a solid four weeks.

So, on Sunday, June 1, I suspect my mom recited the bunny mantra and then hit the road with Buster and the senior Bedfords. That night she wrote: *"Looked at new Dodges and Packard's – talked more specifically about wedding – In Pelham, in church, in evening, white wedding dress, favorite people and reception – Honeymoon – Connecticut."*

It would be like Grampy to respond to Buster's request for a *"little second-hand convertible"* with something a step above.

PVT N.F. Bedford, Fort Devens, Ayer, Mass. – Monday, June 2, 1941

Dearest,

Just my usual little short note for a pre-exam pep-talk. Now dear, I want you to get in there and fight. Remember, this organic is no tougher than you are. Hit it hard. Smack it in the carbon rings and hit low and fast in the opening between the carbohydrate molecules. Don't let up. Drive, drive, drive! Just do your best and you will come out of this game with a big score in your favor.

The exaggerated after-effect of four years of Princeton football, but the chemical structure was impeccable.

With that over, I can now tell you how much I enjoyed being with you this past weekend. It was wonderful, dear, although I am sorry I made you travel so far back and forth. However, if we get our little car out of it, maybe it will have been worth it.

The next land mine to navigate? Consent for leave.

Must run now, sweetheart, but not before telling you not to worry about anything. The Sergeant got his furlough, so I am pretty sure I will be able to get one too. Mother will be alright once she gets used to the idea. Most of all, remember that you mean all the world to me...

As much as Grammy survived the psychological moment, she remained emotionally strained. Her big heart haunted by the adage "your son is your son until he takes a wife."

With Robin's already cluttered mind, a letter from Lelia was about as welcome as a flat tire on the way to the airport.

L.M. Skinner, Rancagua – Sewell, Chile – June 2, 1941 (airmail)

Dearest Roberta,

I'm snatching ten minutes at school to send you this list and say hello. We thought of you so much Sat. Bud said he might get you a birthday cake. He hoped to be able to eat at one of the famous taverns with you. I hope you won't let writing letters etc. to Buster interfere with your reviewing conscientiously for your final exams.

It was permissible for Bud to disrupt her studies, but not Buster?

Please, please work so as not to fail in your graduation. It would be such a blow. Sacrifice good times the next 8 days. We're going to wire for flowers about four days ahead of graduation so you can enjoy them a couple days ahead. I almost weep from disappointment and regret that I can't see your graduation when we have looked ahead for so many years to that event.

What about the wedding?

We will be so proud and happy over your finishing (if you only don't flunk out on some final).

In the Crane Road house, when that kind of catty remark crossed lips, my mom turned to animal violence. An effective warning began with squinty eyes locked on a target. A silent growl grew vocally in a blistering flash. "Wrrrreoww!" It made the "end of discussion" point and, more often than not, kept the peace.

This is only one sheet of the shopping items – will send for about 10 or 12 items on a separate sheet (in our next air letter so this letter won't be overweight).

Russell dislocated his knee again at Cavalry school – in the infirmary about 3 wks.

Awkwardly dismounting from a horse? No room for explanation. Lelia got back to the checklist.

You can see by this shopping list that you can't hurry the shopping so much in New York. Dorothy said <u>all the trips</u> she had to make to Braden Office, and to Chilean Consul's office for getting your passport vised, to the Steamship Co., etc. took so much time and with the heat in N.Y. you just <u>can't</u> rush. You will have to make various trips to Miss Otterstrom's office – getting things arranged. Daddy is ordering a movie Kodak for your graduation present. So you can take pictures on your trip.

Love, Mother.

...Write us just a note to tell us if you are still coming on Santa Lucia. You can't possibly make the Clara on June 20.

With respect to exams, this "snatched" hello was tardy to the party. By the time my mom tore open the envelope she'd turned a fast corner bound for graduation and wedding bells. Unbeknownst to Lelia, half a laundry list of shopping for Campamento Americano would wait. No hurry on the embossed seal of the Chilean Consulate either. Robin would board neither the *Santa Clara*, nor the *Santa Lucia*.

PVT N.F. Bedford, Fort Devens, Ayer, Mass. – Tuesday morning, June 3, 1941

My beloved,

I talked to Dad last night over the telephone. He suggested that Mother would <u>love</u> to help you with your plans for the wedding if you asked her. As a matter of fact, I suppose that she would be broken hearted if you didn't ask her.

Soup to nuts, Grammy prided herself in social-ability.

I am afraid that her coyness last Sunday was due more to my impetuosity than to any distaste for having to help plan the wedding. She just thought that I was forcing you to ask her help and she wanted you to make your own free choice in the matter since planning the wedding <u>is</u> the privilege of the bride and her mother. I think that she might have been a bit hurt that you didn't insist that you would "<u>love</u> to have her help, my dear" – you know the sort of thing women like.

Simple enough. Robin had no choice but to close the door on her own mother and open the window to Grammy. Mother of the bride *and* groom? It would be transformational tonic to perform *two* leading roles.

The Major seems pretty amenable to the (furlough) *idea, so I am certain that everything will be all right.*

Buster cut this note short, packed up and left *"on another overnight problem."*

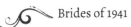

Roberta Skinner, Haven House, Northampton, Mass. – Monday, June 2, 1941

My dearest husband - :

I'm sure you have never seen a happier looking little girl than Robin today – I've just hummed everywhere I've gone – and have had a chronic case of butterflies in my tummy every time I think about you, or see someone I've told the "big secret" to... I don't see how I can possibly be any happier, even on my wedding day - (the only exception is when Junior's born – 'cause then I know you'll be so happy and proud, too.)

It's just everything I've dreamed of for years and years – and not even in my wildest dreams did I think anybody as wonderful as you would ever exist to be my husband.

After I got back, I found an invitation from Caddie and Martie, who are being married the 21ˢᵗ at 4:00. I guess all our friends will have quite a bit of weddings and such – 'cause Fuzzie's and the Smithereens will be in Short Hills and Caddie's and Princetonians at Vassar. June is certainly a wonderful month, isn't it?

Your own, forever and ever, Robin

Would you like it if my cousin gave me away?

Grasping at twigs in a far-flung family tree, my mom would recruit Roy.

I wrote to Mother tonight – everything's all settled.

Game, set, match. Would Lelia read it and weep? The "special attention" expended on Bud and Dottie would distract her.

In the first seventy-two hours of June, the bunny mantra paid off. On the evening of June 3 my mom wrote: *"Nifty Chem exam – sure I passed it. Flowers from Buster - Gardenia and roses and card enclosed. Called tonight."*

Auntie Rhea was the first to chime in with congratulatory graduation correspondence; then let loose like a jumping spider with poor eyesight.

Mr. Nathaniel Forrest Redford

Dearest, Just a little something to cheer you up after your last exam and start you off right on one of the happiest weeks of your life. See you soon.
Love, Buster.

A sweetly scripted turning point sentiment accompanied gardenia and roses.

She tried not to complain, but sixteen weeks after Frank died, Roy insisted on the sale of the Huntington's forever home in Amsterdam. It was an asset, yes, but the monthly overhead was an impossible liability. In short order Rhea relocated south to Alexandria, Virginia and moved in with her son.

Mrs. Frank Huntington, 212 E. Howell Ave, Alexandria Va., Tuesday, June 3, 1941

Dear Roberta –

Congratulations girlie, your Auntie is proud of you and wishes you every joy and happiness for the future.

Roy is planning on seeing you get your "sheep skin." Don't know as I can say that much, even though I should like to see you graduate.

I have been laid up with an infected heel since April 1ˢᵗ. To make it worse I fell down these horrid stairs here on top of the infection and bruised the heel bone. Have been chasing Drs. and doing everything – have had to keep off from it almost entirely. I only just the past few days could even fit on an old shoe – a bruised bone is much worse than a broken one. Afraid you would not be very proud of your auntie's appearance. I do hobble out and get in a car once or twice a week with an old slipper on and Roy has taken me to the grocery store – but I have not been able to get over into Washington since the last of March so haven't a dud to wear.

Roberta I am writing this to ask you what you would like us to get you for a graduation gift, might just as well get something you would like and can use and would be so much easier on me than to attempt to chase around...

G-Pa H died suddenly Apr. 24ᵗʰ and Roy has to go up to Amsterdam and meet a lawyer to see about his things and he may have to be there next wk. Thurs. so make a prompt reply please.

Roy, by default, had managed the earthly affairs of his father just a year ago. Now it's his grandfather Huntington. While "G-Pa H" is off fishing with Frank, rejoicing in the reward of the hereafter, Rhea struggled to keep up appearances in ashes to dust living with Roy, proximate to the nation's capital.

Wish I could give you a $100.00 check. We are still living here in this horrid little dump and with housing conditions as they are in Washington and all places near I doubt if we can find anything else. People just flocking in here by the thousands every month, yes every week – can't even find single rooms. This Defense work calling so many! Lord I have been so ashamed of this place – have been scared to death for fear some of my friends would drop in here. We near froze to death here when Dixons were here.

Auntie Alta and Uncle Dix passed through for a visit in February, after first meeting Buster and the senior Bedfords. Warm and welcoming as Rhea tried to be when her sister and brother-in-law stopped in, the poor dear remained chilled with hand-wringing anxiety.

Heavens don't you ever pop in here with any of your friends. I haven't been able to do one tap of spring cleaning and it is the dirtiest location I ever saw! R.R. Freight yards a quarter mile away and the fire engine house right back of us burns soft coal and we just have to eat the dirty black soot and cinders. Roy knows I despise it here but don't tell him I have complained to you. I know he tried to do what he thought was for the best last Sept. Now please answer this question – when are you going to leave for Chile and where are you going when college closes?

Two million-dollar questions. Rhea, too, is unaware of the holy matrimony about to unfold.

Please destroy this as soon as you read it for would not look good to have around your room. My eyes have given me so much trouble. I can't even use them to sew. Guess I am a poor stick.

A big hug and kiss, Auntie Rhea

Rhea was true to the facts with respect to the industrialized character of Alexandria. I imagine her in a flowered housedress, rag tied around her head. She limped in a slipper and swiped with a feather duster. It was impossible to keep up with soot and cinders in the kitchen, let alone those settled on the coffee table, dressers and nightstands. The place was a pit compared to the clean and green landscape of her home in Amsterdam. It's a safe bet her big sister, Alta, silently took pity on Rhea's lot in life last February. The heel infection had since made matters worse.

The Fire Station on Windsor Avenue, just out their back door in 1941, remains an active player in providing emergency services still today. The "Pot Yard," (an innocent moniker for the Potomac rail hub) was the place where thousands of freight cars converged, sorted and redirected daily. According to strict timetables, this bewitching space was an enormous north meets south transition point; in a Mason Dixon way. Located three blocks east of Rhea and Roy's red brick Howell Avenue home, it consumed a swath of land six miles long, just shy of a half-mile wide. As silent as the soot and cinders were, steel wheels on steel rails, with train whistles blowing, added up to a whole lot of noise annoyance.

Presently, it's the site of smart growth redevelopment.

As much as Auntie Rhea was not enamored with locomotives, it's impossible to ignore the romance of the railway. Is it too cliché to suggest worker spirits were lifted around the Pot Yard singing "fee-fi-fiddly-i-o," *I've Been Working on the Railroad?* Despite its racist underpinnings, it lived in songs for children one generation to the next immortalized by the likes of Pete Seeger, Alvin and the Chipmunks, and Raffi.

Enough digression on Auntie Rhea's Pot Yard. Lelia is yet to receive Robin's letter postmarked June 3. The one that unilaterally made it so *"everything's all settled."* But the word is out amongst friends. That smart-ass Mary Liz prepared to forgo the rice tossing; symbol of fertility. Instead, she was selecting shoes to throw, in keeping with a common, though ancient, rite of passage. Robin scribbled rapid-fire thoughts Wednesday night in a note to be posted first thing in the morning.

Roberta Skinner, Haven House, Northampton, Mass. – Wednesday, June 4, 1941

My dearest –

A goodnight note to tell you that I had Edna's phone no. wrong – it's Rehoboth *98 – and that I just can't wait to see you again, dear – It seems longer than ever this week. Your picture looks so nice sitting on my dresser, sweetheart. I bought an album today and started a Robin-Buster scrap-book. I'm going to take just loads of pictures of you this summer.*

Mary Liz just walked in and says she's going to be very happy on the 22nd to throw her old shoes at you (that's her way of congratulating you).

Was she familiar with the insult it represented in Arab culture, like we are today?

Dottie Davies says she can't possibly come on the 22nd 'cause her job starts the 20th in St. Pete. However, she says there isn't any other ceremony she'd rather be at, than seeing us married.

All my love my dearest, and a thousand and one kisses –

Your own, Robin

Considering my mom's stingy letter writing reputation, *two* notes to my dad postmarked the same day were nothing less than notable. As she packed, she pondered, then paused to reveal her innermost thoughts.

Roberta Skinner, Haven House, Northampton, Mass. – Thursday, June 5, 1941

My dearest –

Just a little note, 'cause I just started thinking about you, as I was packing. You know, sweetheart, I am much too happy about this whole thing. I just can't believe that after June 22nd, I shall be an honest-to-goodness wife "officially." And every time I look around this room, and think "from now on, no more of this roaming around the countryside" – but instead a place that I can call home, even if it's only one room – I get a wonderful thrill.

Compared to the hundreds of thousands of souls without safe haven in 1941 (and still today) she's led the life of a *blessed* refugee. In the grand scheme, my mom was grateful but looked forward to so much more.

I guess I never stopped to realize or let myself think about having a legal residence or home, dear. But I'm getting awfully happy about it now... Honey, I'm going to do everything on earth, to make you the happiest man alive...

Chin up, my mom marched through the month. There was nothing superstitious about Friday the 13th when she wrote: *"Buster arrived tonight with Ben Wood. Had a last reunion at Rahar's – with Van, Dizzy and Gina and Jean."*

Then on June 14: *"Had Ivy Day today – lovely procession."* In the name of Smith tradition, wearing white dresses, they planted ivy. But that night, Robin confessed words that smacked of a Louie lecture: *"Talked to Buster in afternoon. Loves me – but sometimes doesn't like me. Thinks I'm a little immature and undependable."*

A matter-of-fact observation on his part, eight days before their wedding, after which he motored back to Devens with Ben Wood.

That night, one man she might have married made an appearance. Her diary revealed this: *"Had last drink with Louie at Rahar's – He likes Buster."* A capstone-like encounter that closed a four-year growing up chapter for both.

Robin described the content of Baccalaureate the evening of June 15. The grads were sent on their way with Chapel-talk thoughts from the *Book of Proverbs* with a "best set" standard; the price of a virtuous woman is far above rubies. *"After four years of gathering knowledge and virtue (courage) tell them that you learned to face the future laughing. A virtuous woman. Great changes ahead – we like changes – need of keeping Christian virtues, humanity, kindness, less security, sorrows. Life in future still the joy of living."*

There is no better life-lesson: face the future laughing. And to "like changes" when the proverbial cheese moves. As it is about to. Over the next several years.

Mrs. Wm. Dixon, 341 Keith Ave., Missoula, Mont., Saturday, June 14, 1941

Dear Roberta:

I intended to send you a telegram of congratulations Monday – but after receiving a letter from Rhea yesterday I decided to send this air mail – special delivery – so I can write more.

So surprised to know of your wedding June 22 –

Stupefied is more like it. Just like her sisters.

How I wish we could be there. I won't send a wedding present until I hear – what you want – and if you are going to Chile July 4th, etc., etc. You'll have to write me finally.

I started your graduation present last Monday – notice the "hurricane lamps" and that the candle sticks can be used without the glass globes – for candle holders.

I love Auntie Alta's practical gift giving. Then she came clean with the *real* reason she wrote airmail (though not "special delivery" as she claimed). A bald eagle with outstretched wings and a shield in its talons adorned the bi-colored six cent stamp of blue and carmine red. Special delivery was sixteen cents at the time.

Now this is what I want you to do – <u>insist</u> on Rhea going to your wedding. She wrote that she thought the Bedfords would put on such an elaborate affair – that her clothes wouldn't be <u>swell</u> enough. I can't get a letter to her – don't know how to reach her – but she has a new dress – and if she needs a long dress – perhaps she can borrow one of Mrs. Segebarth's or buy a dinner dress – and she can cut it off – later – for a P.M. dress. She wrote she would stay alone in a hotel in N.Y. – next Sunday.

On Sunday? The night before graduation! Even though Lelia maintained *"the jam at graduation isn't any place for Auntie Rhea,"* with a flicker of McLatchey spirit, the poor stick would give it a go.

She has a very warm spot in her heart for you – and it will do her more good to see you married than anything I know of.

I know how busy you are – All my love and best wishes – Auntie Alta

On June 16, 1941, head held high, a tasseled black mortarboard shaded my mom's blue eyes of shining determination. I imagine every young woman who walked the line in the Class of '41 as rosy cheeked, posture perfect. With practiced handshakes, they accepted their diplomas; friends and family nodded approvingly; politely applauded.

Short and sweet, Mom summed up the experience without reflection on sentimental speech nuggets. Words delivered by school officials cloaked like royalty in academic regalia were lost on the breeze.

"Commencement – movies. Lunch with Roy and Auntie Rhea. Packed and left."

Auntie Rhea, with Roy's help, witnessed the momentous turning point with unmistakable family pride. Four years of floundering ended favorably with an A.B. after Robin's Skinner surname. On to the joy of living. Preparations began in earnest to cross the threshold of matrimony.

Robin in B+ posture; showing a little leg with bobby socks and flats.

Action at the New Florence Hotel

Chapter Thirty

The day after graduation, barely stripped of her commencement gown, Robin attended a second fitting of her wedding dress. Bridal lingerie was fitted, as well, to assure an unbroken undie line; a slimming all-in-one bra-to-girdle garment in some combination of sexy silk and Lastex. Functionally (but uncomfortably) designed to firm the hips, flatten the belly, and support "the girls." Snappy garters secured stockings.

Adding to the dress and undie *"fitting"* were *"pictures."* Nothing said about hair and makeup but with sultry eyes and ruby lips revealed in her wedding portrait it was evidently part of her day.

Two days after graduation, June 18, the wedding is t-minus four days and counting. *"Lunch with Gina and Joyce and Mom and Dad at Princeton Club. Looked for Bridesmaid's dresses. Got wedding ring at Tiffany & Co."*

As awkward as it can be when determining what to call future parents-in-law, my mother appeared suddenly content in the familial "Mom and Dad." With T. Wayne and Lelia in absentia, the senior Bedfords bought in literally and figuratively to "gaining a daughter." Perhaps all the more because of the tragic loss of their little Eugenia to a petticoat fire, before Buster's birth.

Evidenced by such flurry over two days, the privilege of pulling off this wedding was fully in the hands of Grammy and Grampy; the wedding party in tow. Proof that Buster's felicitous-written intimation, *"you know the sort of thing women like"* was spot-on.

I forgive those kick-him-in-the-knee sexist words; with a wife and three daughters he was outnumbered and behaviorally modified later in life.

In one afternoon they checked shopping for bridesmaids' dresses off the list. Presumably the purchases were made at a bridal boutique where rush alterations were expected. A dedicated seamstress worked thread-flying magic in a back room. Instructions were left for parcel delivery: straightaway to Pelham Manor.

As much as the whole afternoon smacked of a Manhattan scavenger hunt, Tiffany and Co. was a fine place to end the day. And because I have no evidence of an engagement ring prior to this point, I do believe a "wedding set" was selected. If memory serves me, a platinum band supported a brilliant one-carat solitaire diamond; the trademark Tiffany setting. It paired well with a simpler wedding ring encircled with small diamonds, to be worn "closest to her heart."

As a kid, it made no sense to me why my mom's engagement ring was showier than her wedding band. (Dad never wore a ring, save for a heavy gold unmistakably masculine "Bedford crest." It resembled a custom wax seal stamp and often opened doors for conversation.) Her ring carried "best set" weight. And would lift her up through the war.

We humans are steeped in tradition; symbolic ties that bind. Etiquette, on the other hand, smacks more of social stratification. In the run up to this wedding, Grammy honored both. First edition Emily Post, *Etiquette: The Blue Book of Social Usage*, a best seller in 1922, was pulled from the bookshelf at Pelham Manor and dusted off for consultation. Topically relevant pages, honored for their meticulous rules of conduct, were bookmarked for quick reference. (Emily would agree dog-eared page corners ruin a first edition.)

With a heart-felt wish to be by Robin's side, to assist and witness the big day, Auntie Alta stamped another letter from Missoula. Her pen circled around to signal growing preparatory measures of the U.S. military. Her son, Bill Dixon, Jr. (another of Robin's first cousins) was now thirty-one years old and married to Betty, twenty-nine. For lack of children to care for, Betty was fortunate to be employed by the U.S. Dept. of Forestry.

Mrs. Wm. Dixon, 341 Keith Ave., Missoula, Mont. – June 18, 1941 (airmail)

My dear Roberta –

How I want to be with you and help you. – I can imagine how busy you are. –

I think you have done mighty well to get through college and marry a young man deserving, as Buster impressed us.

Very few girls who haven't their mother go ahead with the plans for their wedding – I feel sure Mrs. Bedford is helping you – otherwise I should have taken the plane and hurried to you – I want to see you "flow" up the aisle at 5:30 mountain time Sunday O-so badly. – Please send me photos of the wedding – will it be written up in N.Y. Times and your picture there? I hope so. I just hope Auntie Rhea feels able to go ahead and take your Mother's place – she is the logical one. She'll do it – if you just insist on it. She lacks confidence in herself – but if she feels able it will do her more good than anything else in the world.

Now, about your wedding present – you must select your silver pattern. I like Towles' and Gorham patterns – maybe your mother wants to give you your flat service – so I don't dare send anything until you write me all about the furnishings in your home – and what you have chosen.

I fear you are not taking any wedding trip – because of Buster's service in camp. We hope he may be free Jan 1st and that you'll come west to visit us then. If I can be of any service to you – do write and ask me.

Why in the world did she think he'd be "free" in six months?

Bill Jr. had to turn in his questionnaire this week. We hope Congress will pass the bill – changing the age right away – so he won't have to go.

Recall FDR's proclamation last September. All young men between twenty-one and thirty-five were required to register for the draft. Discussion in Washington waffled over a modification of the term of service from twelve to eighteen months. For some unknown reason (Ma Grover, social hearsay, newsprint or radio broadcast), Alta prayed Bill, Jr. would age out. That won't happen. And the reason she believed Buster would be "free" January 1? She did not understand his *three-year enlistment*. Only in hindsight do we know the grasp of the draft will grow. Her son will serve within the year.

She continued...

The new Florence Hotel – a beautiful building was opened Monday night with a formal banquet - $15.00 per couple – while there Walter McLeod rec'd a cable from Bud – saying he arrived and Dorothy and Lelia met him. He showed me the telegram.

Recall Bud's words written to Robin a month ago. A fine sample of a twenty-three-year-old's passionate thinking. I conjure a straw-stuffed Ray Bolger, cast as the Scarecrow in *The Wizard of Oz*.

"I'm awaiting a reply to a letter inquiring the date of my call to active service. How truly wonderful it would be if the reply would state sometime in August! Then I could fly to see Dorothy!"

Bud dutifully reported in to his father, Walter H. McLeod, assuring his safe arrival in Chile. Fluky timing. Auntie Alta and Uncle Dix were among the who's who of the Missoula business community when the cablegram arrived.

Auntie Alta went on...

Marsh is just back from school. She is homely as can be – but entertaining – I was seated opposite her.

Marsh, Bud's seventeen-year-old kid sister may not be a looker, but personality goes a long way. The adage, "You can catch more flies with honey than vinegar," is instructive at any age.

Best wishes and congratulations to you children. Uncle Dix would have been glad to "give you away" if he could have been there –

Heaps of love – Auntie Alta

Like the Palmer House in Chicago, the Florence Hotel was restored following a fiery demise in 1936. Walter and others in the local business community pulled together during the Great Depression with the foresight to rebuild. Seven stories of "Art Modern" architecture; horizontal lines and rounded corners, anchored the street front across North Higgins Avenue from the Missoula Mercantile where Walter now presided following the retirement of his father.

Uncle Dix, part owner and salesman in a shoe store, understood the mixed-use commercial advantages of a downtown hotel. Presumably, winter boot sales to unprepared visitors boosted the bottom line; souvenir cowboy boots and boot polish, too.

Meanwhile, back in New York, Robin was swept up in fits and starts like every pre-war bride of 1941. The dress, venue, flowers, cake and champagne were best set standards. Bridal bedlam ensued. Vows to "stress less" were yet to be invented.

Church, Steeple and the People

Chapter Thirty-One

I t follows if the engagement party invites were distinctly hand-en-graved so, too, were the wedding invitations and announcements. An embossed mark hardly bigger than an inchworm, placed subtly under the envelope flap, divulged Grammy's source: Dempsey & Carroll, the finest purveyor of elegant engraved stationery. They set the standard from the time they established their New York venture in 1878. The founders understood correspondence and etiquette, as social institutions, were inextricably linked. A tissue paper insert placed over the four-and-one-half by six-inch slice of rich cotton fiber cardstock ensured the ink didn't smudge.

The guest list of who attended the small ceremony at the Huguenot Memorial Church remains a mystery to me. But Buster's folks, the Reverend, and the bridal party were revealed in a news clipping, dated June 20, published in *The Pelham Sun*.

On reading the text, I cursed my snapping turtle grandfather. He owned fifteen lying words that misrepresented the family lineage. More on that in a minute.

Friends and family sent congratulatory telegrams from near and far. Letters of regret wove a short story of interesting invitees.

For example, Buster's former 150-lb. Tiger teammate, Butts Hansl, responded promptly with a Western Union from his station at Pine Camp, what we know today as Fort Drum. Butts (given name, "Raleigh") was a Cadet Major in the Reserve Officers' Training Corps (ROTC) at Princeton. Over the four-year course, he was celebrated as one who had attained the

Mr. and Mrs. Thomas Wayne Skinner

have the honour of

announcing the marriage of their daughter

Roberta Lelia

to

Mr. Nathaniel Forrest Bedford

Sunday the twenty-second of June

Nineteen hundred and forty-one

Huguenot Memorial Church

Pelham Manor, New York

highest average in military science. In the right place and time, he went on to instruct in the university's Department of Military Science and Tactics. Eventually he served in Italy.

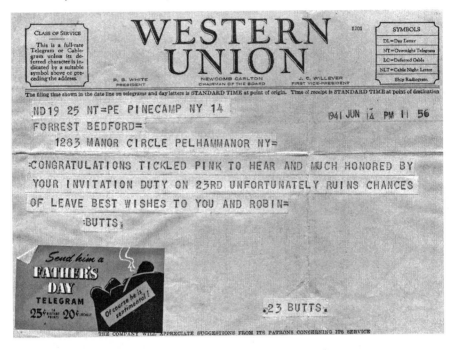

Gordon MacLean "Tiff" Tiffany was a "Yalie;" Yale class of 1935. No doubt Buster gave him crap about that alma mater. Tiff and his wife, Ellie, celebrated their first anniversary this month. He would earn his LLB Degree from Columbia in the coming year.

From Gordon MacLean Tiffany, 402 N. Columbia St. Chapel Hill, N.C. – June 19, 1941

Dear Buster:

Congratulations and best wishes to you both and may I add a hearty welcome to the H.O.B ("Happy Order of Benedicts"). Such a virile muscle-man will indeed be an asset.

I am very sorry that we can't be there to send you all off – it would be a very happy occasion for us were we able to do so – but as you so tactfully put it – it would be a little much for even the newly-discovered Tiffany energy.

A hint that his wife, Ellie, is expecting?

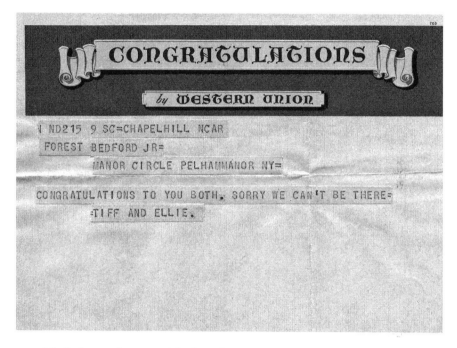

Of all the couples I've wished on their way, I know of none who were better equipped with all the ingredients of a successful and happy married life. You'll find married life is the shining example of "the whole is greater than any of its parts" – you'll soon know what I mean.

Another hint at parenthood.

Maybe I shouldn't speak of this now, but we've given the matter of a wedding present a good deal of thought and the selection down here is, as you can appreciate, rather limited. It would be better I think for us to wait till we return to the city at the end of August where the variety will offer a wider choice. I hope this meets approval because a bale of tobacco on your "present table" might be a little awkward.

During shared time at Columbia Law, the highbrow classmates sampled pipe tobaccos and bonded over like-thinking on the moral foundation of civil liberties. Flash to the 1970s when law students lit fluffy buds of Colombian Gold, like a marijuana mascot, and rehashed the same relevant civil rights themes.

Godspeed and success "attend you," Tiff and Ellie

Bob Driver, the *"nice boy"* Buster introduced to Robin early on in my parents' courtship hadn't seen the betrotheds since the Barrister's Ball. Recall the evening they trouped to the Monkey Bar and made faces in the mirror. Earlier in May he wrote to return two dollars he'd borrowed during a game of *"galloping dominoes."* More commonly known as dice. Bob had come up short in a fast-paced game of craps. Aside from that, he relayed that fellow law students were settling down for pre-exam review... *"none of us have really done the amount of study that we should have at this point. You were called on the other day. When Hamilton heard you were in the Army, he laughed, and said, "I guess I might as well tear up his card."*

Oh Hamilton! Ye of little faith! It was also proof lecture time was too valuable to waste on roll call. My dad was not missed. And even though Bob Driver would serve as usher at the wedding he, too, sent a congratulatory telegram to mark the occasion.

By contrast, Ed and Isabel Smith were fast friends of Grammy and Grampy. They first met through a Martha's Vineyard connection, where Ed was born and raised, and Grammy first worked as a domestic following her immigration to America. Ed was a like an uncle to Buster. In turn, my dad was like an uncle to the three Smith boys.

Ed was descended from a family long associated with whaling and the sea. The Arctic and oceanography were his passion. I mean it as a compliment when I say Edward H. "Iceberg" Smith reminds me of a first-generation Boaty McBoatface. (Do you know the boaties? Three yellow submersibles of UK fame in underwater exploratory mode; fact-finding clues to help solve the puzzle of climate change). Using rudimentary instruments Ed collected data, observed and recorded temperature and salinity readings at various depths. He was the first to map ocean currents, post

Titanic. Once currents were understood, likely paths of icebergs could be projected hence reducing the risk of iceberg/ship collisions.

At this point in his storied career, Ed was commanding officer of the U.S. Coast Guard Cutter Northland and commander of the Greenland Patrol. (Greenland was a Danish colony that had been virtually abandoned following the invasion of Denmark in April 1940.) The Greenland Patrol escorted Allied ships and kept watch over the northern extension of U.S. coastal waters to guard against covert German installations.

Ed's activities symbolized a world at war well before U.S. engagement, while Isabel humanized family life at home. She wrote to explain their circumstances, and marked the day with a telegram, too.

Mrs. Edward H. Smith, 5 Wildwood St. Winchester, Mass. – June 19, 1941

Dear Roberta,

I think it's so fine that you and Buster are being married this weekend. It seems like quite the sensible thing to do – now that times are uncertain.

We would like nothing better than to come to your wedding and reception, Sunday, and it was certainly sweet of you to think of us – but I'm afraid as much as we would like to – we'll have to decline.

Today I took Porter (our oldest boy) into the hospital – to be treated for a severe cold – so they might operate on him for appendicitis as soon as possible. His present condition would not warrant an operation safely – but the surgeon in charge says Port's appendix must come out by the last of the week – probably Saturday. So you can see why we will have to stay close at hand.

Ed came home a week ago Sunday. He was several weeks late – but we've grown to think nothing of that! Right now he's in Washington – and planning to leave again soon for his long cruise – the 1st of July. We don't have him home a great deal.

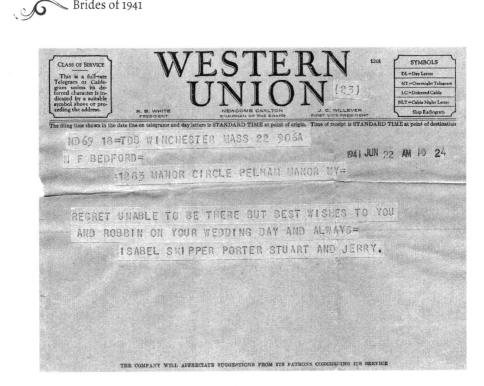

Isabelle's reference to Ed's "long cruise," sounds as though "the Skipper" is about to depart for a relaxing vacation.

I'm so excited about your wedding – It must be lots of fun making your plans and all. If you plan to come up this way at all – do stop with us...

All for now – I know you're busy and have little time to read rambling letters. Congratulations on your graduation and just all the happiness which two dear people can share together, always....Affectionately, Isabel

On the first of July, a distressed letter arrived from Louie.

L.E.B, 17 Gilman St., Holyoke, Mass. – Wednesday, June 25, 1941

Mrs. N. Forrest Bedford
Groton Inn
Groton, Mass. Please Hold.

Dearest Robin,

You will never know how disappointed I was not to be able to see you and Buster married, but there was nothing that I could do about it. Honey you waited too long before you mailed your letter telling me where to come...

I spent a frantic day Sat. trying to find out where Buster lived. Smith said you had not left a forwarding address and the telephone company asked every Bedford in Pelham if they had a son getting married.

Imagine AT&T operators ringy dinging up a home residence to inquire if a son of the household was getting married that day.

Not being at your wedding makes me feel as though I had missed my sister's or my own... I do want to wish both you and Buster all the happiness that life can bring... If after you get settled a bit and can get down to see us, I do hope that you will come.

Best luck to you both, and my love to you Robin.
Love, Lou

On Thursday, June 19, with just days left before church bells, my mom wrote *"Stayed home today to straighten up house."* Presumably she was hanging with Grammy and the hired help, readying Pelham Manor for reception perfection. Meanwhile my grandfather (more likely his secretary) was seeing to it this announcement was placed in Friday's *Pelham Sun*.

ROBERTA SKINNER TO BECOME BRIDE OF N.F. BEDFORD

Miss Roberta Lelia Skinner, daughter of Mr. and Mrs. Thomas Wayne Skinner of Rancagua, Chile will become the bride on Sunday of Mr. Nathaniel Forrest Bedford, son of Mr. and Mrs. Nathniel Lynn Bedford of Manor Circle.

The evening wedding ceremony will take place in Huguenot Memorial Church at 7:30 o'clock with the Rev. Dr. Willard P. Soper officiating. A reception will be held at the Bedford home in Pelham Manor.

The bride, who was graduated this month from Smith College, will be attended by Miss Virginia Solley of Washington,

Conn., as maid of honor. Miss Joyce Thompson of New York City will be bridesmaid.

Mr. C. Benedict Wood of New York will act as best man. Both the bridegroom and the best man are members of Squadron A., 101st Cavalry and are stationed at Fort Devens, Mass. Mr. Robert F. Driver of Washington, D.C., will act as usher.

Miss Skinner prepared for college at Emma Willard School in Troy. Mr. Bedford, who is a descendant of Gen. Nathaniel Bedford Forrest of Civil War fame, is a graduate of Lawrenceville School and of Princeton University 1939. He was a member of the Tower Club at Princeton, is a member of the Princeton Club in New York, and is on leave from Columbia Law School while serving with the army.

On Monday, June 23, a headline in the *St. Petersburg Times* confirmed "*Miss Skinner, Mr. Bedford Wed Yesterday in New York.*"

A picture of the bride fell through the cracks.

Time to rise up and set the record straight over Grampy's fifteen words of fabrication inked in typeset: "*Mr. Bedford, who is a descendent of Gen. Nathaniel Bedford Forrest of Civil War fame...*"

Trust me on these five facts:

1. The General's name is *Nathan*; not Nathaniel.

2. Prior to the Civil war, *Nathan Bedford Forrest,* achieved financial success. As a cotton-picking slave trader.

3. In the fight against the Union Army, General Forrest was a celebrated cavalry genius of the Confederates. A barbarous, merciless savage. (Author Jack Hurst proves it in his top-notch biography about the man.)

4. Forrest was famous for this basic principle of military strategy: "Get there first with the most men."

5. It is widely accepted; Nathan Bedford Forrest was the first Grand Wizard of the Ku Klux Klan.

Not my hero; not my relative.

Forging ahead on bridal bedlam, a June 20 calendar cross-check marked the day my mom might have sailed on the *Santa Clara*. The voyage was the furthest thing from her mind: *"Bought Bridesmaids' presents at Tiffany's. Bridesmaids' lunch at Louis Sherry's – Nancy, Gina, Joyce. Bought shoes, bag and stockings."*

On the summer solstice, Saturday the twenty-first of June: *"Bought riding clothes. Hair set. Got wedding license. Saw gang for a few minutes in Biltmore Hotel. Got car."*

What did this bride do on her wedding day in 1941? Robin summed it up like this: *"Addressed announcements. Packed for honeymoon. Wedding. Lots of pictures. Reception. On to Connecticut."*

I give her credit for writing anything at all but, on that point, I should come clean. Every "diary" entry dated Monday, June 16 through Tuesday,

Buster and best man, Ben Wood, with the newlyweds' 1939 Lincoln Zephyr.

July 8, 1941, was written front and back on a single eight-and-a-half by eleven-inch piece of American Writing Company paper. The color, "eggshell" remained creamy; un-yellowed. The subtle watermark: "Rag Content, Acceptance Bond. USA." Top shelf stationery; perfectly intact nearly 80 years later, found stuffed amongst letters from the back of the closet.

Her diary was somewhere out of reach. Rightly so, for a newlywed. Random squiggles jumpstarted her extravagant Parker "Duovac." Daily notes, comprised of mixed entries in pen and pencil, told a short story.

One sheet of rag bond documented the birth of seventy years of wedlock for this bride of 1941.

A circumspect cable acknowledged the day from the collective cast of characters in Campamento Americano. The message? As truncated as it could possibly be.

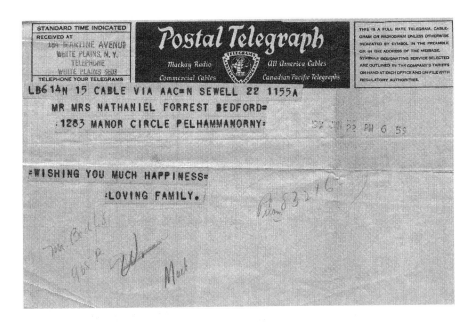

Hair and makeup artist at work circa 1941.

Pre-ceremony bride and her attendants (L to R: Bridesmaid Joyce Fletcher, Maid of Honor Virginia (Gina) Solly and Robin).

On to the church.

Here comes the bride.

Small crowd for a big moment at Huguenot Memorial Church.

Announcing Mr. and Mrs. Nathaniel Forrest Bedford.

Father/son handshake of a thousand words.
(L to R: Grammy, Buster, Robin, Grampy, the Reverend and cousin Roy.)

Glasses raised to the Bride and Groom, Gina offers a toast.

Snappy Grampy poses while Grammy supervises the cake cutting
and the Reverend thinks a prayer.

Buster tenderly feeds Robin while Grammy, Roy, Grampy,
Auntie Rhea and the Reverend attend.

Robin has an intended target?

Today it would be a text message with Gina's fingers more fully occupied.

Rolling Out, Rolling On

Chapter Thirty-Two

On to Connecticut.

A short furlough for Buster made for what appeared to be a two-day honeymoon. Mom gave nothing explicit away about their wedding night. But face it, in 1941, a satin and lace nightie with ribbons and a matching robe were tangled in a bedroom panty scene. On Monday, *"Played tennis and croquet. Swam after nap. Took drive around lake. Saw movie "Blood and Sand."*

This classic 1941 Century Fox Technicolor film combined love and drama; an Academy Award winner for Best Cinematography. Spanish guitars rhythmically matched the action. Tyrone Power mixed it up with Linda Darnell and Rita Hayworth. (A role that brought Hayworth international recognition in her role as a sultry femme fatale.) For Buster, the title might have evoked real-time desert war images. Blood and sand was one way to imagine the Western Desert Campaign nine months before; the Italian invasion of Egypt to fight the British Commonwealth. As it turned out, a colorful toreador twirling around a bullring is a place where blood and sand also mix.

On June 24 the rag bond diary substitute revealed this: *"Slept late. Swam. Played all afternoon."*

"Played?" An innuendo perhaps. Robin's suspiciously subtle double entendre.

That night, Buster wrote his first letter as a married man to his wife.

A letter, two days after the wedding?

Robin was awkwardly holed up with Grammy and Grampy at Pelham Manor. Buster was already apologizing.

PVT N.F. Bedford, Fort Devens, Ayer, Mass. – Tuesday night, June 24, 1941

My beloved,

Oh, sad night! Such a beautiful moon over Robin's Pond and you not here. I certainly do miss you, my dear, even though we have been separated for just a few hours. Well, at least your absence has given me time to ponder my sins a bit, and I have just realized that maybe I have been picking on you too much about a lot of little things this past week. – Not so much the fact that I have had to point out a few things to you, but more the time and manner in which I did the pointing. I'm really very sorry sweetheart, and I have already resolved to be more tender and more discreet in my criticisms after this. Will you please forgive my past manners, for I really do appreciate the magnificent effort you are making towards adapting yourself to a new way of life and the sportsmanlike way in which you have accepted my criticisms so far. I think that you are one in a million.

On the brighter side of things, Frank Bangs and I had three blistering games of badminton after supper this evening in which I barely managed to defeat him by a close score. Afterwards we had a beer at the Post Exchange to relax, and now we are going to turn in early for a good night's sleep.

By the way, I have just hatched one of my screwy ideas for some fun. If you really want to see a sight, do drive up to Litchfield to see the Squadron roll in, but don't hang around afterwards. You see, I have an idea that sometime Friday night at the dance at Haight's place I am going to cut in on a beautiful blue-eyed brunette and be so swept off my feet that I shall elope with her immediately after the dance in spite of the fact that she already has a wedding ring on her finger...

Must heigh me off to bed now, so good night my darling wife, and dream of me just a bit as I shall dream of you.

Your ever loving husband, Buster

P.S. Frank Bangs says to be sure to bring a vivacious young lassie to Haight's dance for him. Ask Gina to see what she can do.

From what I made of it, my dad spent two days on this maneuver somewhere in the Berkshires, ended up at the dance at Haight's place, then took the rest of the week off.

At Buster's suggestion, Robin made her way to Litchfield to document the dust kicking roll-in. Dirty as it was, blood and sand were not a part of the action.

What next?

Honeymoon Part II.

Evidenced by notes on my mom's rag content diary substitute; picnics, swimming, sun baths, sleeping in, taking naps.

Honeymoon essentials.

Buster on honeymoon hiatus.

Witness this historical transition: Cavalry to Mechanized infantry.

M3 Scout Cars in rollout formation.

Ready for action: un-ditching rollers in front, weaponry in back.

"Took canoe out on lake and watched a glorious sunset." Horseback riding *"away up Pinnacle Mountain."* Elevation 600 feet. Was the bad hat invited? They played golf and tennis. *"Read funnies after breakfast on lake shore."*

Not surprisingly, this memorable mark in time included stage and cinema, too.

The hit Broadway comedy play, *The Male Animal* (James Thurber and Elliot Nugent), was on tour. The story centers on a "brains vs. brawn" theme: a woman, her husband and her ex-collegiate football hero. Robin was a lucky girl to find both athletic prowess and intellectual curiosity in the essence of my dad.

Paramount's *I Wanted Wings*, starred Ray Milland and William Holden. A 1942 Oscar winner for special effects, it played like a pre-Pearl Harbor propaganda film. Lofty images of aircraft romanticized the pilot's job in a compelling "Oh beautiful for spacious skies" kind of way. An 18-year old Veronica Lake, and her sexy peek-a-boo sweep of blonde hair, nabbed a role that launched her into stardom.

It's been said box office ticket sales spurred an uptick of young men visiting Air Corps recruitment centers. Patriotism grew as a uniting force in the nation's service, six months before Pearl Harbor would seal the deal.

Scores of Hollywood stars put themselves to use in the effort. In real life, Ray Milland applied, but was rejected by the Air Corps. He stepped up in the Pacific to entertain Allied Troops. William Holden served with the Air Corps, and acted in training films, too. Supporting actor, Wayne Morris, in character as a U.S. Army Air Corps recruit went on to become a decorated WWII "F6F Hellcat" Flying Ace!

Admirable as those pilot trainees were, it never occurred to me that my mom wouldn't know how to pilot their Lincoln Zephyr. Why would she? Neither of my grandmothers ever got behind a steering wheel. They'd have a better grip on rein action, buggy whips and bicycles built for two.

On June 27, five days post-wedding, my mom gave it away: *"Driving lesson."* Presumably my dad coached her through jerky starts, stops and grinding gears, his equanimity in overdrive. It took them a week to get around to lesson number two. The day after, she dropped this line on the rag bond: *"Got dent fixed."* Oops. A toilet plunger can make for a fast and cheap repair, though I have no evidence that's how they went about it.

On June 29, the newlyweds packed up and left their honeymoon hideaway in Connecticut. According to some plan Grampy orchestrated, they settled into their official husband and wife love nest in a small apartment at the familiar Groton Inn. It was a fine place for Robin to sit and knit woolens while Buster was on the march, just over four miles south at Fort Devens.

Three days later, without one breadcrumb of detail, my mom dropped this bomb: *"News that Dottie and Bud were married."*

What? When and where?!

Double-Wedding Delight

Chapter Thirty-Three

Did these young brides of 1941 give up diary notes and pick up knitting needles when they wed? In my mom's case, the answer was yes. The detailed record of events that began September 23, 1938 was abandoned. She closed a long chapter in life with this last entry on the rag bond, dated July 8, 1941: *"Wrote Mom. Got B.W.R. wool."*

In the letter to Lelia, I presume she asked for details on new chapter beginnings for Mr. and Mrs. "Bud" McLeod. Then she described her own church ceremony, reception perfection, and a broad sweep of bits about the Connecticut honeymoon, too.

I was stumped on the B.W.R. wool until the nursery song, *Baa, Baa Black Sheep* flipped this light switch: The British War Relief Society of America sent clothing to aid the masses in bombed-out areas. Robin intended to fashion good karma in the form of woolly garments for the relief effort.

As she knit and attended to Buster's comings and goings, bosom buddies from her footloose years wrote to reveal the direction free birds flew. Buster's chums and family from hither and yon chimed in, too.

If there is one certainty about letter writing in the 1940s that still holds true today, a person can trust a mail carrier to deliver no matter the weather. The big difference is content and volume. Imagine a mail table limited to cards and letters, bills and bank statements. I can't remember a time without third class advertising circulars, direct mail catalogs and credit card solicitations in a heap. No one needed a shredder at the ready, the way we do today.

Friends and family wrote from all points. One way or another they'd learned my folks were settled in with a new mailing address at the Groton Inn.

Former Haven housemate and bridesmaid, Joyce Thompson, dropped a line from her summer post in Maine: Camp Hiawatha. She spoke her inquiring mind.

Joyce – Camp Hiawatha, Kezar Falls, Maine – July 4, 1941

Mrs. Forrest Bedford

Groton Inn,

Groton, Mass.

Dear Robin baby.

Enclosed you will find checks to the tune of $22.50, and I'll send you the rest soon. I had the money all for you and then when you left I forgot to give it to you and spent it right away so we have to do things this way now.

Reimbursement for the price of her exquisite bridesmaid dress?

Camp's fine, etc. Please write me and tell me where you are and what are your plans and all about you and Buster and how you like him.

Like under the covers? A dangerously leading question crossed the line into nuptial secrets. A veritable lovers leap from the list of attributes my mom and Joyce bulleted last March, Buster's *"sweet nature, clean mind, high ideals, gentleness and fine moral values."*

And honey I'm sorry this money's so late. Patience in all things.

Dress shopping took place just two weeks ago. Repayment terms were, apparently, etiquette based.

My love to Buster and to you. Please keep us posted and write soon.

Bye dear, love, Joyce

Auntie Alta played it safe writing care of Pelham Manor.

Mrs. Wm. Dixon, 341 Keith Ave., Missoula, Mont. – July 8, 1941 (airmail)

Dear Roberta –

Where are you anyway? I supposed you were at Pelham Manor but Rhea wrote you were going to Groton.

I didn't receive any announcement – so I know nothing about the wedding or you – except that Rhea wrote me.

Surely Robin mailed an announcement first class to the Dixon's Keith Avenue home, with others she hastily hand-addressed on her wedding day.

Did you decide on your silver pattern? If so just what pieces have you?

I haven't heard from Chile in so long. Bud expects to stay until the last of July – I was at a party with Mrs. McLeod last week.

Bud's wish for a delayed call to active service came true, so he could *"fly to see Dorothy!"* Mrs. McLeod didn't have the full scoop, but at least her ear was to the ground and Auntie Alta caught informative tidbits.

Maybe Dorothy will be coming back about that time. Your mother wants her to enter some school for home economics – or interior decoration – or something along that line.

Lelia held out hope that Dottie would find a career path beyond that of homemaker. Not that Grandma understood the "joy" of work, but happiness had a price tag. Besides, Dottie needed something to occupy her time while Bud served.

Now please send me a return air letter – so I will know where you are and what you want, etc.

Love to both, Auntie Alta

Did you receive my wire – the afternoon of your wedding?

An incorrect address possibly delayed the delivery, but there was certain proof of its arrival.

Robin's chemistry classmate, Edna Mann, was enthusiastically at work in a lab in Baltimore; Johns Hopkins. Dream job for a recent Smith graduate who (bless her heart) spent hours with my mom in the Burton Hall science building bonding over beakers and bacteria.

Edna Mann – 1811 Park Ave., Baltimore, Md. – July 10, 1941

Robin dear,

How is married life treating you? It's hard to believe that you've been married almost three weeks! I was really terribly disappointed not to have gotten down for the wedding. As it turned out I probably could have come – for the Friday before the wedding I had a wire from Miss Hill deferring me for another week. But the same afternoon I had a hurried call from friend Richard saying he just had to come out Friday night – but I was going down to Camp Edwards which brought forth an urgent request for a date Saturday morning at 9:00 A.M. Then I went into Providence with him and saw him off on the 11:05 train! Some scramble!!

With beauty and brains, Edna would be a catch for any eligible young man. Recall the lab scene Robin recapped for Buster last February when the girls posed as laboring chemists for the yearbook photographers. *"Two <u>very beautiful</u> photogenic models equipped in earrings, brilliant make-up and long sleeved silk blouses."*

Since I was deferred for a week I've been there [at Hopkins] *the sum total of 5 days – working only 4, and so far I love it! Although routine lab work may sound rather dull, it's really very interesting to trace the course of different people's ailments. I'm in the Brady Urological Institute of Johns Hopkins right under Miss Hill. There are only five of us in the lab including Miss Hill. I go in at 9:00 A.M. and am usually out by 4:30 anyway! On my way in I pick up what specimens there are on the first floor and take 'em up to the lab and put them into the icebox and mubato* (an incubator) *– straight routine urine cultures in the former and gonorrhea in the latter. There's one poor woman who seems to have every kind of bug imaginable in her kidneys and bladder – strep, staph, aerobacter and pyocyaneus, poor woman! However, today only the pyo showed so she seems to be getting better!*

The pitiable woman Edna spoke of had, among other things "aero-bacter" and "pyocyaneus." Aerobacter is an impressive word, but represents normal flora found in the intestinal track of people. Pyocyaneus is a flowery name, but not pretty. It's a bacterial species found commonly in clinical specimens at Edna's fingertips. It causes the blue or greenish color in pus.

Then there's another woman who came in yesterday! The intern came tearing into the lab – roaring his head off. He handed Mrs. T a swab – to examine for Gc. A woman had come into the dispensary – was sure she had gonorrhea – she'd just finished reading deKruil's article in Readers Digest and was sure she had all the symptoms (note: examination by intern revealed she'd never had any intercourse!)

After lunch we collect any more specimens and centrifuge, smear and plate. Mornings we spend reading plates and identifying organisms. It's really a lot of fun. If I'm fairly rapid I can find a few minutes here and there to read journals, etc. Miss Hill has given me a bunch of very interesting ones which lead up to what she is doing. When all the vacations are over – she says I'm going to be helping her. She's really doing some very interesting work with sulfonamide derivations and how they work on bacteria.

As much as "Sulfa" drugs are generic today, how fortunate was Edna to help with research on "sulfonamide derivations" used to treat staph and gonorrhea? In 1941, the application was directed toward military medicine in treating infected wounds.

Auntie Rhea would have killed for it!

She says she thinks it would be interesting for me to be working with her since she is doing some of the work in collaboration with Miss Burt and Miss Anstow. After I finish what I'm doing tomorrow morning I'm going over to the library and do some reference work for Miss Hill. Honestly, she is the most enthusiastic person about her work – she's got me all pepped up!

I have a wonderful room. It's almost huge! I have a big double bed, a couch, chiffoniers, bureau, desk and chair, and an easy chair, and three large windows.

I live with two sisters – one about 65, the other about 50. Then a third sister is here most of the time. They are awfully nice and they certainly feed me well! I've never in my life have eaten such huge breakfasts!

Three sisters? Meaning spinsters? Possibly nuns. No matter, Edna was well-treated, evidenced by this bubbly share:

Miss Hill took us to dinner Sunday night when I arrived – Dinner complete even to the sparkling Burgundy! There's an awfully nice girl in the lab – Elizabeth Packard (Lib). She took me to dinner and the movies Tues. Then last night we went bicycling in the park which is only about four blocks from where I live.

Oh, there's so much to say about Baltimore and the lab, I can't begin to tell you all in one letter! Let me hear from you soon – I still love to get letters, and I'm dying to hear how you are keeping yourself occupied! You'll probably hear more about every-thing as I gradually tell you in future notes – but in the meantime – please write. Give my best to Buster.

Love, Edna

P.S. Five Gram stains used to seem like a lot in good old Burton Hall... but yesterday I made 47 in 35 minutes! Then transferred 24 cultures to various media!

Next, the buck stopped with "Daddy" Skinner presiding over taboo talk. There was trouble in the treasury. He wrote to square dollars and cents. They added up to declassify the cost of my parents wedding, just shy of $2,000. Of course, it is the honor of the bride's parents to foot the bill; so, in keeping with etiquette, they did just that.

L.M. Skinner, Rancagua – Sewell, Chile – July 15, 1941 (airmail)

Dear Roberta –

We have your air letter of the 8th with the bridal picture, telling us that the camera, light meter, filters, film, etc., had arrived safely, but that you were still look-ing for a Braden draft from me for $450.00. There isn't any for $450.00 (Mother and I had a misunderstanding over this and she unintentionally misinformed you. She thought it was for $450.00 but it was really only for $400.00) This $400.00 draft was requested about a month ago to be made out to Miss Roberta Skinner and sent *to Haven House, Smith College, Northampton, Mass. Are you sure you left a good clear forwarding address at Smith?*

The truth is it's been two months since Lelia wrote in her letter of May 14 to say, "*Daddy is sending a Braden Copper Co. Draft this A.M. (having the N.Y. Office send it to you at Smith) of $450.00 (I think it is) to take care of expenses.* Oops. Evidence, in their slow-moving world, it took painful patience, *months*, to correct a financial misstatement.

If you went to the Braden Office in New York last Thursday you doubtless have all this information by now and we hope you have the $400.00 as well. In addition to this, I sent you Braden drafts for $100.00 each, the first of May and the first of June. Did you get both of these? Tell us definitely, as we have had a couple of drafts go astray, and it takes months to trace them, and in the meantime the money is lost so far as we are concerned.

Snap. How lucky are we to live in a brave new world of mobile banking?

Mother also sent you her personal check for $300.00 on May 8th and another for $300.00 more on June 10th. Did you get both of these?

We are now requesting another $500.00 Braden draft to go by air mail to Mrs. N.F. Bedford, Groton Inn, Groton, Mass., together with a $70.00 Braden one from mother, for both of which we would appreciate a definite acknowledgement; not a note to the effect that you got the checks and drafts all OK, for then we have no idea which ones you are talking about; as we feel that we have been sending them rather thick and fast, and are beginning to worry if you are receiving them all.

We are assuming that you have the $400.00 by now, which with the above $570.00 will cover the $969.00 you need to pay off everybody; on the basis that the previous $800.00 (300 + 300 + 100 + 100) is all washed up.

Affectionately, Daddy

Then T. Wayne added a matter of fact note, scouting the best bang for the buck on steamship fare. The fifty-percent student discount would soon expire for the new graduate.

How about catching the Santa Elena leaving N.Y. Aug. 29, arriving Valpo Sept. 16th – Mother would be on vacation then and could come to Valparaiso with me to meet you... if purchased before Sept. 13th, could you get a round trip ticket good for 6 mos., say, at the half fare rate?

When it came to discourse on finance, Grandpa Skinner was all business. Joyce, Edna and Joanie, on the other hand, kept her socially afloat.

Joanie, now situated on Long Island, was *"filthy dirty and hot as anything."* A bandana tied around her head in tough-chick chic, did she model Rosie the Riveter? Six weeks ago, at Smith, the Senior Supper "wanted ads" called for a nearer Army base for Robin. Joanie and her affectionate "puss-puss" (Nat) were on that list, too. He was presently on the march in South Carolina.

J. Fleischer, 664 E. Beech St., Lido Beach, L.I., N.Y. – Friday, July 18, 1941

Robin dear,

Gosh, I was glad to hear from you! It all sounds so wonderful and you sound so happy and I'm so happy for you both, lambs.

But I don't see how you have the steel courage to get yourself up at 5:30 in the morning. It just doesn't sound possible! I can't believe that you, Robin Skinner Bedford, rise with the sun every morning.... And I wonder to myself, would I be able to do that if we married while Nat is still in the Army? But I never get an honest answer!

Recall this request Robin made of Buster in a letter at the end of May: *"Try and find out whether you could get away from camp at night this summer, dearest. It would be awfully lonely seeing you only on weekends..."* Joanie substantiated that Robin clocked practice hours behind the wheel between Groton and Devens, making it possible for the newlyweds to land in each other's arms most nights.

Wish I could tell you something about our plans. I'd adore saying Robin – baby, we're being married in September and you must make immediate arrangements to be there! But gosh – I can't say it any more than when I left school, though perhaps it seems a little bit closer now 'cuz he's a Pfc. with specialist rating and that might get us somewhere – I don't know.

Puss-puss was up for a Fourth of July furlough, still wishing the bestest of every-thing to you, and it was swellegant but over very quickly... I want you both very, very much to come down for a weekend... 'course there isn't very much to do except beach...

I love working. I'm filthy dirty and hot as anything, but I just love doing it. It makes me feel so helpful. I wonder now how I could have loved so lying on the beach all summer.

"Beaching it" was a marker of the "best set." Joanie's return address, Lido Beach, was a fine resort town to do just that. A college graduate in the wait to wed, Joanie reaped the rewards of feeling *"helpful"* at a job that seemingly had little to do with her Smith diploma. A position to support the U.S. Navy from the coastal hamlet would be up-worthy, though I have no evidence her position involved the war effort. I do know the Beach Club held a children's aluminum party, in support of the national drive for strategic metal. Little boys wore pots on their heads like army helmets.

Oh, but I've forgotten to tell you the latest rumor - it's persisted so long that we think it may be more than just a rumor: that the 8th Div. will be transferred to Devens very soon. I'd die of happiness if it were true.

Love and happy-wishes to you both, Joanie

Five days after "Daddy" Skinner wrote to set money matters straight, Lelia replied to Robin's letter with details of Bud's visit and then some.

As if a double-wedding could span two continents, Buster and Bud married the Skinner sisters *on the very same Sunday,* June 22, 1941.

Much ado about getting Dorothy's carnet (a permit for crossing national boundaries) and passport ensued out of necessity. It would boast her new marital status and certify her married McLeod surname.

L.M. Skinner, Rancagua – Sewell, Chile – July 20, 1941 (airmail)

Dearest Roberta and Forrest,

Last Sunday we returned from Santiago from seeing Dorothy and Bud take off for Bueno Aires. It was, as the weather reporter at the airport told us, the most perfect day in two months for a Trans-Andean flight, very clear, sunshiny and calm. We had an air letter Thursday from Bud, saying it was a beautiful and thrilling flight. They had three days there and were to have five in Rio de Janeiro (are still there today). From there they go on to Belem – Trinidad – along the Northern Coast of S.A. to Panama. Bud wants two days there to see the canal and fortifications, then they go northward through Central America with another two days stopover in Mexico City, one at Guatemala City, and four days at Los Angeles, for Dorothy to get her trousseau – then on to San Francisco where Bud wants his California relatives to get acquainted with Dorothy.

That beat a two-part honeymoon in Connecticut that Robin now regretted writing home about.

We have had a very rushing time ever since Bud arrived at the Santiago Airport June 16. We have made three trips to Santiago – so the time he was here in Sewell with us seemed like only a passing moment. It was a very happy four weeks (lacking three days). Every minute so precious! They were married with a civil ceremony – here, June 22, at home with some of our most intimate friends.

Evidence it took Bud less than a week to put a ring on Dottie's finger. As a bride, her wedding portrait looked nothing more than civil.

We served refreshments and went direct to Santiago... and began at once getting Dorothy's passport, public record, her carnet and her Argentine Vise (which we could get on her carnet before passport was issued.) The rest of her Vise's as well as Buds could not be obtained until 10 days later when her passport would be ready. (We can obtain a passport here more quickly than in the U.S.) So we all came back up

Dorothy Skinner McLeod Bridal Portrait June 1941.

to Sewell for the 4th of July dance and celebration. We had invitations to attend the "American Society of Chile" dance in Santiago, but Bud had made so many pleasant acquaintances here in Sewell – he preferred to patronize the Teniente Club dance here in camp.

Like Skeeter, Bud took a liking to the Teniente Social Club.

They were then with us until the following Wed. during which time Dorothy was packing her trunks (to be sent by boat) and then, they returned to Santiago to finish up their necessary vise's. Dad and I again went down last Sat. A.M. and all of us attended a wedding of one of Dorothy's friends here – at 4:00 P.M. and a big dinner celebration at 9:00 P.M. It was 11:45 when we said good-night and we all arose at 6:00 A.M. to get ready to drive to the airport at 7:15. They took off at 8:15 A.M. – 10 min. ahead of schedule, as all the passengers were on hand.

And although overhead compartments were first introduced in the DC-3, no one delayed the flight by trying to shove a trunk up there.

I never will get over being cheated out of our last 10 minutes together!

I'd wager Dottie was thrilled to get the hell out of dodge.

To go back to their wedding, the civil ceremony is the only one that is recorded in S.A. – A church wedding, by a minister, is not recognized and is not binding in this country. People (foreigners like us) have them if they choose – but they must first have the civil ceremony where the family lives, so Bud and we talked it over and he and Dorothy preferred to postpone their church wedding until they arrive in Missoula. Auntie Alta can arrange for it and have Bud's pastor marry them and I have asked her to give a reception at the New Hotel Florence, which opened in June...

Where, on June 16, Walter McLeod showed Auntie Alta the cable from Bud, with news of his safe arrival in Chile.

... Bud has so many relatives on both sides of the house that I imagine it will be a large wedding. And what I feel happiest about – is that his parents will not be cheated out of seeing their only son married and always feel as disappointed as I was, over not seeing you married. We all felt that would take care of the whole situation and both families would feel we had all taken part.

Grandma deconstructed the double wedding conundrum. A June 10 cable from Bud informed of his planned arrival in Santiago. Shortly *after* Bud's cablegram, Robin's *"everything's all settled"* letter, airmailed June 3, arrived. Lelia paraphrased the content... *"saying you were going to push your wedding ahead to the Sunday following graduation."*

She continued... *I then began to talk that I was going to hop a plane and get up there to see you graduate and married and be back here in about three wks. Dorothy said "If you want to go I can manage the maids and the house – I don't want you to feel that Bud's trip prevented you from being at Roberta's wedding."*

But our invitation to come to Chile having been extended to Bud nearly a year ago, I didn't feel quite right to pull off for the states and leave him, even though I didn't have any idea he was going to be married before Dorothy had finished college. Before Bud arrived, Dad told Mr. Turton one day, that I was all jazzed up to go up for your wedding and he replied to Dad "She just can't go – her place is right here, if Bud and Dorothy decide they want to get married, she will be needed here." Dad and I both told him, he and everyone else, who thought Bud was coming to be married, were absolutely crazy – just as though Bud couldn't come down for a trip to see Dorothy and go back without getting married! But they all had a laugh on us, and as it turned out it was a good thing I didn't go - though I will just never get over the fact I didn't get to see you and Forrest married.

So she'd said, more than once. Since *"all had a laugh on us"* Grandma used the humor in it to brush away the hurt. As much as it weighed on her, it's doubtful my mom really cared.

We would have preferred that you wait until December and Dorothy two yrs. to finish College – but we tried to be broad minded and weigh the pros and cons and view things through Bud's and Forrest's eyes. If you each can have – even a year – of happiness together before the boys have to go into active service it will always be a great comfort to you in case the seas separate you later.

And it's true the war would do just that.

We wouldn't want any objection from our side of the family to interfere with your happiness. From the broadcasts it looks as though Forrest will not be released after Dec. I hope Bud won't have to go to training camp for another year. He expects to know soon after he reaches Montana, whether he can get into business for a year. We are hoping they can enjoy the happiness of a little apartment and a taste of their own home life, before he is called.

Your wedding as Auntie Rhea described it, seemed very nice. She expressed it as "Beautiful – Simple - Yet lacking nothing." I think you, as well as us, owe a great deal to Forrest's father and mother for carrying it through for us. It was too bad all the details were heaped upon them. In fact it was rather embarrassing to us and that's why we preferred that you wait until Dec. when I could have assumed the responsibility.

The only person it was *"too bad"* for was Lelia. The senior Bedfords, while mindful of traditions, got to do it up big for their only son. Their way!

I hope we'll be able soon to get the bills for your wedding straightened up as well as what you borrowed from Mr. Bedford! We're waiting for you to reply to Dad's letter of the past week to see if you finally received the $400.00 Braden draft that should have been forwarded you from Smith.

T. Wayne made that clear. Was this the subject of pillow talk?

We want to get both you and Forrest, as well as Dorothy and Bud, your flat sterling service for our wedding gift. We will get cuts of different patterns... but I think both you and us will be fully satisfied handling it that way.

It would gratify Lelia. The "best set" newlyweds would expect it.

We've enjoyed the snapshots you mailed us of yourself and Forrest and are waiting for the album of wedding photo's coming through Braden. We thought the Herald's "bride photo" of you was splendid. You must have been a very sweet bride! I'll be anxious to see your wedding gown when I get back to the States. It looks very attractive in the Herald.

I have no evidence of my parents' wedding announcement, with bridal portrait, in the *New York Herald Tribune*; competitor to the *New York Times* in 1941. I shudder to think the Nathan Bedford Forrest myth was perpetuated through the larger circulation base of the *Herald*. However, her eleven by fourteen Bachrach Studio branded bridal portrait loomed prominently above my dad's dresser in the Crane Road house. Its decorative frame measured nearly two feet tall, a foot-and-a-half wide.

Looking up at her face with my little girl eyes, she appeared to me beautiful as a bride could be.

I'd like to give you both a big kiss. I think we're very fortunate parents to have acquired two such wonderful sons. Wouldn't it be grand if we could all live close together?

My Grandma Skinner's wishful thinking had evolved; "*...making a home for our children...*" was re-fantasized to this impossible dream: "*Wouldn't it be grand if we could all live close together?*"

Roberta Skinner Bedford Bridal Portrait June 1941.

Dad and I had such a happy time palling around with Dorothy and Bud. He seems as though he had always been "one of us," and I'm sure it will be that same way with Forrest. Bud wrote back from Buenos Aires, "It took only a minute for us to create our close friendship – I do feel that I have known you for a much longer time than just a brief period of four weeks."

Four weeks of flitting around did wonders for Grandma. What son-in-law today would find time to walk that line?

Have you gotten your birth certificate, so you can start right in getting your passport and make application for your S.S. reservation?

Minding the business of surrendering her maiden name, there was no debate. For generations the women in our family had followed social norms and shifted their maiden name to the middle, tagging the end with a new surname. My near-Irish twin kept the Bedford name after her marriage in 1985. In my alphabetical experience, Bedford is a name of privilege. It holds a sequential spot toward the front of a line.

The passenger lists are crowded both by boat and air for 6 – 8 weeks ahead. I don't know how many times I have asked about your birth certificate.

For the record, she'd asked *once* about the birth certificate. Her busy mind obsessed over certificates, and they had nothing to do with educational achievement like they do today. She continued:

You will also need a police certification with your finger prints. Health certificate. Vaccination certificate. They don't tell you about the latter, but if you don't bring one they will vaccinate you on ship-board just before reaching Valparaiso.

She'd lectured about the typhoid and small pox injections in her letter of May 12.

Dad wants you to come on the "Santa Elena" sailing form New York Aug. 29th and if you don't begin right soon you won't be able to get passage.

Well a big "abrazo" for you both and all our love to you, Mother

Bubbles and Blues

Chapter Thirty-Four

F amily can be one reason to be grateful for friends a person can horse around with. Take Bill Futch for example, one of Buster's closest childhood chums from St. Pete. As kids, the two boys sharpened their humorous wit like pointed sticks. A life skill I happened to know served them both well into their nineties.

From W.D. Futch Box #3513 Orlando, Fla. – July 22, 1941

Dear Buster and Robin,

Buster, before I get started please explain to Robin that the reason that I write my letters on the typewriter is because I am such a poor penman. Robin, I do realize that it is pretty bad form and is decidedly frowned upon by Emily, to say nothing of Mother. So please don't hold it against me. And besides, consider the paper I save, which is not to be sneezed at in these times of National Defense...

Presently, Bill is an intern in medical school, where poor penmanship is perpetuated.

I have just come back from St. Pete where I spent the weekend. As you probably already know, Bubbles was married on Saturday afternoon. The wedding was held at the Suwannee Hotel (why, I shall never know).

The reason was scandalously obvious. A hotel wedding was appropriate for a groom twice divorced. Their mutual friend, Bubbles, was wife number three to Henry Gassaway Davis, III, a class of 1924 Princeton grad with engineering and business degrees from Columbia. A lucky heir to a mining fortune with presumably no student loan debt.

...Bubbles made a beautiful bride, as everyone expected.

Bubbles, aka Florence Dean Crump, was a Vassar graduate class of 1939 and a Power's Model in New York; a beauty with brains, roots in St. Pete with ties to a prominent Pittsburgh industrial family.

Her husband, Henry Gassaway Davis $$$ (I'm sorry, I meant III), seems to be a pretty nice fellow and quite young considering he has been a husband twice before and a father once...

The inescapable celebrity truth? He was the ex-husband of *two* Vanderbilt heiresses: Grace Vanderbilt (with whom he fathered a daughter) and her cousin Consuelo Vanderbilt Smith.

He won't be caught in the draft, tis rumored. The chawming couple left immejutly after the wedding on an extended trip and will make their home in New York after the first of September.

Now for the final chapter in that thrilling drawmer The Love Life of a Young Interne, entitled There Ain't None. And I ain't kiddin'...

Confiding in Buster, he'd called it quits on his girl.

So it's off and away, high-diddle-day, more fish in the sea, new worlds to conquer... I would have given my right arm to have been at your wedding... please tell me whether married life is all that it's cracked up to be.

Your pal, Bill

Fit to be tied, Auntie Alta wrote my mom again. A wedding announcement was yet to arrive in the Dixon's mailbox. Alta broke with etiquette posting a letter before the courtesy of a reply to her last letter was received.

Mrs. Wm. Dixon, 341 Keith Ave., Missoula, Mont. – July 23, 1941 (airmail)

Dear Roberta:

Why don't you write me – I didn't receive any announcement of your wedding. I wouldn't have known whether or not you are married if Rhea hadn't written me – and if Mrs. McKenzie and Mrs. McLeod hadn't said they rec'd announcements.

Well did Bud and Dorothy surprise you – I thought they might if Bud felt he could assume the responsibility of a wife – with his military duties claiming him.

Was Auntie Alta privy to Bud's intention? Robin recalled Dottie's words of New Year cheer, *"I know we'll be married now as soon as we can."* But I wonder this. In June of 1937, when Auntie Alta and Dix took in their wayward sixteen-year-old niece for the summer, did a nineteen-year-old Bud appear at the stoop like a big-eyed puppy dog? Who had who on a long leash across time zones, September to May, until they reunited in June 1938 and again in 1939? For three Montana summers, Walter and Olive McLeod and the Dixons observed embers of love between Dottie and Bud. Then came the *"huff"* in May 1940; and that triangle with Jack.

Auntie Alta continued with breadcrumbs of insider information:

Neither McLeods nor I know definitely how they are coming but Mrs. McLeod thinks by San Francisco. Dorothy sent me a cable after they were married – said they would be in Missoula August 10.

Circling back to emphasize the real reason for this letter, Alta continued...

Now – <u>I want to know</u> if you have selected your silver pattern – Do tell me what it is and what you have – and <u>all</u> about your wedding presents. If I don't buy yours before Dorothy gets here – I may be broke – Please tell me what you are doing. What are your plans for housekeeping, etc?

Her way of asking where they planned to live?

It won't seem natural for Dorothy to arrive in Missoula and not be at 341 Keith – I know McLeods will be very nice to her. Bud waited to write his parents and ask if they had any objections and they said "none."

Auntie Alta spoke like a forlorn mother, but knew firsthand Dottie's in-laws were good, kind people. At twenty-three, Bud didn't need "permission," but asking for *"objections"* played like a "speak now or forever hold your peace" maneuver. What's a parent to say from six-thousand miles away? Mistakenly I presumed Bud's dad, Walter, paid the airfare and father and son had discussed the plan, man to man. Just as Buster sought an "approved union" from his dad nearly a year ago, Bud looked to Walter for the same.

Fortunately for Alta, the grown Dixon children remained close at hand. Her daughter, Lois, would return from Minneapolis, *"Sunday on the train."* She'd been at the University of Minnesota for a summer course. Also close to home were Bill Jr. and his wife:

Bill and Betty are usually here about two nights per week for dinner. Betty still holds her civil service with U.S. Forestry Dept. She has a good job – several girl assistants. She looks after the purchasing of supplies for the field men.

Auntie Rhea has been about helpless with her foot. She is taking treatments now at a Washington hospital. I feel so sorry for her – she has no one to do anything for her. Do you write her? Please do so. She feels so alone – your letters will cheer her up.

Love to both, Auntie Alta

We have a new DeSoto sedan – a large tropical tan –very light – almost creamy – "fluid drive" etc. We like it very much.

As much as Auntie Alta suggested they may go broke over sterling flatware, the new four-door family DeSoto (a division of Chrysler) was nothing to sneeze at. At $1,085, it was one of the bestselling medium-priced cars on the market. With a sleek rocket-body and trademark "waterfall" chrome grille it was a looker on the outside and something for gearheads to behold under the hood, then and as a classic car today. Powered by a straight six-cylinder engine, with the optional two-speed Fluid Drive and

"Simplimatic" Transmission, it rolled smoothly out of the garage onto Keith Avenue, Uncle Dix behind the wheel.

Did they have an inkling Chrysler would suspend civilian operations in the coming year, until the war ended? The timing of their purchase was impeccable.

Back in the northeast, Robin and Buster, too, were grateful to have their '39 Zephyr. Unbeknownst to Auntie Rhea, Robin's energy for letter writing was enthusiastically invested in Pelham Manor.

Mrs. Nathaniel L. Bedford 1283 Manor Circle, Pelham Manor N.Y. – July 24, 1941

Dear Robin:

You and Buster have been wonderful about writing to us. We appreciate it very much for we can never hear too often. I hope that this does not sound selfish – It really is not, for parents are just that way. They naturally are interested in every <u>thing</u> that concerns their children. We are always anxiously waiting to hear and hope that life shares its best with you.

Tuesday we mailed news and pictures (newspaper) of the Crump-Davis wedding.

Bill Futch's humorous commentary on Bubbles Crump's nuptials was far superior to the clipping Grammy sent. The formal news narrative was a weighty best set 1941 social statement naming all names on the guest list, worthy of extra postage. Nearly a full page in the St. Petersburg Times was occupied with a collage of dramatically lit black and white photos circling a dwarfed passport size mug of Henry G. Davis III, who sported an unceremonious necktie. In bridal portrait pose, a striking dark haired, red-lipped Bubbles wore pearls and a girdle that pinched under a gown of white satin. It made her head look big. Chantilly lace bodice, hooped skirt and long train defined 1941 fashion. In another pose, set upon a wicker love seat the bride was flanked stage right by her flower girl, who fingered a ruffled basket filled with white rosebuds. To her left, a half-pint ringbearer sported a white satin sun suit. Under the brides nose he displayed a satin box sized for a vest pocket he lacked. Smiling bridesmaids wore poufy short-sleeved frocks of white marquisette and (rather corny, but apparently chic) white net heart-shaped bonnets. Luckily oversized bouquets became fashionable in the 1920s and remained popular up until WWII. Mid-sections hid behind colonial bouquets of gold and silver sea oats. No one would notice their belly bloat from a buffet luncheon at the Chatterbox just hours before the ceremony.

All the fuss over fashion led Bubbles to an improvised altar banked with palms and white candles. A décor that explained why Bill Futch called the choice of venue at the Suwanee into question.

Grammy's letter of July 24 continued with a subject shift to more personal overarching family concerns.

We rec'd a letter from Buster written in the field. I do hope his transfer will arrive shortly for these trips are going to get longer and harder. Have him phone as soon as he hears.

Future phobia? That fear of the unknown to come. The senior Bedfords wont for company.

If Buster gets a 4 day furlough let us know what you two want to do. Come home or go on a trip with us.

Does my mom hold her breath, wishing for time alone with Buster? She is unaccustomed to parents so close at hand. It was logistically simple to ignore her own controlling mother who ran her life by letter for so long.

We are interested in all the little things that in any way concern you however small they may seem to you. Our only wish is for your happiness and success in all your married life. Love from us both. Your loving, Dad and Mom

Mrs. Frank Huntington, 212 E. Howell Ave, Alexandria Va. – July 26, 1941

Mrs. Roberta Bedford

Groton Inn

Groton, Massachusetts

Dear Roberta –

Seems strange to address an envelope to you as Mrs. I don't know Buster's first name so will have to address it Roberta.

Emily Post was haunting Auntie Rhea with a difficult choice. Nowadays no one thinks twice about addressing correspondence using a married woman's first name. Not so in 1941. Stationery at the ready, Rhea reasoned it was reprehensible to use a nickname like *Buster*. She uncomfortably penned *Mrs. Roberta Bedford* and wasted the first sentence explaining her decision to do so.

You must still consider the Huntington's your guardians.

Do brides have guardians? That's a push-me-pull-you moment. In her heart, Rhea was as protective of Robin as the senior Bedfords were of Buster but hadn't the means to offer more than anemic emotional support. A poor stick of a widow in person and in pocketbook.

Was glad to get your stingy little note and know you had such a nice "honeymoon." Hope such happiness will always be in store for you.

The senior Bedfords would see to that.

Alta writes me Dottie has followed her Sister's example... expects them in Missoula August 10th, Bud has to go to camp Sept. 1st... does not know where. I wish the future looked more settled for both of you girls. Such an upset world as we are living in and every day makes it seem as the U.S. is getting in deeper and deeper. I wish we had a few more, or many more like "Wheeler and Lindy."

Time out to pick apart that turn of phrase. Both Burton K. Wheeler, democratic senator from Montana, and Charles Lindbergh, aka "Lucky Lindy" were vocal isolationists. Aunt Rhea's desire was not out of the norm, wishing for a few more years of *"Wheeler and Lindy."* She and Roy sensed the tension at the heart of the nation; the whirl in Washington.

Then Rhea put the hammer down on my mom's lack of written correspondence.

Roberta, why don't you write Alta – said she wrote you two letters to Pelham Manor and I think she sent one to Groton Inn and never a word. Why didn't you acknowledge her graduation gift? She is writing you trying to find out what you would like her to send you for a wedding gift. If you treated me that way I would just forget all about you.

Then this extra poke:

Roberta please do not think I am trying to tell you what you must do, but I wonder if you have even written Bill Charles about your marriage.

An obliging boy who lived with his parents in Amsterdam, Bill Charles never ranked on the man score. He was acknowledged once in a blunt diary entry nearly three years before. It was the day of Orson Welles' *War of the Worlds* radio broadcast: *"Breakfast with Bill. Walked for a while then put him on bus. Thank God! He is so uninteresting – grrr."* But, Auntie Rhea made this point:

You know he was so nice to you as well as his family and they were so thoughtful of Uncle Frank and Roy during all our trouble of sickness and deaths last year. If you haven't written him may I suggest you send him a friendly little note telling him, as long as you did not send out any announcements? He will hear of it sometime and I am sure coming direct from you will make a better feeling.

The poor stick continued, oversharing more on the heel saga. It's not pretty. Nor is the housing market in a mushrooming D.C. area, revealed by this eye-witness account:

I am still having trouble with this foot – almost three weeks ago I went to the hospital, they made an incision and burned the side of my heel off and on with an electric needle and it just will not heal up. Wish I had left it as it was when up to your wedding, I could hobble around with an old shoe on, now can't wear any kind of a shoe. I am so discouraged over the thing. This whole summer has been spoiled on account of this. I can't get out to look for a house and there is nothing to be had here or in Washington - about 5,000 new people coming here every week for this defense work. Hotels are all full and can't even get a room. Men and women gov't employees are doubling up four in a room. This place is up for sale. I have thought some of storing furniture and going to Montana with Alta, yet I know I would not be satisfied and happy there. I just despise it down here. So hot in summer and cold and damp in winter.

Not to mention their proximity to sirens and soot of the fire station and that hot mess of the Pot Yard.

Roy is kept busy, so much writing and chasing legal people trying to settle up Daddy H's wee, small estate. Talk about red tape – that is a case where it sure comes in. He did not leave a will and everything has to go through court proceedings.

At least Roy had the brains to manage it. Had his own father, Frank, not finished the game so fast, he'd be first in line for the task.

I don't hear a word from your mother. Did you write her all about your wedding? I wrote her I liked Buster very much. I tried to tell her how efficient a woman Buster's mother was and how everything was just perfection. She deserves credit for putting over such a wonderful wedding in such a short time.

Witnessed before God, family and friends, there would be no run-of-the-mill "furlough" wedding under Grammy's watch. Her imprint: tasteful, intimate, memorable.

Roberta you looked so sweet and pretty the night of your wedding. Don't think ever again that Dottie has anything on you for looks. If you could and would try to improve your (B+) carriage you would just be handsome. Such a pity your own parents could not have had your wedding for you or at least been present. I thought all that week maybe Lelia would hop a plane and be there, but I suppose Dottie and Bud took all their time and attention.

Yes. They did.

Pity a heavy-hearted Rhea in this next bit of narrative. On a side trip to their former hometown of Amsterdam, she had visited with the neighborhood network.

I have been so blue and unhappy ever since being up around Segebarths and old friends. They have their house fixed up so nice now. Just brought back old memories of Frank's and my happiness. Roy thinks I ought to be able to just think of them as of the past but I can't.

Roy was too young to appreciate old connections and comradery as an aging person would. But I can attest it is the bullseye explanation of why my parents eventually retired to the continuing care complex of Franciscan Oaks, just over a mile from the Crane Road house. They were able to retain friends, the Community Church connection, their membership in the Mountain Lakes Club, familiar doctors and shopping habits of a lifetime. These next generation "old folks' homes," are everywhere today with excellent food and plenty of activities. Strategic marketing targets the "best set" often with the (literal) buy-in of successful children. Guilt-free peace of mind for every member of the family.

Personally, I'm a proponent of aging in place.

This pesky heel has worried me almost "dippy." I have had visions of having to have my whole leg amputated.

More than stinky feet, are there other odors due to tissue breakdown? In addition to Edna's enthusiasm for "sulfonamide derivations" at Johns Hopkins, it was hopeful (but not helpful) that human trials on the use of penicillin for treating bodily infections were underway in 1941. The poor stick was nearly four months into this nasty infection with no relief in sight. Chronic pain was reason enough to be *"blue and unhappy."*

It hurts me so when the doctor dresses it. Roy has been a peach to wait on me, but I know he is getting tired of it after all these weeks and months.

Love, Auntie Rhea

On a bubbly note, and true to my mom's word, lots of weddings had taken place since graduation day. Corny as a 1941 classic movie scene, recall she wrote Buster: *"June is certainly a wonderful month, isn't it?"* A thank you note from former housemate, Fuzzy, revealed a best set wedding gift of a silver plate. Then bosom buddy Ruth Smith confessed this:

August 1, 1941

Dear Robin,

It is good to hear news from the eastern part of the state and to know that so far no ardent M.P.'s have captured you and dragged you away because you are driving without a license. Frankly, I have been doing the same here all summer, and so far I have escaped detection – and detention.

Naughty newlyweds. Mark my words someone is going to get caught.

I don't suppose one writes a letter of thanks for the party, when the "party" was a wedding. But Walter and I both had an awfully good time and we wanted to tell you so. Unfortunately I had misbehaved so badly over the champagne at Fuzzy's wedding that I didn't dare go to extremes at yours. Emily Post is right in her description of the "bridal glow."

Hopefully Ruth was a happy drunk, not too sloppy. It's fair to say no one is exempt from life lessons learned from personal experience they'd just as soon forget.

I can tell you *Jose Cuervo* is no friend of mine.

Ruth continued her assessment of the way Robin was living, and insightfully shared how she survived as a married woman.

You certainly are living a strenuous life with the double existence Buster shares between camp and town. I suppose when you get used to it six o'clock in the morning isn't so unlike any other hour of the day, but I still think of it as the "quiet time" when only truck drivers and farm hands are on the road.

Personally, I prefer being on the road alone with truckers. They know *how* to drive. My mom and Ruth lack so much as a learner's permit.

As a new bride, Ruth also confessed this: *"I have found the secret of feeling less inly."*

"Inly," an old expression? Meaning inward and obligated. How does a wife in 1941 free her spirit? In the equanimity of ironing her linen largesse from a bridal shower two year ago?

Nope!

Surround yourself with a dozen books half-read and forget the letters to be written, and the mending to be done. Have you read Maurois' biography of Shelley or any of his others? It is the pleasantest way of getting familiar with famous people I know.

She went on to ask if my mom was reading *"Kant's list."* Immanuel Kant, a German philosopher, wrote of perpetual peace in an essay dating to the year 1795. *"The law of world citizenship shall be limited to conditions of universal hospitality."* His philosophical thought was on point in 1941. Forty-four years later, in 1985, recall the Grammy Award winner for African Relief written by Michael Jackson and Lionel Ritchie. *"We are the world, we are the children, we are the ones who will make a brighter day so let's start giving."* Same Kant-like message delivered with hopeful heart nearly two centuries later.

Call me an aging hippie, but it's impossible to ignore the worth of social consciousness taught through song.

Moving from one subject of millennia to another, recall that Grampy Bedford, at age sixteen, made a reasoned decision to leave the Georgia home of his step-father and, sadly by association, his own mother Katie. I believe his cornbread-fed half-brothers grew to dislike their father. They, too, moved south to Florida. Like a shadow, my great-uncle Bill took a job with the American Book Company where Grampy, thirteen years his senior, showed him the ropes.

Where am I going with this?

Somehow Buster's wedding announcement, published in the St. Petersburg Times, made its way north to Jacksonville. Busybody Bill sent the clipping further north to Savannah where Grampy's cousin "Phete" lived.

Phete, in turn, flipped this reminiscence. To match his words with a drawl, conjure the multi-award winning classic film set in the 1940s,

Driving Miss Daisy. Generalizing the level of intelligence of people with a southern accent is not uncommon but it is ignorant at best. Nudging my attention past the dialect to the subject matter, the literacy of his letter is irreproachable.

Mr. Nathaniel L. Bedford
Manor Circle
Pelham Manor, N.Y.

August 5, 1941

Dear Nat, -

In a round-about way, we received, a few days ago, the first news that we have had of your family in a long, long time. It was a clipping from a Jacksonville paper telling of Buster's marriage.

When I think of other days (and I am getting old enough to think of them quite frequently now!) it seems passing strange that the word of so auspicious an event in which <u>you</u> are so vitally concerned should have had to reach us in that way.

By his insinuation of age, my grandfather must be his cousin removed a degree or two.

How is it possible that the baby boy – the first grandchild of that old family circle – welcomed so tenderly and doted on through babyhood to manhood – could get so out of touch with that ever-narrowing circle? Those three families of the Patot sisters were always just like one, you know, until your generation came along.

For me, Phete raised this question. In sands shifting through the hourglass, are we all born to sell the next generation short due to differences in values and attitudes? Hopefully Grampy looked at Phete through a generational lens and laughed.

And who were the Patot sisters?

Catherine Patot, my great-great grandmother, was mother of the widowed Katie, my Grampy's birthmother. She was the eldest of four Patot daughters: Catherine, Mary Isabel, Emma and Sophia. They also had a younger brother, Stephen. I have no evidence anyone along that line ever left the Peach state, but everyone who knows the geography of the eastern seaboard understands it's a straight shot south from Savannah to Jacksonville. Residents of either state bear distinctive southern charm and character.

Provided they govern themselves with civility.

Whatever the cause, whether intentional, or due to pressure of many things, I want you to know that the love of the older ones who can still <u>remember</u> is ever yours; and I am sending for them all our felicitations to the young couple, and to you and (my Grammy) Ethel. May you, indeed, be only gaining a daughter – the happiest wish I could make for you!!

Lovingly, Cousin Phete

Partial as I am to my Yankee roots, Phete's verbal anointing was a lesson in the expected courtesies of the American South. Whether Grampy cared to hear from his cousin, I have no idea. But one thing for certain, Phete was a novelty. His genteel voice was like no other boxed in the back of the closet.

Hot, Cold and Dizzy

Chapter Thirty-Five

Mrs. Forrest Bedford, Groton Inn, Groton, Mass. – Wednesday 5:00 P.M., August 14, 1941

Dearest -:

It's been so warm over here today – Jeannie and I have just sat around – with both cars in the garage. Ours is getting simonized for $4.50 – 'cause it's so new and most of the dirt is just dust.

Presumably "the garage" is air conditioned and came as a relief from sticky August heat and humidity. As for simonized? At the time the auto cleaning product line, Simoniz®, had been "verbified" as much as Google (verb form "googled") is today. America's first car wax company was a household name. An effective print and radio ad campaign had motorists everywhere talking about the remarkable new Liquid Simoniz® Cleaner in 1941. The paste form required old fashioned elbow grease. Liquid or paste, this was a man's job, and Robin had shopped around to find the best price at the Socony station... *"two other garages wanted $6.00 and $7.50."*

For those too young to know, <u>Socony</u> was the abbreviated name for <u>S</u>tandard <u>O</u>il <u>Co</u>mpany of <u>N</u>ew <u>Y</u>ork. Socony was born of a 1911 anti-trust ruling of the U.S. Supreme Court calling for dissolution of John D.

Rockefeller's Standard Oil empire. Thirty-four "baby Standards" flew out of the monopoly bust like baby spiders parachuting after a hatch. Standard Oil of New Jersey was smartly branded Esso (phonetic version of the oil giant's initials, S.O.) The *Happy Motoring* service station, near the Crane Road house, was dear to my folks. Esso's bicep flexing Bengal championed the "Put a Tiger in your Tank" ad campaign in the 1960s. The mascot alone would earn my parents' patronage, but the service was exceptional, too. With every fill-up a cheery attendant would wash the windshield and check under the hood: oil, hoses and belts.

I decided I'd forgo the puppy, honey – I talked to Mrs. Carter – and she told me of her experiences with one out in the Philippines where they had tile floors. She said it kept one houseboy busy all the time keeping little puddles mopped up. But she said if I could keep it out of doors it would be alright.

My Bedford grandparents often wrote news of their dog, Rancy. Pets were a warm and fuzzy part of the family fabric. It explained how I captivated Grammy and Grampy with my cemetery tours in the woods bordering the Crane Road house. The desire to invite a four-legged furry into my parents' newly-created family nest came as no surprise.

Presumably Mrs. Carter was the Groton Innkeeper, and rental restrictions around pet ownership were yet to be invented. She effectively poured cold water on this moment of puppy-love without saying no. Mom vacillated. Would Buster be disappointed? She signed off with this:

I saw a carpenter today in Groton. Maybe he'd fix us a dog house out of an orange crate or something... The other morning en-route home (from Devens) *at 6:20 I went to see how the puppy slept and they just put a piece of canvas over 'em. Guess I'll go see him.*

Could she see past her nose? A dog housed in an orange crate outside in a Massachusetts winter?

Lelia, who was presently afflicted with cabin fever, might set her straight on that point. With Robin's trip to Campamento Americano still on the table, there would be no one to care for the pup.

L.M. Skinner, Rancagua – Sewell, Chile – August 14, 1941 (airmail)

Dearest Roberta –

We are just emerging from one of the worst blizzards Sewell has ever known. We had just such a winter in 1914 then again in 1926 and now again in 1941.

It's true. A winter storm had pounded central Chile for the last eight days. Three Chilean workers were killed, and several houses were demolished when an avalanche struck the El Teniente camp.

Who dared shovel the stairs?

We are so thankful Bud and Dorothy got started just when they did so as to avoid it and it will be the beginning of spring when you arrive in September. We haven't had a letter from you saying you were definitely coming and therefore there are two things that make us anxious about just what your plans are.

Here we go again.

First Buster's Mother didn't mention you coming in her letter last week and yesterday I received one from Auntie Alta and she said she had just had a letter from you (after she had written you twice) and she didn't mention it either. It will be a disappointment to us if you aren't coming. Since Dorothy and Bud left we are counting on having you with us. There is one thing I want to impress upon you in this letter. In case you aren't coming on the Santa Elena you must be advising Grace and Company, so you won't be charged for your passage. They have a waiting list of passengers and in case someone cancels the first on the waiting list gets their reservation, but anyone in the waiting crowd needs time to get their papers etc. in order.

Did they wait for word by telephone, or telegram? Lucky us with our text messages today.

We haven't received a letter from you for at least 21 days. Your last was written July 25. Where we thought we had impressed upon your mind to keep in touch with us, we thought you would send us at least a note on each airplane – keeping us posted as to your plans, Buster's plans, and how you were making out with all your preparations.

Robin <u>was</u> busy. She proved herself to *new* parents with notes and letters, kept house, cooked, knit, had the car simonized, drove Buster to and from Devens, and waffled over a puppy. Was she dogged by the decision? Yes. She was caught in a procrastination trap. Lelia went on like my mom would step off the steamship tomorrow.

When your boat is pulling up alongside of the dock in Valpo – have your packing done ahead of time so you can be out on deck. It took about ½ hr. before we could go on board when Dorothy and Russell's boat pulled in and all the other passengers were up on deck and Russell and Dorothy never did get up out of their staterooms – they were packing. We thought sure one of them was ill. (Lelia, at least, convinced herself that was the case.) *We had to go hunting down the hallways for their rooms.*

I have been wondering whether there could have been a second sheet to the typewritten sheet of shopping I sent you last June... Based on recall, items were missing. Brand loyalties came to light as she repopulated the list. Mentholatum®, an aromatic ointment of menthol and camphor, is still around today. A salve topically used for muscle and joint pain, and as a chest rub to relieve congestion. She specified a *large* jar.

Then another thing I've thought of since writing you is a birthday card for Bud and one for Auntie Alta, both their birthdays come in Oct... if you aren't coming get those and send them boat mail right away, will you? You won't need to bring any Arrid – nor nail polish. Dorothy left a lot of those. If you have any extra space you might bring Kotex. I wrapped them in tissue paper and tucked in corners.

Curse, the curse! Worse than the Kolax pads was the stringy pin-and-belt harness used to hold them in place. When I received my first *You're a Young Lady Now* pamphlet, compliments of Kimberly Clark, I redefined mortified. Later in my teens, The Boston Women's Health Book Collective published my go-to guide, *Our Bodies, Ourselves*. That publication has since circled the world informing and uniting women in multiple languages.

Daddy would like a box of Beemans pepsin gum...

Recall I learned firsthand Juicy Fruit was Grampy Bedford's chewing gum of choice. Now I discover Beeman's pepsin was my grandfather Skinner's top pick. Whether or not Lelia prescribed it as a digestive aid for acid reflux doesn't matter anymore. What's important is the synchronicity of their taste buds in my world. Those wrappers, folded in amongst others, contributed to my colorful thirty-or-so-foot origami gum wrapper chain. It occupied the nightstand drawer next to my bed in the Crane Road house with other especially important papers; an impressive collection of too many to name concert ticket stubs.

Teens can be so weird in their normalcy. Presumably my sister Dianne chucked the contents of that drawer without a second thought to make room for her own grownup stuff, the year she moved back into the Crane Road house.

We could use several boxes of Sucrets or Luden's cough drops. I wrote to Miss Gluck in the Corset Dept. at Bloomingdales and told her to have an artist's model girdle #36 waiting for you to pick up for me. You pay for it, I don't know exactly how much they are now. The ones last year were $10.00 each. You might bring a box of Elizabeth Arden paste rouge – Blond. Also two bottles of Chlorazene gargle tablets (100 to a bottle) from any drug store. When you pack turn my girdle inside out so the brocade doesn't show up so plainly, as there is a heavy duty on anything with silk threads in.

Grandma put my mom up to girdle smuggling!

Keep your cases in your stateroom until the Braden man comes on board. He helps get all Braden peoples things through the customs. Declare all your baggage as personal effects. Don't list things as dutiable on the customs sheet you have to fill out.

Love to both, Mother

P.S. Dorothy and Bud arrived in Missoula Monday. Mr. McLeod gave them a car and they were going to drive from San Francisco. Mrs. McLeod and Olive (Bud's sister) are giving a big reception for Dorothy today from 3-6. Auntie Alta is going to give an evening reception for them.

Robin's twenty-one-day gap in correspondence with Campamento Americano was validated by the fact she often wrote to my dad at Devens.

Opening lines revealed just how young and in love they were: *"How are you, sweetheart? I miss you terribly – it seems like ages since you left this morning."*

She'd best adopt bosom buddy Ruth Smith's advice and surround herself with a dozen books, to include a self-help on defeating procrastination.

"I wrote Mother a long letter this morning – answering all her questions – those she's asked for the past month – then did some shopping for her in Fitchburg – little odds and ends on her list."

How else did my mom occupy herself? Visiting with friends: *"Nancy and I will probably drive in and see Jeanie tomorrow afternoon – and I'll even try to wiggle my ears for the baby like you do."*

My mom was not gifted like my dad (and me) with the ear-wiggling gene.

She continued, imagining Buster in the field on maneuvers.

"It's almost time for you to come home now – I'm going to miss you terribly tonight – You're such a wonderful husband Buster – and so good to me that I'm awfully lonely when you're not around. Married life is just so happy with you, dear – and I love you more and more every day."

The truth is she would miss Buster terribly more than a few nights. Snap. She had left for Pelham Manor. The long-debated trip to Chile was set.

"I paid for my ticket, ordered film which they are tropically wrapping for me, got my vise from the consul O.K., found $300.00 more from the family waiting for me – along with a few more things to get – and having worn myself out thoroughly – came home to pack one trunk. Your Daddy is just wonderful about packing trunks – he kept me moving 'till it was packed."

Like so many other things, I wager Grampy Bedford's trunk packing was self-taught. He gained experience alongside shipmates. Did he avert his eyes or leave the room when she tucked Kotex in the corners?

"It was wonderful to hear your voice over the phone – yet awfully sad too – 'cause I do so want to be with you. Even if you could get away for Friday, honey – it would seem like a dream where I'd only wake up to find you gone again."

A well-meaning Haven-mate sent *"a tremendous box of pecan nuts – to prevent my feeling miserable on board. Mother says that's an excellent remedy for such ills."*

Like many nuts, pecans are packed with nutrition, but for motion sickness? Maybe better for bowel function... *"also crackers – I'll give you one guess what I'll be eating the first 2+ hours out."*

Pray she sticks with crackers. Starchy and salty. Personally, I prefer ginger.

Her next letter to Buster revealed Lelia was spot on when it came to moving about in New York. *"I went into town on the train today – and did a little more shopping – the way things look now I'll have to come back down on Monday, dear. This shopping really takes days and days in New York City honey – you've no idea how tired I was today after just three hours of it – standing around waiting for people to wait on you."* She went on to say: *"Gina phoned and wants to have lunch with me tomorrow. She and Diz want to give me a party before I sail – I do hope your orders come thru this weekend and then you'll be able to see me off."*

The clock was ticking, Buster wrote back fast c/o Pelham Manor:

PVT N.F. Bedford, Fort Devens, Ayer, Mass. – Tuesday afternoon, August 19, 1941

My Beloved,

Here I am, "somewhere in New Hampshire," thinking of you. So far our manoeuver has not been too good, our battle against General rain having occupied more of our time than our enemy.

Then this hint of mother-in-law trouble. More psychological moments?

How is life at Pelham proceeding? Are we doing any better now? I sincerely hope so, for it would complete my happiness if you and Mother could become accustomed to each other and get along together well. Please make every effort, dear.

No more news yet about my transfer. I think that you had better come up Friday in time to meet me at 5:30. If my transfer comes through we can drive down together, if not we can have the weekend to ourselves and also Monday and Tuesday of next week...

Buster on field radio detail, summer 1941.

Till Next We Meet

Chapter Thirty-Six

PVT N.F. Bedford, Fort Devens, Ayer, Mass. – Wednesday, August 27, 1941 (special delivery)

My beloved,

My brain is still in a whirl, dearest, and I don't know just what to tell you. This whole business of you having left for Chile still seems unreal to me – I can't believe it. Even though I know the odds are against it, I just can't imagine not being with you in New York tomorrow night. Not until days without you close around me and leave me with a bare existence will I fully realize my loss. It is like the setting of the Polar sun – you can't believe it is gone, really, and that it won't be back for long, long months. I'm waiting for the sunrise.

I have no idea what he personally knew of the polar sun. But in his mind's eye it was the upper edge of the sun disappearing below the horizon into the polar night. And the darkest hour just before dawn? To date, it would be longer than any other in his life.

Symbolically referencing her changing latitude, he continued...

But while the Polar sun is down below the horizon, as you will be, the deepness of the night is made unbelievably beautiful by the Aurora Borealis, the flashing of the Northern Lights. Just so, my sweetheart, I do hope you will keep my night occasionally beautiful by your letters and the excellence of their contents.

Have a good time, my dear, but do gain something permanent from your trip and every second of your absence keep my heart locked within your own so that you will think of me and will know that I am thinking of you.

Then falling far short of my expectation for a romantic close: *More practical advice to follow later by air mail, but keep this note of my undying love close to you always.*

Your own loving Buster

He wrote to his parents at Pelham Manor early the next morning:

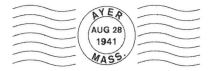

PVT N.F. Bedford, Fort Devens, Ayer, Mass. – Thursday, August 28, 1941 (airmail)

Dear Folks,

Here it is shortly after 6:00 A.M. and already we are out in the field. I'm afraid that all hope of my getting down to see Robin off is gone. It doesn't look as though I would even be home again until I am moved down to Monmouth.

The Signal Corps School at Fort Monmouth was a nerve center of the new U. S. Army in Red Bank, New Jersey. It was located just north of where my folks played in the waves a year ago in Long Branch, on the day Buster proposed. Men like my dad were selectively chosen and sent to learn tactics and techniques of signal communication and the transmission of messages by radio. And carrier pigeon! (In fact, it was the only pigeon breeding and training center in the country.)

Upon completion of their Officer Candidate Course, the men trained at Monmouth were assigned to military units all over the country. How lucky would my dad be to rate a trip to a post so close to home?

He continued with reassuring words for Grammy and Grampy:

Don't worry about me, though. I am feeling fine except for the fact that I already miss Robin very much.

What did he miss exactly? Anyone who's been truly in love has experienced that irrational, magnetic pull when separated from their one true love.

So far we are off to a good start as far as the weather is concerned and our manoeuver shows signs of being an interesting one. I'll write as often as I can and will telephone as soon as I hear any news.

Must get this letter in the mail now. Will write Robin via Air Mail care of her ship. Kiss her good-bye for me and tell her to take good care of herself.

Your loving son, Buster

PVT N.F. Bedford, Fort Devens, Ayer, Mass. – Thursday, August 28, 1941 (airmail)

Mrs. N. Forrest Bedford
S.S. Santa Elena
Grace Lines Pier
New York, N.Y.

My beloved,

I'm sorry that I couldn't make the boat, dearest, but even the Major could not do anything for me this time in the face of a Regimental order forbidding all passes and furloughs except in emergencies. The sergeant major of the regiment thought you sailing wasn't an emergency.

In the bigger scheme of the *new* U.S. Army, other than my dad, who would argue that point?

As long as you are on your way, we might as well try to make the best of it. Don't worry about me, dear, for I will get along all right even though I do miss you terribly already. Have a good time, keep your eyes open, and, as long as I can't be with you, try to make your trip as enjoyable as possible for me by your word pictures of what you see and do. I, in turn, will try to be with you as much as possible in my thoughts and my letters.

If you don't get at least as many letters from me as there are air mails you will know that I am out on manoeuvers where I can't reach a mail box.

Take good care of yourself and remember that you are more precious to me than anything else in this world. I don't know what I would do without you.

Your own loving Buster

Onboard S.S. Santa Elena - Grace Lines – Friday, August 29, 1941

Dearest One –

Here we all are, on board deck and missing you very, very much. Your beautiful roses just make Cabin 128 a paradise in comparison to a cell – and every time I look at them I get an awful lump in my throat.

Buster's calling card accompanied the flower delivery. His handwritten note read: *"With <u>oceans</u> of love to <u>Mrs.</u> Nathaniel Forrest Bedford from <u>Mr.</u> Nathaniel Forrest Bedford...Bon Voyage, sweetheart, and may these show just a small part of my love for you."*

Robin's letter continued...

Darling I do so wish you could be here, but I know it would be just heartbreaking. Trains get out of sight so much faster – and you don't feel that awful wringing at your heart strings as you wave goodbye to someone you love. Maybe it was better this way – 'cause I'm an awful cry baby.

Mommy and Dad (Bedford) have been just wonderful to me – getting packed and finishing shopping – I don't know how I'd ever have gotten here today if it hadn't been for them. Mother brought a tremendous basket of fruit and jelly, etc. on board for me – and Daddy gave me a corsage of gardenias – he's such a great guy.

Oh honey I miss you so – but you've been so sweet about writing letters. I hope I can do as well – I'll try real, real often –

New York Harbor bustled that Friday, August 29. It was the new normal, as supplies were frantically loaded aboard boats of all sizes for transport to the European allied powers. Explosive-laden vessels filled with ammunition and fuel were afloat, within easy incendiary reach of the *Santa Elena*.

The ship pushed away from Pier 57, then churned past Ellis Island without incident. Lady Liberty, that universal symbol of freedom and democracy, soon disappeared in the distance.

In news out of Tokyo that day, United Press reported that the Premier Prince of Japan had reached out to Washington. He considered negotiations between the U.S. and Japan necessary to "usher in a permanent peace in the Pacific."

Yet the attack on Pearl Harbor was exactly one-hundred days away.

In the hills of Massachusetts and New Hampshire, Buster gave his all to the war games. Men on the move with horses and mechanized units fought by day and night. They tested strategic reconnaissance, artful methods of camouflage, and after-dark operations. Thousands of army vehicles used "blackout lights" on backcountry roads. Unlike real warfare, it was another short-lived sham. Back at Devens on Sunday night, he wrote... *"I doubt if that empty feeling in my heart will ever be gone until you have come back to me."*

As safe as Campamento Americano was, under the thumb of Lelia and T. Wayne, my mom would test the equanimity of her *"wonderful husband."* Buster had told her point blank she was *"a little immature and undependable"* just eight days before their wedding. Now, nearly ten weeks into the evolution of holy matrimony, this bride of 1941 was about to prove him right.

Possibly the untold reason she advised me to "think about it" when a man proposed.

Acknowledgements

The author acknowledges the brilliant individuals who made this publication possible. My editor and friend, Stacy Dymalski, "The Memoir Midwife," for her inspiration to shape this book (and its sequels) from the moment she recognized the story behind the letters. To Katie Mullaly, who tackled her own mid-life career-changing leap from the public sector to excel as an author and publisher, I credit the interior design of this book with gratitude for her savvy technical direction. To Michelle Rayner, Cosmic Design, thank you for working your creative magic, releasing the soul of written words straight through to the cover design.

Credit also goes to the Internet provider *Ancestry.com*, and the far-flung Ancestry members who contributed to the research of my family simply by digging up their own roots, especially my brother, Dr. Bob Bedford, and distant cousin, Shane McLatchey. To my sister, Dorothy, thank you for your critical eye and thoughtful encouragement with respect to this book and our life paths in general. With the game afoot, priceless discoveries have popped from my laptop in the searchable archives of *Newspapers. com, History.com, Allmusic.com*, YouTube, the Smithsonian Institution and the National Institutes of Health. Leonard Maltin's *Classic Movie Guide*, in combination with the online database of *IMDb*, linked me to the world of my film-loving mother.

Finally, I salute my husband Pete, a true World War II aficionado. The battles and campaigns, to which he devotes his attention and collections of military memorabilia, are altogether different but relevant to my stories. It is with hard-won lessons of history we keep the faith our progeny will succeed, where other generations have failed, in advancing a socially and environmentally conscious future.

About the Author

When New Jersey born Bonnie Ann Bedford picked Park City, Utah, as a place to settle in the 1970s no one expected the old silver mining boomtown, turned ski town, would evolve to become a 2002 Winter Olympics host city and, later, a world-class destination resort. Fresh out of grad school, her first full-time job with the Park City Chamber of Commerce (then housed in the former Sheriff's office on Historic Main Street) placed her in a non-profit position to convince visiting travel agents and press writers "This is the Place!" It was a tough sell, especially with Utah's weird liquor laws. But it's how she met her husband of thirty-six years, Pete *Park*. Did his forebears own the city? No.

Fast forward. With two young sons underfoot, she began a public service career as a local government Parks and Recreation administrator, large as life like sitcom character Leslie Knope (Amy Poehler) in *Parks and Rec*. Though when it came to public meetings with citizens of one neighborhood or another, it played more like bad reality TV. The Recreation District magically launched like a rabbit out of a hat from a home office in the family laundry room. Bonnie navigated through a world of NIMBY's (not in my back yard) and BANANA's (build absolutely nothing anywhere near anything) to provide opportunities for public parks and recreation facilities, non-motorized trails, and open space preservation.

When she left the public sector in 2013 after seventeen years of service, Bonnie received the Utah Parks and Recreation Association's "Lifetime Achievement Award" for "outstanding accomplishments." She was equally humbled when Park City Rotary Club named her *Professional Citizen of the Year* ten years before that. Known as one to keep an unending list of "to-do's" the hiatus from punching a clock gave her a minute to begin the painstaking process of transcribing old family letters. But then home life took a hairpin turn and came to a screeching halt. She became a caregiver. Not for her aging parents, Robin and Buster (they'd already passed), but for her firstborn son, then twenty-four years old. Along one of Utah's Scenic By-ways, out of cell range, he rode shotgun as a passenger in a Honda Civic head on into a pickup truck. His survival was nothing short of a miracle. In her Christmas letter of 2014, Bonnie wrote "the angels are among us." Conceivably those angels were the very family members who were cast, like it or not, into this book.

Before anyone looked to Internet meme's and life coaches for empowerment, Robin and Buster Bedford fashioned Bonnie's future with words like this: "*You can do anything you put your mind to!*" Proving they were right, she helped her son help himself to get back on his feet. As much as her path has wandered in unexpected ways, it's finally time to introduce the first book of three in a trilogy. Personal stories delivered in the context of significant events in U.S. history. A legacy derived from hard-working, church-going middle-class people who identified as Republican in a time when "civil discourse" in party politics sought to better our country, our democracy and our national security.

Made in the USA
San Bernardino, CA
13 November 2018